THE CAMBRIDGE BIBLE COMMENTARY

NEW ENGLISH BIBLE

GENERAL EDITORS

P. R. ACKROYD, A. R. C. LEANEY,
J. W. PACKER

LEVITICUS

LEVITICUS

COMMENTARY BY

J. R. PORTER

Professor of Theology
University of Exeter

CAMBRIDGE UNIVERSITY PRESS

CAMBRIDGE

LONDON · NEW YORK · MELBOURNE

Published by the Syndics of the Cambridge University Press
The Pitt Building, Trumpington Street, Cambridge CB2 1RP
Bentley House, 200 Euston Road, London NW1 2DB
32 East 57th Street, New York, NY 10022, USA
296 Beaconsfield Parade, Middle Park, Melbourne 3206, Australia

First published 1976

Printed in Great Britain
at the
University Printing House, Cambridge
(Euan Phillips, University Printer)

Library of Congress cataloguing in publication data
Bible. O. T. Leviticus. English. New English 1976. Leviticus.
(The Cambridge Bible Commentary New English Bible)
Bibliography: p.
Includes index.
1. Bible. O. T. Leviticus – Commentaries. I. Porter, Joshua Roy.
II. Title. III. Series.
BS 1253 . P67   222′. 13′077   75–20831
ISBN 0 521 08638 8 hard covers
ISBN 0 521 09773 8 paperback

GENERAL EDITORS' PREFACE

The aim of this series is to provide the text of the New English Bible closely linked to a commentary in which the results of modern scholarship are made available to the general reader. Teachers and young people have been especially kept in mind. The commentators have been asked to assume no specialized theological knowledge, and no knowledge of Greek and Hebrew. Bare references to other literature and multiple references to other parts of the Bible have been avoided. Actual quotations have been given as often as possible.

The completion of the New Testament part of the series in 1967 provides a basis upon which the production of the much larger Old Testament and Apocrypha series can be undertaken. The welcome accorded to the series has been an encouragement to the editors to follow the same general pattern, and an attempt has been made to take account of criticisms which have been offered. One necessary change is the inclusion of the translators' footnotes since in the Old Testament these are more extensive, and essential for the understanding of the text.

Within the severe limits imposed by the size and scope of the series, each commentator will attempt to set out the main findings of recent biblical scholarship and to describe the historical background to the text. The main theological issues will also be critically discussed.

Much attention has been given to the form of the volumes. The aim is to produce books each of which will be read consecutively from first to last page. The introductory material leads naturally into the text, which itself leads into the alternating sections of the commentary.

The series is accompanied by three volumes of a more general character. *Understanding the Old Testament* sets out to provide the larger historical and archaeological background, to say something about the life and thought of the people of the Old Testament, and to answer the question 'Why should be study the Old Testament?'. *The Making of the Old Testament* is concerned with the formation of the books of the Old Testament and Apocrypha in the context of the ancient near eastern world, and with the ways in which these books have come down to us in the life of the Jewish and Christian communities. *Old Testament Illustrations* contains maps, diagrams and photographs with an explanatory text. These three volumes are designed to provide material helpful to the understanding of the individual books and their commentaries, but they are also prepared so as to be of use quite independently.

P.R.A.
A.R.C.L.
J.W.P.

CONTENTS

THE FOOTNOTES TO THE
N.E.B. TEXT

The footnotes to the N.E.B. text are designed to help the reader either to understand particular points of detail – the meaning of a name, the presence of a play upon words – or to give information about the actual text. Where the Hebrew text appears to be erroneous, or there is doubt about its precise meaning, it may be necessary to turn to manuscripts which offer a different wording, or to ancient translations of the text which may suggest a better reading, or to offer a new explanation based upon conjecture. In such cases, the footnotes supply very briefly an indication of the evidence, and whether the solution proposed is one that is regarded as possible or as probable. Various abbreviations are used in the footnotes.

(1) Some abbreviations are simply of terms used in explaining a point: *ch(s).*, chapter(s); *cp.*, compare; *lit.*, literally; *mng.*, meaning; *MS(S).*, manuscript(s), i.e. Hebrew manuscript(s), unless otherwise stated; *om.*, omit(s); *or*, indicating an alternative interpretation; *poss.*, possible; *prob.*, probable; *rdg.*, reading; *Vs(s).*, Version(s).

(2) Other abbreviations indicate sources of information from which better interpretations or readings may be obtained.

Aq.   Aquila, a Greek translator of the Old Testament (perhaps about A.D. 130) characterized by great literalness.

Aram.   Aramaic – may refer to the text in this language (used in parts of Ezra and Daniel), or to the meaning of an Aramaic word. Aramaic belongs to the same language family as Hebrew, and is known from about 1000 B.C. over a wide area of the Middle East, including Palestine.

Heb.   Hebrew – may refer to the Hebrew text or may indicate the literal meaning of the Hebrew word.

Josephus   Flavius Josephus (A.D. 37/8–about 100), author of the *Jewish Antiquities*, a survey of the whole history of his people, directed partly at least to a non-Jewish audience, and of various other works, notably one on the *Jewish War* (that of A.D. 66–73) and a defence of Judaism (*Against Apion*).

Luc. Sept.   Lucian's recension of the Septuagint, an important edition made in Antioch in Syria about the end of the third century A.D.

Pesh.   Peshitta or Peshitto, the Syriac version of the Old Testament. Syriac is the name given chiefly to a form of Eastern Aramaic used by the Christian community. The translation varies in quality, and is at many points influenced by the Septuagint or the Targums.

Sam. Samaritan Pentateuch – the form of the first five books of the Old Testament as used by the Samaritan community. It is written in Hebrew in a special form of the Old Hebrew script, and preserves an important form of the text, somewhat influenced by Samaritan ideas.

Scroll(s) Scroll(s), commonly called the Dead Sea Scrolls, found at or near Qumran from 1947 onwards. These important manuscripts shed light on the state of the Hebrew text as it was developing in the last centuries B.C. and the first century A.D.

Sept. Septuagint (meaning 'seventy'; often abbreviated as the Roman numeral LXX), the name given to the main Greek version of the Old Testament. According to tradition, the Pentateuch was translated in Egypt in the third century B.C. by 70 (or 72) translators, six from each tribe, but the precise nature of its origin and development is not fully known. It was intended to provide Greek-speaking Jews with a convenient translation. Subsequently it came to be much revered by the Christian community.

Symm. Symmachus, another Greek translator of the Old Testament (beginning of the third century A.D.), who tried to combine literalness with good style. Both Lucian and Jerome viewed his version with favour.

Targ. Targum, a name given to various Aramaic versions of the Old Testament, produced over a long period and eventually standardized, for the use of Aramaic-speaking Jews.

Theod. Theodotion, the author of a revision of the Septuagint (probably second century A.D.), very dependent on the Hebrew text.

Vulg. Vulgate, the most important Latin version of the Old Testament, produced by Jerome about A.D. 400, and the text most used throughout the Middle Ages in western Christianity.

[. . .] In the text itself square brackets are used to indicate probably late additions to the Hebrew text.

(Fuller discussion of a number of these points may be found in *The Making of the Old Testament* in this series.)

LEVITICUS

✳ ✳ ✳ ✳ ✳ ✳ ✳ ✳ ✳ ✳ ✳ ✳ ✳

THE CHARACTER OF THE BOOK

The word 'Leviticus' comes from the title of the work, *Liber Leviticus*, in the Vulgate, the Latin version of the Old Testament made by Jerome about A.D. 400, which in turn is a translation of the name given to it in the Septuagint, the Greek version of the late B.C. period. So the name is descriptive, 'the Levitical book', that is, concerned with the temple personnel, all of whom were supposed to be descended from Levi, the third son of the patriarch Jacob. In one way, the description gives a good idea of the work's character. It was produced in the circles of the priesthood that survived and regrouped themselves after the fall of the kingdom of Judah to the Babylonians in 587 B.C. It is also in part a manual to instruct the priests in the correct performance of their liturgical duties, especially about their part in carrying out the increasingly elaborate ritual of sacrifice, but in other areas of the cultus, that is, the whole sphere of official public worship, too. From another point of view, the description is inadequate. Priests in Israel always had a responsibility for ascertaining the divine will for individuals and the nation in general, for teaching and explaining God's commandments to the people from generation to generation and for seeing that they were observed in the actual administration of justice and the conduct of ordinary life. These duties became increasingly important with the disappearance of the monarchical state-system at the exile and from that time, the priesthood, and especially the high priest, gradually emerged as the leaders of the nation. So Leviticus also contains a great deal of instruction addressed directly to the laity, to teach them both their religious and civil obligations and to bring

I

home to them how important it was that these be observed.

At a first reading, the book of Leviticus may seem a confused and disorderly collection of unrelated materials. We have to remember that ancient literature often does not follow the methods of logical arrangement which seem so natural to us and also that, as will be seen, the work can only be properly understood as part of a much larger whole. In fact, a fairly clear shape can be discerned in it. Its kernel is chs. 8–10, which are in narrative form, and which continue, originally from the end of the book of Exodus, a great priestly narrative in which all the collections of laws are now set. But because these chapters recount the beginning of Israelite sacrificial worship, the section chs. 1–7 was prefixed to them, giving the necessary details of how sacrifices were to be performed. The distinctive mark of the worshipping community thus constituted was its 'holiness', that is, its being set apart from all other peoples to belong solely to God: so there follow chs. 11–16 which give directions for maintaining and preserving holiness. Finally, what is involved in the summons to be the holy nation is spelled out for ordinary life in the remaining chapters of the book.

THE PRIESTLY WORK

Leviticus was not originally a separate and self-contained unity but formed part of a continuous whole comprising what are now the first five (or, more probably the first four) books of the Old Testament. This great work is primarily a collection of a vast amount of material with very different dates and backgrounds but it has been given a definite shape and arrangement by the priestly circles mentioned above. Many scholars think that the priestly school first produced its own document, covering much the same ground as the other sources which can be discovered in Genesis–Numbers, which is usually known by the letter 'P'. The priestly writers later joined this to the other sources and made it a framework into which they were all fitted. Other scholars believe that 'P' never existed as a separate document but that the parts of the Old Testament which are assigned to it represent rather the editorial activity of the priestly school as it collected and arranged the older materials and stamped them with its distinctive outlook. From the point of view of our understanding of the books in question, it perhaps does not matter a great deal which view is adopted. It would be generally agreed, first, that at least Genesis–Numbers as they now exist are the product of the priestly writers, who meant them to be understood from their own point of view and, secondly, that what is contained in Leviticus in particular is much more distinctively priestly in character than most of the other sources in those books.

The final result of the activity of the priestly writers was a lengthy narrative, relating the history, first of mankind as a whole and then of Israel, from the creation of the world in Gen. 1 to the death of Moses, the priestly account of which is to be found in Deut. 32: 48–52 and 34: 1, 7–9, although it once probably stood at the end of what is now the book of Numbers. But it is history in a special sense, for what interested the priestly editors were the statutes and commandments which God had given in the past. So, in their particular work, the collections of laws are by far the most prominent feature and the narrative only an accompaniment to them, to explain when and how they were given. Above all, their special interest, to which all the previous history leads up, was in the constitution of Israel as a national and religious community at Mount Sinai on the basis of the divine laws and regulations received there. So the core of the distinctively priestly material is formed by the enactments of Exod. 25–31; 35–40, by Leviticus, and by similar laws comprising a large part of Numbers. According to the priestly concept, as we see very clearly in Leviticus, Moses is not so much the great national leader and founding-father, but rather the recipient of the divine law which he then has to transmit exactly to the Israelites.

This does not mean, however, that by any means all the legal collections were actually formulated by the priestly writers responsible for the narrative framework. Sometimes this is the case and sometimes, too, they have worked over and expanded older material with their own legal teaching. Often, however, they simply incorporated virtually unchanged into their narrative of the giving of the law at Sinai a number of collections of laws, stemming from different historical periods and different areas of Palestine. This is very markedly true of Leviticus, which contains at least two such older, independent collections, chs. 1–7 and 17–26. Even when the priestly editorial activity is more obvious, as in the collection in chs. 11–16, yet even then it is often largely a case of systematizing and interpreting very ancient regulations. Indeed, strictly speaking, there is comparatively little of the immediate and direct work of the priestly school in Leviticus, although the book can only be properly understood in its setting as part of the priestly source as a whole.

WHEN AND WHERE WAS THE PRIESTLY WORK WRITTEN?

In trying to discover the date when the priestly work assumed its final form, we may begin from the fact that neither the historical and prophetical books written before the exile nor the other sources in the first five books of the Old Testament show any trace of the distinctive language and religious outlook which so clearly stamps the priestly source. Since that language and outlook had so great an influence on subsequent literature – for example, on the books of Chronicles – and indeed on the whole character of later Judaism, it is difficult to believe that the priestly work would not have affected those other writings had it been in existence when they took shape. On the other hand, the priestly work has close affinities, in its aim and theology, with Deuteronomy and Ezekiel, both of which come essentially from the period of the exile. Further, as will be seen below, the most probable reason why the priestly writers ever embarked on their great task was to meet the challenge posed by the trauma of the exile and to provide a structure for the community which was slowly rebuilding itself in Palestine in the years following the catastrophe.

We may suggest, then, that the priestly work was later than Deuteronomy and Ezekiel, at a time when a restored community in the Promised Land was a practical possibility, perhaps even as early as the late sixth century B.C. This is supported by the fact that often the priestly source seems to presuppose ritual practices which only become normative with the building of the second temple and also by its special picture of the figure of Aaron, which is quite different from how he appears in the other sources of Genesis–Numbers. In the priestly source, Aaron is both the high priest and the ancestor of the whole priesthood: both these features reflect developments which only occurred after the return from exile (cp. p. 60). Whether the actual work of the priestly school was carried out in Babylonia or in Palestine is not easy to decide. Certainly, the priests of Jerusalem who had been taken into exile were among the contributors, for specifically Jerusalem cultic traditions, which they would have preserved, play an important part in it. But the priestly work also incorporates a much wider range of cultic traditions and, if the position adopted in the succeeding commentary can be accepted, it took them over as collections which were only formed on the soil of Palestine after 587 B.C. Perhaps, then, it is most likely that the priestly work was a result of the united priesthood, formed between the old Jerusalem priests when they returned from Babylonia and the priests from other Israelite shrines who had replaced them during the exile, and that its background is Jerusalem from the period of Haggai and Zechariah onwards (cp. p. 16).

But the question of the date of the priestly work is a subtle one: it is really only possible to speak of the date of the material which the priestly writers themselves produced or of the final great whole for which this provided the arrangement and the interpretation. When we go on to consider the origin of the material which they incorporated into their narrative and which, as has been seen, forms so large a part of the total product, the problem becomes much more complicated. On the one hand, the priestly editors took over previously existing legal collections, which probably represent the traditions of various Israelite sanctuaries during the monarchical period. But, on the other hand, these collections themselves are made up of still smaller collections and even separate individual laws, which were generally passed on by word of mouth. Many of them go back to the days before there was such an entity as 'Israel'. They may even be originally Canaanite. Since they remained in force from age to age, it is impossible to date them: they are timeless. Hence the process by which a book like Leviticus reached its present form is a long and complicated one. The work contains legal material from many centuries which, because laws deal with real-life situations, throws much light on the nature of Israelite society at different stages in its development.

The difficulties in translating Leviticus are not caused by textual problems – since the text was written and transmitted in a single scholarly circle, it is generally in a good state – but from the occurrence of so many ancient, rare, and often unique, words and expressions of whose true meaning and significance scholars are still quite unsure.

THE PURPOSE OF LEVITICUS

The structure of Leviticus is thus highly complex but, fortunately, the reason why it was composed as part of the priestly work is not hard to see. Although the laws it contains are placed within a historical narrative and represented as being given in the distant past, yet the priestly work is in fact not directed to the past but to the present and future. It was undertaken as a direct response to the destruction of the northern and southern kingdoms which, as the ancient Near East saw things, could be expected to mean the end alike of Israel's God and his people (cp. 2 Kings 18: 33–5). Other writings in the Old Testament were produced to meet the same situation, notably the so-called 'Deuteronomic History', running from Joshua to the end of 2 Kings, and the book of Ezekiel. Another example of such a response to the catastrophe of the exile, earlier than the priestly source, but, like it, the work of priests and having a very similar outlook on events, is 'the law of holiness' which now forms chs. 17–26 of Leviticus itself.

The priestly school sought to cope with the shock of national disaster in various ways. First, it was concerned to preserve the fundamental laws, which were the basis of the people's life, by fixing them in writing (cp. e.g. p. 25). Many of these were ancient customs, handed on orally, as we have seen, and because of the disruption caused by foreign invasions, were in danger of being lost and forgotten. In this, the priests were only extending their traditional function as guardians and transmitters of law. But they now went further. In their work, all law was represented as the direct commandment of God himself, given for all time at the very beginning of Israel's existence as a nation (cp. the comment on 27: 34). The law-giving at Mount Sinai was the time of perfect communion between God and people, just as the wilderness period was in the message of the prophets.

Secondly, the priestly writers tried to understand and explain to their people the reasons for the tragedy which had happened to them. Here, like the writers of Deuteronomy, they adopted and developed the teaching of the great prophets before the exile, which had largely gone unheeded, and we must never forget that it was Judaism after the exile, the creation of the priesthood, which preserved and put into

writing the prophetic oracles. It was not that God was powerless to defend his people, as the whole of the world surrounding Israel would have believed. Rather, disaster was actually
sent by him, with foreign conquerors as no more than his
agents, as a just punishment for Israel's constant disobedience
to the terms of the covenant they had once accepted. The
distinctive way in which the priestly school presented this
message was by setting out in detail the laws and commandments which gave practical expression to the covenant
obligations, to bring home how often and in how many ways
the Israelites had failed to observe them.

But if the law represented a judgement on the past, to the
priestly school it was also a warning and a promise for the
future. For, thirdly, another aim of the priestly work was to
show that God's commandments remained in force and that
they could become the foundation for a reconstructed community, if only they were observed faithfully as they had not
been before. So reiterated teaching and exhortation, to
emphasize the importance of keeping the law if Israel was to
revive and survive, is a marked feature of the priestly source.
In Leviticus, this is especially true of 'the law of holiness',
which can be seen as an extended sermon on this theme. But
the priests also endeavoured to make the keeping of the law
a practical possibility for the people of their own time.
Partly this was done by reinterpreting ancient regulations
whose original significance was no longer understood, and
by extending and developing them, through decisions in
actual cases of difficulty, to meet changing social and economic
circumstances (cp. pp. 196–7 below). More importantly, it was
done through a new emphasis on elements which had been
present in embryo in the faith of Israel before but had not
previously been sufficiently appreciated. So, in Leviticus, we
find a heightened awareness of sin and guilt as things that
destroy the bond between God and his subjects, accompanied
by a new interpretation of the sacrificial system, and the one
sanctuary where it is carried out, as the means by which sin

can be taken away and as the focus of divine forgiveness (cp. p. 11 below). In these ways, we see the beginnings of scholarly and scribal commentary on the law which was to develop into the massive intellectual achievement of rabbinic Judaism.

THE THEOLOGICAL VALUE OF THE BOOK

At the outset, it must be stressed that Leviticus, and the priestly work generally, take for granted the basic covenant faith of Israel. This needs saying because there are still some who try to draw a sharp distinction between the 'priestly' and the 'prophetic' outlooks in the Old Testament, almost as though they were two different religions. But we have already seen several examples of the essential similarity in the way both priests and prophets understood the nation's relationship with God and interpreted the course of its history. The priesthood after the exile was the heir to the message of the great prophets and one reason why the particular writings which make up the Old Testament were selected from a much larger body of ancient Hebrew literature was that they all express a common faith in God's choice of Israel and the consequences which flow from this fact. The covenant with Israel and the canon of books in the Old Testament are inseparable.

Nevertheless, there are some distinctive features and particular emphases of priestly theology, especially as found in Leviticus, which often cause difficulty for a modern reader. One is the insistence on the keeping of the commandments of the law as ensuring a right relationship with God. Much religious thinking today would feel this to be an artificial, even a legalistic, understanding of that relationship; for Christian thinking, it seems at variance with Paul's teaching in the New Testament. But here two points need to be borne in mind. First, there is the religious outlook of the wider world in which Israel lived. There, gods were usually arbitrary and capricious: they were bound by no rules and a man could never be sure what attitude they would take to his actions. It was therefore a great advance when Abraham could ask God, expecting a positive answer, 'Shall not the judge of all the earth do what is just?' (Gen. 18: 25), that is, act in accordance with a standard which he himself has set and which man can know. Secondly, all the individual regulations were viewed as stemming from the covenant made by God with Israel; they were a gift of God, part of his great work of grace by which he had freed the Israelites from Egypt and settled them in the Promised Land. So the divine mercy is expressed by a word which means 'keeping faith' (cp. Exod. 20: 6): as God was faithful to his side of the covenant, his people were expected to be faithful to theirs.

Again, the priestly outlook can be condemned as inward looking. It saw the law as Israel's possession which separated it sharply from all other nations who had no share in the covenant. It is easy to see the dangers in this attitude and its exclusiveness did not go unchallenged after the exile, as we can see from the Old Testament itself in such a protest as the book of Jonah. Once again, however, we have to try and see the priestly achievement against the background of its own time. The priestly teachers succeeded in preserving Israel as a religious community, even when it had lost its national independence. In so doing, they also preserved the revelation of the one true God, as the basis of the new community's life, to be shared eventually by other peoples, through the witness of later Judaism, which attracted many thoughtful men of the Graeco-Roman world, and through the mission of the Christian church.

A further problem is raised by the priestly emphasis on ritual and the centrality of the sacrificial system, which is more obvious in Leviticus than in any other book of the Old Testament. The offering of sacrifice was a universal characteristic of all the religions of the ancient world and the priestly circle inherited an age-old system which they took for granted. What is important, however, is the way in which they gave a new and greater significance to a number of old sacrificial concepts. These are discussed below (pp. 19–21) in the opening comments on 1: 1–17 but perhaps two may be singled out here as having abiding religious value. On the one hand, the ancient idea of the sacrifice as a gift to the deity came to be seen as a recognition that everything that man enjoyed was first of all a gift from God and sacrifice was an act which recognized this truth. A similar view underlies the great importance given to the sabbath and the sabbath year in Leviticus, for these are signs of God's lordship over life and time and of man's complete dependence on him. The same profound truth probably underlies the purity laws in chs. 11–15, which are perhaps the part of Leviticus which the modern reader finds hardest to understand. Whatever their original purpose and significance may have been, in priestly thought they are intimately linked with the doctrine of God's creation of the world. To observe them is to live in accordance with the divine ordering of nature. The priestly writers taught that man's power over his environment was certainly great but it was not unlimited and ultimately man must learn to live in a world ordered and directed by God.

But perhaps the most characteristic understanding of the purpose of the sacrificial system which was developed by the priestly compilers of Leviticus is that it was the normal way of expiating sin and restoring the right relationship with God which sin had interrupted. In turn, this idea rests on the priestly view of sin and guilt, which was much wider than ours usually is. Sin is whatever disrupts the proper order of things in a society where every facet of life is governed by the precepts of the divine law. So it is an objective reality and if a person does something that infringes the law, understood in its widest sense, he incurs guilt, whether or not he intended his action and even if, from our point of view, he could not help it. So, too, the effects of sin can go far beyond the immediate circumstances of the wrong-doing, for they inevitably destroy that perfect holiness which God demands of his people. Hence the sacrificial system, in its various aspects, came to be presented as an objective means, ordained by God, by which all the effects of sin were nullified and the offender restored to full fellowship with the Holy God and the holy community: and the temple, where the sacrificial ritual took place, came to have as its most sacred part the cover over the Ark, where supremely expiation was made. In Leviticus, the old original ideas about what sacrifice was supposed to achieve have been so completely overlaid by this over-riding concern that it is now not easy to recover them. But the view in Leviticus of sin, guilt and sacrifice is the mould which enabled the New Testament writers to understand the death of Christ as the all-sufficient sacrifice to atone for the sin of the world. Since the final destruction of the temple and the cessation of sacrifices, Jewish tradition has seen Leviticus primarily as the key to the life of purity, so that children's instruction in Scripture began with this book. As a Rabbinic saying puts it, 'let it be the pure which the pure begin to study.'

✻ ✻ ✻ ✻ ✻ ✻ ✻ ✻ ✻ ✻ ✻ ✻ ✻

Laws concerning offerings and sacrifices

✻ Chs. 1–7 form an independent collection which was incorporated into the narrative of the priestly source, but it falls into two originally independent sections. 1: 1 – 6: 7 is addressed to 'the Israelites' (1: 2; 4: 2) and lays down ritual directions for the main types of individual sacrifice. Thus it has often been considered as a manual for the layman, to instruct him on the correct procedure when he brought his offering to the sanctuary. But this is hardly correct. A great deal is said about the priests' specific role in the ceremonies, while much of importance that the layman would need to know is omitted: this is especially marked in the case of the shared-offering (cp. the comment on ch. 3). What we have here, therefore, is rather a memorandum for the priesthood about the ritual to be followed when a sacrifice was offered by an individual (1: 2), which of course included details about the latter's part in the proceedings. There are several lists of the sacrifices to be offered to the various deities of the Canaanite pantheon among the texts discovered at the city of Ugarit on the North Syrian coast and it is probably on this type of material that 1: 1 – 6: 7 is ultimately based.

The second section, 6: 8 – 7: 38, is much more markedly concerned with the priests: it seems to be designed to provide a supplement to the first section and is consequently later than it. It is much less systematically arranged than the first section and contains a number of miscellaneous provisions whose position may be simply due to the fact that they were couched in phraseology similar to that of the material with which they were connected (cp. the comment on 7: 23–7). But the main concern of the section is with the priests' dues from the sacrificial offerings. From Phoenician colonies at Carthage and Marseilles between the fourth to the second century B.C., we have lists of sacrificial priestly dues and probably an old Israelite list of a similar kind is the basis of the greater part of the material in 6: 8 – 7: 38.

Many of the ritual practices in both sections are obviously extremely old and the duplications and contradictions in them show that their origin is diverse. Probably they represent the practices of a number of different shrines in ancient Israel, which have been gathered together in a single collection. That is to say, this collection is comparatively late – its date will be discussed further later – and stands at the end of a long process of development. This development was the work of the priests, who taught the people who came to worship at the shrines the ritual and significance of sacrifice and who gradually expanded their teaching by deriving general rules from decisions they gave in cases of difficulty that arose. Such activity is recognizable in Lev. 1–7 when we consider two literary – although originally oral – forms in these chapters. First, there are the old basic commandments, which are absolutely binding: they are in what is called 'apodictic' form, that is, admitting of no exception and employing the formula, usually in the singular, 'you shall' or, more commonly, 'you shall not'. Secondly, however, there are regulations which modify, explain or extend the basic laws and how these came about can be seen from the fact that they are in 'casuistic' form, that is, they describe a case, 'if a person does so and so', 'if a man's sacrifice is so and so', and then give a direction as to what is to be done (cp. also the comment on 2: 1–16).

But chs. 1–7 are more than a simple collection. The priests who put the material together have imposed on it a liturgical and theological unity. On the one hand, they produced a scheme or pattern of 'sacrifice'. Rites of originally very different character have all been given a common framework, so that the features which had once made them distinct appear now as variants of the general pattern. On the other hand, if these rites once had different forms, they also had different purposes and meanings. Now they are all given the same significance and function: all are gifts to God and all 'make expiation' (cp. the comment on 1: 1–17). Again, sacrifice becomes predominantly a matter for the priests, as it had not always been (cp. Judg. 6: 26–7). They alone can perform the basic rituals and the major part of almost all sacrifices goes to them for their upkeep, as God's representatives. Hence sacrifice comes to have a 'value' which can be expressed in financial terms and we find in Leviticus the beginnings of the process by which it became possible, and indeed, usual, to give a monetary equivalent rather than to present an actual sacrifice (cp. the comment on 4: 1 – 6: 7).

When, where and how did this collecting and systematizing take place? The probable answer is Jerusalem after its capture and sacking by the Babylonians in 587 B.C., where it is generally agreed that some form of cultus continued during this period. Josiah's reforms (2 Kings 23: 8) and the widespread desolation caused by the Babylonian invasions (cp. Lev. 26: 27–39) left Jerusalem as the sole sanctuary of God (cp. Jer. 41: 4–5). With the deportation of the official royal priesthood to Babylon, the priests of the other sanctuaries would have congregated in Jerusalem, as the author of Deuteronomy expected them to do (cp. Deut. 18: 6–8) but which the exclusiveness of the Jerusalem priesthood had prevented (cp. 2 Kings 23: 4; Ezek. 44: 12–14). They would bring their own religious usages and customs with them and it would be a practical necessity for these to be unified in a single cultic pattern. Other motives too would be at work in this development. In view of the collapse of the national life, the people's basic traditions would need to be preserved, and perhaps written down, to prevent them disappearing for ever. Preserving such traditions would also be necessary as a charter to rebuild the nation should it ever be restored in the future. But there were also the needs of an existing worshipping community to be met and chs. 1–7, while no doubt looking backward and, to some degree, forward, are primarily concerned with an actual situation.

This view of the background of these chapters helps to explain several other features in them. The priestly theology saw the doom that had befallen the nation as the punishment of Israel's sins, not least in its failure rightly to carry out the cultic worship of its God, which for them was the channel of communication, and the bond of union, between him and his people. Thus the viewpoint of the priesthood was essentially the same as that of the prophets, who also saw the destruction of Israel as a punishment for its failure to keep the divine commandments. It was the situation in which Israel found itself which led the priests to see sin as the central concern and to explain the purpose of the whole sacrificial system as 'expiation', annulling sin's consequences and restoring a right relationship with God. Again, in part, the role of the 'Tent of the Presence' in these chapters is as a link with the normative wilderness period, when Israel's pattern of worship was given for all time by God through Moses. But the Tent here need not be the elaborate 'Tabernacle' of later priestly theology (Exod. 35–8), modelled on reminiscences of the first temple. It could be much more like the simpler structure of Exod. 33: 7–11 (and cp. the link between Lev. 1: 1 and the closing verses of Exodus which depend on Exod. 33: 7f.), which had had actual successors in Israel's history (cp. Josh. 18: 1; 2 Sam. 6: 17; 2 Chron. 1: 2–3). As Israel had been satisfied with a tent as God's dwelling-place before the temple was constructed (cp. 2 Sam. 7: 6–7), so the old Tent of the Presence was restored in actuality at a time when the temple no longer existed and could not yet be rebuilt. Also in chs. 1–7 the priesthood is descended from Aaron. Probably, at least in most instances, this is due to a later recension of these chapters, to conform to the situation of the second temple (see below). But it is very likely that the ascription of priesthood after the exile to the descendants of Aaron alone is the result of a sort of concordat between the former Jerusalem priests, who viewed the priesthood as confined to the descendants of Zadok (cp. Ezek. 44: 15–16), and the priests from other shrines, who had replaced them at Jerusalem during the exile and who, in many cases at least, claimed Aaronic parentage (e.g. the Shiloh priesthood, 1 Sam. 2: 27–8). As a result, Zadok came to be regarded as descending from Eleazar, Aaron's eldest surviving son (cp. 1 Chron. 24: 1–3). It may well be, then, that behind the references to the Aaronites in these chapters lies a real historical situation of a body of priests constituted in Jerusalem during the exile.

Although chs. 1–7 thus comprise, essentially, old cultic

material that has been collected and reinterpreted at different stages of the period of the exile, when they were incorporated in the priestly work, further changes and additions were made, to fit the outlook of that work and to answer to a later situation (cp. e.g. the comments on 6: 9; 7: 1–7). With these, the chapters reach their existing form. *

THE WHOLE-OFFERING

THE LORD SUMMONED MOSES and spoke to him **1** from the Tent of the Presence, and said, Say this to 2 the Israelites: When any man among you presents an animal as an offering to the LORD, the offering may be presented either from the herd or from the flock.

If his offering is a whole-offering from the cattle, he 3 shall present a male without blemish; he shall present it at the entrance to the Tent of the Presence before the LORD so as to secure acceptance for himself. He shall lay 4 his hand on the head of the victim and it will be accepted on his behalf[a] to make expiation for him. He shall slaughter 5 the bull before the LORD, and the Aaronite priests shall present the blood and fling it against the altar all round at the entrance of the Tent of the Presence. He shall then 6 flay the victim and cut it up. The sons of Aaron the priest 7 shall kindle a fire on the altar and arrange wood on the fire. The Aaronite priests shall arrange the pieces, includ- 8 ing the head and the suet, on the wood on the altar-fire, the entrails and shins shall be washed in water, and the 9 priest shall burn it all on the altar as a whole-offering, a food-offering of soothing odour to the LORD.

If the man's whole-offering is from the flock, either 10

[a] Or by him (*the* LORD).

from the rams or from the goats, he shall present a male
11 without blemish. He shall slaughter it before the LORD at
the north side of the altar, and the Aaronite priests shall
12 fling the blood against the altar all round. He shall cut it
up, and the priest shall arrange the pieces, together with
13 the head and the suet, on the wood on the altar-fire, the
entrails and shins shall be washed in water, and the priest
shall present and burn it all on the altar: it is a whole-
offering, a food-offering of soothing odour to the LORD.
14 If a man's offering to the LORD is a whole-offering of
birds, he shall present turtle-doves or young pigeons as
15 his offering. The priest shall present it at the altar, and
shall wrench off the head and burn it on the altar; and the
blood shall be drained out against the side of the altar.
16 He shall take away the crop and its contents in one piece,
and throw it to the east side of the altar where the ashes
17 are. He shall tear it by its wings without severing them
completely, and shall burn it on the altar, on top of the
wood of the altar-fire: it is a whole-offering, a food-
offering of soothing odour to the LORD.

✳ The 'whole-offering' is so called because the entire animal
was burnt on the altar and none of it was eaten by any
human being: only the skin went to the officiant as his
perquisite (7: 8). The Hebrew term, '*ōlāh*, describes the ritual
and means 'what goes up', either on the altar or to God in
smoke. Verses 3–9 give the main details of the ceremony for a
victim from the 'cattle': these are repeated in more summary
form for a victim from the 'flock' in verses 10–13. In the
case of 'birds' (verses 14–17), a somewhat different ritual is
prescribed and verse 2 shows that this section is a later,
secondary addition (see below).

In this chapter we find various ideas about the meaning and purpose of sacrifice which are important for the outlook of Leviticus as a whole.

(i) A sacrifice is an 'offering' (verse 2), Hebrew *qorbān*, literally, 'what is brought near' as a gift. This word describes all sacrifices in Leviticus. In the ancient Near East, it was unthinkable to approach a superior without a present if a favourable reception was hoped for and the same idea applied to God (cp. the ancient law in Exod. 23: 16*a*). Already, however, in the expansion of the old regulation in Deut. 16: 17, the sacrificial gift is not so much to win God's favour but rather the offerer gives as much as he can as a thankful recognition of God's blessings to him. That this idea is present also in Leviticus is suggested by such verses as 5: 7; 12: 8 and 14: 21, which echo the deuteronomic passage.

(ii) The offerer is directed to 'lay his hand on the head of the victim' (verse 4), a rite common to all the animal sacrifices. This may mean that by this act he identifies himself with the animal. Two interpretations are possible: the worshipper, through the animal, gives himself wholly to God – we may compare the Israelite practice of the 'ban', by which defeated enemies were given over to God by complete destruction (cp. e.g. I Sam. 15: 3) – or the animal becomes a substitute for the worshipper and suffers the penalty of death in his place. There are numerous Babylonian rituals which employ this means to cure a sick person and in Israelite legal practice the witnesses laid a hand on the head of the wrong-doer to transfer to him the guilt they had incurred by witnessing his crime (cp. 24: 14; Daniel and Susanna 34). While this latter explanation would fit in well with the sin- and guilt-offering (see p. 38), it is not so appropriate for the whole-offering, which could be offered on occasions that had no connection with sin. However, the compilers of Leviticus tend to assimilate the theory and practice of all sacrifices to the sin- and guilt-offerings, which were their prime interest, and such may be the case here. Another possible view is that the laying-on of the hand was simply to designate it as the offerer's own gift. In any event, the laying-on of the hand had different meanings on different occasions and the significance here is perhaps not the same as in the Day of Atonement ritual (cp. 16: 21).

(iii) God's acceptance of the animal (see p. 21) is in order 'to make expiation' for the offerer (verse 4). The original sense of the Hebrew verb *kipper* is not wholly clear, but in Leviticus it means to neutralize the consequences of sin or of uncleanness (cp. 14: 7; 16: 15–20), as far as any real distinction can be drawn between them. Expiation is effected by means of the animal's blood applied to the altar, as 17: 11 states. As this verse makes clear, there is an inherent power in the blood, the 'life', but to expiate it must go on the altar, that is, it must be transmitted to God. So, in Leviticus, all animal sacrifices make expiation. However, this idea seems more appropriate to the sin-offering and, once again, we may have here an example of the compilers' tendency to subsume all sacrifices under their primary concern with sin: that this is so is strongly suggested by the fact that, in case of necessity, in spite of 17: 11, a grain-offering too can make expiation; cp. 5: 11–13.

(iv) If the blood of all sacrifices is expiatory, that part of any sacrifice which is burned on the altar for God is also propitiatory, that is, it averts the divine anger and restores good relations between God and the offerer. This concept is expressed by the phrase a 'soothing odour to the LORD' (verse 9). Originally, this implied that the deity actually smelled the fragrant smoke of the burning offerings, and this caused him to look favourably on the one who had provided them (cp. especially Gen. 8: 21, and 1 Sam. 26: 19, where the Hebrew is literally 'may he smell an offering'). Leviticus here retains an ancient cultic expression, but its original anthropomorphism has long disappeared and it now serves to indicate that the due performance of the sacrificial ritual is the means of renewing and strengthening fellowship with God (cp. Ecclus. 35: 1–11, especially verse 6).

1. This is part of the narrative framework of the priestly source, in which its laws and regulations are set. It follows on from the last verses of Exodus, where God has taken up his dwelling in the sanctuary. For *the Tent of the Presence* in Leviticus, see above p. 16.

3. That the victim should be *a male* exclusively is only required in the case of the whole-offering. It is an ancient prescription, reflecting masculine predominance in a patriarchal society: note that with the sin-offering (ch. 4) the requirement of a male victim is confined to the upper ranks of society. By contrast, the victim must always be *without blemish*. For the meaning of this, cp. 22: 17–25 and cp. Mal. 1: 6–14. Only at the one authorized sanctuary of the LORD may sacrifices be made; cp. 17: 1–9. *to secure acceptance for himself:* the last two words could equally well be translated 'for it'. The animal must first be checked for ritual purity: only after the offerer has laid his hand on it (verse 4) does the question of his own acceptance arise.

5. *the Aaronite priests:* in this chapter and elsewhere, there is a somewhat curious alternation between this expression (verses 5, 8, 11) and 'the priest' in the singular (verses 9, 12, 13, 15). The latter represents an earlier stage in the development of the material and suggests conditions before the exile, while the mention of the Aaronites reflects the situation after the exile, when there was an elaborate hierarchy, with the priesthood confined to the descendants of Aaron. *fling it against the altar all round:* this is a different rite from the placing of the blood 'on the horns of the altar' in the sin-offering (4: 25) and before the codification of Leviticus did not have expiatory significance. The altar was the means by which offerings were conveyed to God and so to throw blood there is to give it to God (for the antiquity of the custom, cp. 1 Sam. 14: 31–5), perhaps originally as food (cp. Ps. 50: 13 and below p. 22). Hence this is the task of the priest, while

the preliminary preparation of the victim is left to the layman (verses 3, 4, 5, 6). The altar on which animal and grain offerings were burned stood outside the Tent in the open air.

8. *the head and the suet:* in all animal sacrifices, certain fat parts of the animal, carefully defined in 3: 3–4, were God's due and had to be burned on the altar. It was strictly forbidden to eat these (7: 25). Here, the entire animal goes to God and so an inclusive term, *suet*, is used to denote this. For the same reason, the head is specifically mentioned. As with the blood ritual, the burning of the dismembered animal is the function of the priest.

9. *the entrails and shins:* these were the filthy parts of the animal. But the motive for the regulation in this verse is not hygienic but cultic: dirt of any kind meant ritual uncleanness (cp. Zech. 3: 3–5). *burn:* this is not the ordinary word for burning, which implies destruction, but *hiqṭīr*, a technical ritual term meaning 'to cause to smoke' and so produce the *soothing odour*. *food-offering:* the meaning of the Hebrew word *'ishshēh*, which is applied to the parts of all sacrifices which were given to God, is disputed. There seem to be three possibilities:

(i) the N.E.B. translation links the term with a Sumerian word meaning 'food'. Thus, originally, the sacrificial smoke, with its *soothing odour*, would have been the means of conveying actual food to the deity. In the world surrounding Israel, sacrifices were primarily thought of as food for the gods (cp. e.g. Deut. 32: 37–8) and there are traces of this idea in the Old Testament. It is noteworthy that, in Israel, only domestic animals could be offered in sacrifice and the material of the grain-offering (ch. 2) and the libations (23: 13) consisted of the basic food of ancient Palestine. Again, the sacrificial offerings are called 'the food of God' (cp. 21: 6, 8; 22: 25). However, it is doubtful if this ancient concept still had much vigour by the time of the compilation of Leviticus, when, as has been seen, the dominant theory of sacrifice was that of a gift: the offerings were what a man could give to God because they were his own possessions.

(ii) *'ishshēh* may be connected with a root meaning 'to bring about friendly relations', i.e. with God. This would well express the propitiatory effect of sacrifice as defined in Leviticus.

(iii) usually, the term has been connected with the Hebrew word for 'fire' and rendered as 'an offering by fire'. This is probably the way in which the compilers of Leviticus understood it. It is the burning of the offering which produces *soothing odour* and so brings about fellowship with the deity.

10–13. The ritual in these verses is identical with that in verses 3–9, but it was not felt necessary to repeat all the details.

11. *at the north side of the altar:* an additional detail. In the Old Testament, the north has a double significance. On the one hand, it is the sphere from which death and destruction come (cp. Jer. 1: 14; 4: 6; Ezek. 9: 2). On the other hand, it is the dwelling-place of God from which he comes (cp. Ps. 48: 2; Ezek. 1: 4). In view of the phrase *before the LORD*, it is likely that the latter idea is uppermost here. In Israelite religion, the 'north', *ṣāphōn* in Hebrew, has a religious, rather than a geographical, reference. In Canaanite religion, Baal's seat was on 'the mountain of the north': cp. also Isa. 14: 13.

14–17. An indication that verses 14–17 are later than the rest of the chapter is that almost all the ritual is performed by the *priest*, for the priestly body increasingly took over, after the exile, sacrificial functions originally belonging to the layman (contrast Lev. 1: 5 with Ezek. 44: 11 and Lev. 1: 6 with 2 Chron. 29: 34). Permission to offer *birds* may reflect a situation of poverty during and after the exile. *drained out:* the bird's body was squeezed against *the side of the altar* since there was not enough blood for the full ritual of 1: 5. *the crop and its contents:* again the filthy, unclean part of the animal, which had to be thrown away on the rubbish-heap. *without severing them completely:* another ancient ritual prescription (cp. Gen. 15: 9–10), the meaning of which was probably as obscure to the compilers of Leviticus as it is to us. ✳

THE GRAIN-OFFERING

2 When any person presents a grain-offering to the LORD, his offering shall be of flour. He shall pour oil on it and

2 add frankincense to it. He shall bring it to the Aaronite priests, one of whom shall scoop up a handful of the flour and oil with all the frankincense. The priest shall burn this as a token on the altar, a food-offering of soothing

3 odour to the LORD. The remainder of the grain-offering belongs to Aaron and his sons: it is most sacred, it is taken from the food-offerings of the LORD.

4 When you present as a grain-offering something baked in an oven, it shall consist of unleavened cakes of flour mixed with oil and unleavened wafers smeared with oil.

5 If your offering is a grain-offering cooked on a griddle, it shall be an unleavened cake of flour mixed with oil.

6 Crumble it in pieces and pour oil on it. This is a grain-offering.

7 If your offering is a grain-offering cooked in a pan, it

8 shall be made of flour with oil. Bring an offering made up in this way to the LORD and present it to the priest,

9 who shall bring it to the altar; then he shall set aside part of the grain-offering as a token and burn it on the altar, a

10 food-offering of soothing odour to the LORD. The remainder of the grain-offering belongs to Aaron and his sons: it is most sacred, it is taken from the food-offerings of the LORD.

11 No grain-offering which you present to the LORD shall be made of anything that ferments; you shall not burn any leaven or any honey as a food-offering to the LORD.

12 As for your offering of firstfruits, you shall present them

to the LORD, but they shall not be offered up at the altar as a soothing odour. Every offering of yours which is a 13 grain-offering shall be salted; you shall not fail to put the salt of your covenant with God on your grain-offering. Salt shall accompany all offerings.

If you present to the LORD a grain-offering of first-ripe 14 grain, you must present fresh corn roasted, crushed meal from fully ripened corn. You shall add oil to it and put 15 frankincense upon it. This is a grain-offering. The priest 16 shall burn as its token some of the crushed meal, some of the oil, and all the frankincense as a food-offering to the LORD.

∗ Here, the grain-offering is treated as a sacrifice in its own right, but this chapter probably owes its present position to the fact that this offering regularly accompanied the whole-offering and the shared-offering (cp. Num. 15: 1–13). The ritual is old, for it represents what was done at an ordinary meal (cp. Gen. 18: 6–8; Judg. 6: 19–21, for ordinary meals which are also sacrificial offerings). The chapter is a good example of the priestly function of giving 'precepts and law' (cp. Deut. 33: 10). First, the general rule is laid down (verses 1–3). This is then expanded by directions given by the priests to meet cases which arose and which it did not cover (verses 4–10; 14–16) and by the re-affirmation of ancient taboos which were perhaps in danger of being neglected (verses 11–13). No doubt originally these priestly teachings were given orally and then written down and attributed to Moses in order to preserve them in the disruptive situation of the exile.

1. *grain-offering*: this represents the Hebrew word *minḥāh*, which usually means a gift from an inferior to a superior (cp. Gen. 32: 13; Judg. 3: 15; 2 Kings 8: 8, where 'present', 'tribute' and 'gift' are all translations of *minḥāh*). But in

sacrificial terminology the word was narrowed down from
an early period to mean an offering of grain.

2. As with the whole-offering, the worshipper makes the
preliminary preparations. What distinguishes the gift from
ordinary food is the addition of *frankincense:* probably this
was to make a *soothing odour*, as the burning fat did in the case
of animal sacrifices. This was the essential element in the
token (cp. 24: 7): note that *all* the frankincense has to be burned
for God. The token represented the entire offering and so the
remainder could then be released to be eaten by the
priests.

4–10. These directions would be given in answer to a
worshipper's question: 'is it permitted to offer *baked* or
cooked bread, as well as simple flour?' Since they deal only
with this point, there is no need to repeat all the ritual details,
which are taken for granted.

10. *most sacred:* the word is the same as that elsewhere
translated 'holy'. Its basic meaning is 'setting apart from
profane use' and one of the characteristic features of Leviticus
is its awareness of different degrees of holiness, depending on
the extent of the limitation placed on the use of the object
in question. The grain-offering is of the highest degree because
all of it, strictly speaking, belongs to God (cp. 7: 5–6): therefore it may only be eaten by his representatives, *Aaron and
his sons*, that is, the priests proper. The concern of Leviticus
to preserve carefully the holiness of the cultus is in part
because it sees Israel's worship as the means by which the
nation's distinctiveness, based on its unique relationship with
its God, was maintained.

11. *anything that ferments:* another ancient taboo. The point
is that *leaven* and *honey* could not be burned. What ferments
appears to have a life of its own and so must not be destroyed:
in the same way, the life-force of an animal, which is in the
blood (cp. 17: 11), was not permitted to be burnt.

12. This is a priestly direction in answer to the question:
'does the preceding regulation prohibit the offering of leaven

and honey as firstfruits?' The answer is 'no', but they are not to be burned on the altar: the implication is that, after being presented to God, they become the priests' due. The Hebrew word for *firstfruits* here means literally 'beginning' and this indicates their significance. In Hebrew thought, the first member of a series contained all that followed (cp. 1 Cor. 15: 22). So when the first produce of herds or crops was offered to God, he in fact received the whole, his rightful due as the giver of all increase, and the remainder was then available for human use. It is the same idea as that lying behind the 'token' (verse 2).

13. *salted:* another ancient ritual practice. There seem to be two ideas in this verse:

(i) The effect of salt was to consecrate: the salting of a devastated city (cp. Judg. 9: 45) was part of the ritual of the 'ban', which prevented any further human use of the site and consecrated it to the deity, and the same notion lies behind Elisha's action in purifying a spring (cp. 2 Kings 2: 20–2). Thus, as the further note at the end of the verse makes clear, all sacrificial gifts to God had to be salted (cp. Exod. 30: 35; Ezek. 43: 24).

(ii) The second idea is expressed in the phrase *the salt of your covenant with God.* A covenant created a bond of union between the contracting parties and it was often sealed by a sacrificial meal (cp. Gen. 31: 54). Salt was the regular accompaniment of a meal in the ancient Near East, as it is among the Arabs to this day. According to the priestly outlook, 'a covenant of salt' meant a 'permanent covenant' (cp. Num. 18: 19; 2 Chron. 13: 5). So here the ancient ceremony is transformed into a sign and memorial of God's unbreakable covenant with his people.

14–16. This is a further explanatory addition to make it clear that the regulation in verse 12 did not apply to the offerings of firstfruits from the grain. Following the systematizing tendency of Leviticus, these are classed with the grain-offering, but they are in fact treated in a distinctive way, in

that they are *roasted* (verse 14). This is a very ancient rite
(cp. Josh. 5: 11, where 'parched grain' represents the same
Hebrew word as *roasted*), a harvest ceremony to free the
new crop for human consumption (cp. 23: 12–14), and is
certainly of Canaanite origin. ✳

THE SHARED-OFFERING

3 If a man's offering is a shared-offering from the cattle,
male or female, he shall present it without blemish before
2 the LORD. He shall lay his hand on the head of the victim
and slaughter it at the entrance to the Tent of the Presence.
The Aaronite priests shall fling the blood against the altar
3 all round. One of them shall present part of the shared-
offering as a food-offering to the LORD: he shall remove
the fat covering the entrails and all the fat upon the en-
4 trails, the two kidneys with the fat on them beside the
haunches, and the long lobe of the liver with the kidneys.
5 The Aaronites shall burn it on the altar on top of the
whole-offering which is upon the wood on the fire, a
food-offering of soothing odour to the LORD.

6 If a man's offering as a shared-offering to the LORD is
from the flock, male or female, he shall present it without
7 blemish. If he is presenting a ram as his offering, he shall
8 present it before the LORD, lay his hand on the head of the
victim and slaughter it in front of the Tent of the Presence.
The Aaronites shall then fling its blood against the altar all
9 round. He shall present part of the shared-offering as a
food-offering to the LORD; he shall remove its fat, the
entire fat-tail cut off close by the spine, the fat covering
10 the entrails and all the fat upon the entrails, the two
kidneys with the fat on them beside the haunches, and the

long lobe of the liver with the kidneys. The priest shall 11
burn it at the altar, as food offered to the LORD.

If the man's offering is a goat, he shall present it before 12
the LORD, lay his hand on its head and slaughter it in front 13
of the Tent of the Presence. The Aaronites shall then fling
its blood against the altar all round. He shall present part 14
of the victim as a food-offering to the LORD; he shall
remove the fat covering the entrails and all the fat upon
the entrails, the two kidneys with the fat on them beside 15
the haunches, and the long lobe of the liver with the
kidneys. The priest shall burn this at the altar, as a food- 16
offering of soothing odour. All fat belongs to the LORD.
This is a rule for all time from generation to generation 17
wherever you live: you shall not eat any fat or any blood.

* In Leviticus, the ritual of the 'shared-offering' has plainly
been made to conform as closely as possible to that of the
burnt-offering. The pattern on which both are presented is
determined by the general direction of 1: 2: both are gifts
(verse 1), the presentation and the blood-ritual are the same
(verse 2), both are primarily concerned with what is burnt on
the altar and so both are 'a food-offering of soothing odour'
(verses 4–5). Nothing at all is said in this chapter about the
special feature of the shared-offering, which explains the
N.E.B. rendering, that the lay offerers consumed those parts
of the animal left over when God and the priests had had their
share: this is only stated incidentally elsewhere (7: 20–1).
Originally, however, the 'shared-offering' was a distinct
type of sacrifice. It was essentially a meal, in which both the
deity and the worshippers joined, so creating a bond of
fellowship between them, and we see its ancient character in
the Passover rite (cp. Exod. 12: 8–10) and in such early passages
as Exod. 18: 12; 24: 9–11. But in Leviticus, the clear differen-

tiation between the portions of the victim that belong to God, priest and worshipper respectively has destroyed the old communal character of the shared-offering and made its significance virtually the same as that of the other animal sacrifices.

1. *shared-offering:* this expression represents two Hebrew words. The first is *zebaḥ*, which simply means 'what is killed'. It probably indicates the period when every slaughter of a domestic animal was for the purpose of a meal in which the deity had his share: only with the restriction of sacrificial offerings for God to one or more sanctuaries was non-sacrificial killing for food permitted (cp. Deut. 12: 15) and the directions for the offering of the blood in 17: 3–4 show that the older idea was never completely lost sight of. It is not surprising, therefore, that the *zebaḥ* seems to have been the commonest sacrifice in early times. The second word is *shelāmīm*, apparently an abstract plural, qualifying *zebaḥ*. The meaning of this term is not wholly clear, but probably it is a specifically ritual expression, borrowed from Canaanite religion: in the Ugaritic texts, the equivalent word means gifts that bring about 'reconciliation' or 'agreement' between two parties. It is this latter idea which came to predominate in the Israelite shared-offering and is primary in the description of it in Leviticus. *male or female:* in contrast to the whole-offering (cp. 1: 3). The difference reflects the origin of the shared-offering in the slaughter of any domestic animal for food.

3–4. *One of them:* this is not in the Hebrew (cp. verses 9, 14) and by analogy with the whole-offering, what is laid down in these verses would be done by the offerer, not by the priest. The very careful directions for the dismemberment of the victim were for his guidance. The extraction of the parts specified, especially *the long lobe of the liver*, may originally have been for purposes of divination, as was common in the religions surrounding Israel (cp. Ezek. 21: 21): but all trace of this has disappeared in Leviticus.

5. *on top of the whole-offering:* this seems to suggest that a whole-offering always had to accompany a shared-offering and the Old Testament shows that the two were regularly offered together on the same occasion.

9. *the entire fat-tail:* an additional item of especially tasty food to be offered to God, appropriate only in the case of this particular breed of animal.

11. *food:* this is the word for ordinary human nourishment, to be clearly distinguished from the 'food-offering'. It indicates how the shared-offering has its roots in a meal.

16. *All fat belongs to the LORD:* this refers to the specifications of verse 3 and is another very old taboo. The entrails were considered to be, like the blood, the seat of life and so the eating of either was strictly prohibited (verse 17; cp. 7: 23–7).

17. *a rule for all time:* a formula used in Leviticus to mark especially solemn prohibitions (cp. 17: 7; 23: 14). *wherever you live:* it has been suggested that this phrase envisages a situation in which many Israelites were living outside the Promised Land. They could not offer sacrifice, but they had to observe the taboos on eating the fat and the blood. Probably, however, the words mean the same as 'inside or outside the camp' at 17: 3, i.e. anywhere in Palestine (cp. Ezek. 6: 6, 14). *

THE SIN-OFFERING AND THE GUILT-OFFERING

* The sacrifices that are specifically concerned with putting right the effects of 'sin' and 'guilt', which are described in 4: 1 – 6: 7, form the heart of the ritual system in the eyes of the compilers of Leviticus, for, in their view, the entire purpose of that system was to bring back the whole nation, which had incurred the divine punishment by repeatedly going astray, into a restored relationship with God and to keep it in that relationship for the future. Particular emphasis, therefore, came to be placed on these sacrifices during the

exile and after, and their scope was extended and their significance transformed.

In Leviticus, the 'sin-offering' and the 'guilt-offering' are closely assimilated and the description of them is confused by the addition of different blocks of priestly instruction (note the various introductions marking originally distinct sections at 4: 1; 5: 14; 6: 1, and the distinctive formula 'if a person' in 5: 1 – 6: 1). Yet enough indications remain for us to distinguish, however tentatively, the character and purpose of each of these sacrifices.

The material in these chapters may be analysed as follows:

A. The section 4: 1 - 5: 13 is concerned with the sin-offering, but in two sections, determined by the offences with which each deals: (i) ch. 4 treats of inadvertent sins (4: 2); (ii) 5: 1–13 deal with the more complicated case of a man whose primary sin is inadvertent but who realizes what he has done and then commits the further sin of concealing it. This section looks like additional priestly teachings (cp. the comment on 2: 4–16), perhaps in answer to the question, 'if a man has concealed his wrong-doing, can he avail himself of the procedure of the sin-offering?'

B. The section 5: 14 - 6: 7 is about the guilt-offering, but again under two heads: (i) in 5: 14–19, the offences are cultic and inadvertent, but (ii) in 6: 1–7, the crimes are social and obviously consciously committed (cp. 6: 2–3).

The sin- and guilt-offerings are certainly old and probably always belonged closely together, but originally they may not have been animal sacrifices. The Hebrew terms *ḥaṭṭā't* and *'āshām* do not in themselves contain any idea of 'offering' – they simply mean 'sin' and 'guilt' – and, at a comparatively early period, sins may have been dealt with by means of a money-payment, a sort of fine. This is strongly suggested by 2 Kings 12: 16, which could equally well be translated, as in the Authorised Version, 'the trespass money and sin money', while, at 1 Sam. 6: 3, *'āshām* is rendered in N.E.B. as 'a gift... by way of indemnity' (cp. 1 Sam. 6: 8), which consisted of valuable gold objects. But, in the priestly circles, as we have seen, it was primarily the blood which had expiatory power, and this was increasingly emphasized as the consciousness of sin became more acute in the face of the disasters falling on Israel: the mysterious power of the blood permitted the widest application for all kinds of defilement both of persons and objects, and for sins which might have been committed quite unconsciously but which yet had serious consequences. Thus, probably not long before the exile, the *ḥaṭṭā't* in particular developed into a sacrifice, distinguished by a special blood ritual, the 'sin-offering', and its wide range of effectiveness is clear from ch. 4. Because of this and because of the centrality of the concern with sin in priestly sacrificial theology, the sin-offering gained a very prominent part in the official cultus after the exile. Sin-offerings were now made, often in large numbers, at all the major festivals and on other important occasions (cp. Num. 28: 15, 22, 30; 29: 5, 16–38; Lev. 16: 3, 9).

By contrast, the *'āshām* always retained much more of its original character. It, too, was assimilated to sacrificial ritual, but it became much less important, and remained much more closely linked with the individual's sins, than the sin-offering, as the material about it in these chapters shows. In particular, it kept its character as primarily a monetary compensation (cp. the comments on 5: 15–16, 18; 6: 4–5), helped by the increasing tendency to commute sacrifices for money after the exile (cp. pp. 14 f.). *

INADVERTENT SINS

The LORD spoke to Moses and said, Say this to the **4** 1, 2 Israelites: These are the rules for any man who inadvertently transgresses any of the commandments of the LORD and does anything prohibited by them:

If the anointed priest sins so as to bring guilt on the 3

people, for the sin he has committed he shall present to the LORD a young bull without blemish as a sin-offering.

4 He shall bring the bull to the entrance of the Tent of the Presence before the LORD, lay his hand on its head and
5 slaughter it before the LORD. The anointed priest shall then take some of its blood and bring it to the Tent of the
6 Presence. He shall dip his finger in the blood and sprinkle some of the blood in front of the sacred Veil seven times
7 before the LORD. The priest shall then put some of the blood before the LORD in the Tent of the Presence on the horns of the altar where fragrant incense is burnt, and he shall pour the rest of the bull's blood at the base of the altar of whole-offering at the entrance of the Tent of
8 the Presence. He shall set aside all the fat from the bull of the sin-offering; he shall set aside the fat covering the entrails
9 and all the fat upon the entrails, the two kidneys with the fat on them beside the haunches, and the long lobe of the
10 liver with the kidneys. It shall be set aside as the fat from the ox at the shared-offering is set aside. The priest shall
11 burn the pieces of fat on the altar of whole-offering. But the skin of the bull and all its flesh, including head and
12 shins, its entrails and offal, the whole of it, he shall take away outside the camp to a place ritually clean, where the ash-heap is, and destroy it on a wood-fire on top of the ash-heap.

13 If the whole community of Israel sins inadvertently and the matter is not known to the assembly, if they do what is forbidden in any commandment of the LORD and so
14 incur guilt, then, when the sin they have committed is notified to them, the assembly shall present a young bull as a sin-offering and shall bring it in front of the Tent of

the Presence. The elders of the community shall lay their 15
hands on the victim's head before the LORD, and it shall
be slaughtered before the LORD. The anointed priest shall 16
then bring some of the blood to the Tent of the Presence,
dip his finger in it and sprinkle it in front of the Veil seven 17
times before the LORD. He shall put some of the blood on 18
the horns of the altar before the LORD in the Tent of the
Presence and pour all the rest at the base of the altar of
whole-offering at the entrance of the Tent of the Presence.
He shall then set aside all the fat from the bull and burn it 19
on the altar. He shall deal with this bull as he deals with 20
the bull of the sin-offering, and in this way the priest shall
make expiation for their guilt and they shall be forgiven.
He shall take the bull outside the camp and burn it as the 21
other bull was burnt. This is a sin-offering for the
assembly.

When a man of standing sins by doing inadvertently 22
what is forbidden in any commandment of the LORD his
God, thereby incurring guilt, and the sin he has com- 23
mitted is made known to him, he shall bring as his offering a he-goat without blemish. He shall lay his hand on 24
the goat's head and shall slaughter it before the LORD in
the place where the whole-offering is slaughtered. It is a
sin-offering. The priest shall then take some of the blood 25
of the victim with his finger and put it on the horns of the
altar of whole-offering. He shall pour out the rest of the
blood at the base of the altar of whole-offering. He shall 26
burn all the fat at the altar in the same way as the fat of
the shared-offering. Thus the priest shall make expiation
for that man's sin, and it shall be forgiven him.

If any person among the common people sins inad- 27

vertently and does what is forbidden in any command-
28 ment of the LORD, thereby incurring guilt, and the sin he
has committed is made known to him, he shall bring as
his offering for the sin which he has committed a she-goat
29 without blemish. He shall lay his hand on the head of the
victim and slaughter it in the place where the whole-
30 offering is slaughtered. The priest shall then take some of
its blood with his finger and put it on the horns of the
altar of whole-offering. All the rest of the blood he shall
31 pour at the base of the altar. He shall remove all its fat as
the fat of the shared-offering is removed, and the priest
shall burn it on the altar as a soothing odour to the LORD.
So the priest shall make expiation for that person's guilt,
and it shall be forgiven him.

32   If the man brings a sheep as his offering for sin, it shall
33 be a ewe without blemish. He shall lay his hand on the
head of the victim and slaughter it as a sin-offering in the
34 place where the whole-offering is slaughtered. The priest
shall then take some of the blood of the victim with his
finger and put it on the horns of the altar or whole-
offering. All the rest of the blood he shall pour out at the
35 base of the altar. He shall remove all the fat, as the fat of
the sheep is removed from the shared-offering. The priest
shall burn the pieces of fat at the altar on top of the food-
offerings to the LORD, and shall make expiation for the
sin that the man has committed, and it shall be forgiven
him.

✻ 2. *inadvertently transgresses:* in view of such passages as
5: 1–16; 6: 2–3, this general direction cannot simply refer to
sins which a man is unaware he has committed, although it

36

includes them. Rather, it seems to mean offences which were not so serious as to put a man outside the covenant relationship with God and so outside the nation. There were such sins, those committed 'presumptuously', and for them the punishment was death (cp. Num. 15: 30-1; Deut. 17: 12). As Leviticus makes clear (7: 37-8), the sacrificial system was part of the covenant obligations given on Sinai: hence, if anyone put himself outside the covenant, sacrificial expiation was not available for him. Such presumptuous sins certainly included murder, adultery and apostasy; and possibly any breach of the Ten Commandments, as a breach of the basic covenant stipulations, was considered to merit the death penalty. On the other hand, inadvertent transgressions also included occasions of ritual impurity. In the priestly theology, sin is an objective, quasi-physical thing – hence, even if committed inadvertently, its consequences cannot be avoided – and so not sharply distinguished from defilement or uncleanness. Thus, sin- and guilt-offerings are made on occasions where 'sin', in our usual understanding of the word, is hardly involved (cp. 5: 1-3; 14: 1-20; 16: 16).

3. *the anointed priest:* under the monarchy, the leader of the Jerusalem priesthood was usually called simply 'the priest' (cp. 2 Kings 16: 10). After the exile, he was always called 'the chief priest' (cp. 2 Chron. 26: 20) or 'the high priest' (cp. Zech. 3: 1). Here we seem to have an intermediate state taking place in Palestine, from the actual period of the exile. The Davidic king was both the head of the state and of the cultus: with the disappearance of the monarchy, the head priest increasingly took over the old royal position, and this process is seen beginning in this verse. Originally, only the king was anointed and there is no evidence that priests were, but here the leading priest has assumed the position which the royal anointing conferred. At a later date, all the Aaronite priests came to be anointed (cp. 7: 36). *to bring guilt on the people:* here another characteristic of the king has been transferred to the priest. The king embodied the whole nation and

37

in 1 and 2 Kings, representing deuteronomic theology, the welfare of the people is directly dependent on the righteousness of the king (cp. 2 Kings 23: 26–7). So the priest's sin brings guilt on the people because he is their representative: note also that the sin-offering ritual for the whole community (verses 13–21) is identical with that for the anointed priest. *a young bull:* the most prized animal.

4. *lay his hand on its head:* here, this rite would appear to effect the transference of the sin to the animal (cp. the comment on the whole-offering on p. 19). This is suggested by verses 11–12: the sin-laden animal is unclean and thus must be taken 'outside the camp' to avoid contamination and destroyed. Only the blood and the fat which, because of the life-force in them, are immune to the defilement of sin, can be offered to God.

5–7. These verses describe the central and distinctive act of the sin-offering. The *sacred Veil* divided the holiest part of the Tent, containing the supreme religious object, 'the Ark' (cp. 16: 2), from the rest. The setting of the ceremony is fixed by the concept of degrees of holiness (cp. the comment on 2: 10): in the case of the priest, it all takes place within the Tent and as close as possible to the spot where God appeared (cp. 16: 2), while for all other individuals it took place outside. The careful manipulation of the blood would appear to be for the purpose of conveying it to God (note the repeated *before the LORD*, verses 6, 7). So it is sprinkled in front of the Veil behind which he dwells: *seven* appears as a sacred number in the Old Testament and also throughout the ancient Near East. Again, it is put on the *horns of the altar*. The horns were four protuberances, one at each corner of a square altar and its most sacred part. They probably derive from the stone 'pillars'of Canaanite religion (cp. Exod. 23: 24), which were symbols of deity: so anyone who takes hold of the horns of the altar is under God's direct protection (cp. 1 Kings 2: 28). *where fragrant incense is burnt:* cp. Exod. 30: 1–10. *pour the rest of the bull's blood:* only the comparatively small amount of blood used for the expiatory rite is of significance in the sin-offering. The rest is simply disposed of reverently (contrast 1: 5).

10. *at the shared-offering:* evidence of the systematizing and assimilating of Leviticus. All the fat must be offered to God and this is to be done identically in the shared-offering and the guilt-offering, since, in neither case, unlike the whole offering, was the entire animal given to God (cp. verses 10, 26, 31, 35).

14. *is notified to them:* cp. verses 23, 28. It is significant that sin must be recognized and accepted before the sacrifice is offered.

15. *elders of the community:* these were the tribal leaders, who returned to prominence among the people left in Judah after the exile with the collapse of the organized state of the monarchy (cp. Ezra 5: 5, 9).

20. *the bull of the sin-offering:* this refers to the bull of the anointed priest and to the disposal of the fat as detailed in verses 8–10. *they shall be forgiven:* cp. verses 26, 31, 35; 5: 6, 10. Expiation is not automatic. There must also be an act of divine forgiveness.

22–35. These verses perhaps represent a comparatively early form of the sin-offering ritual, while verses 3–21 are the result of developments during the exile. Here there are just individual sinners, *the priest* simply (verses 25, 26, 30, 31, 34, 35) and only one altar (verses 25, 30, 34). On the other hand, from the standpoint of Leviticus, a layman would not be permitted to enter the sanctuary, as not having a sufficient degree of holiness, nor would he need the services of someone as important as the anointed priest. A *man of standing* has to offer a male animal (verse 23), a member of the *common people* the less valued female animal (verses 27–8, 32). *

INADVERTENT SIN DELIBERATELY CONCEALED

If a person hears a solemn adjuration to give evidence as 5 a witness to something he has seen or heard and does not declare what he knows, he commits a sin and must accept responsibility.

2 If a person touches anything unclean, such as the dead body of an unclean animal, whether wild or domestic, or 3 of an unclean reptile,[a] or if he touches anything unclean in a man, whatever that uncleanness may be, and it is concealed by him although he is aware of it, he shall incur 4 guilt. Or if a person rashly utters an oath to do something evil or good, in any matter in which such a man may swear a rash oath, and it is concealed by him although he 5 is aware of it, he shall in either case incur guilt. Whenever a man incurs guilt in any of these cases and confesses how 6 he has sinned therein, he shall bring to the LORD, as his penalty for the sin that he has committed, a female of the flock, either a ewe or a she-goat, as a sin-offering, and the priest shall make expiation for him on account of his sin which he has committed, and he shall be pardoned.[b]

7 But if he cannot afford as much as a young animal, he shall bring to the LORD for the sin[c] he has committed two turtle-doves or two young pigeons, one for a sin-offering 8 and the other for a whole-offering. He shall bring them to the priest, and present first the one intended for the sin-offering. He shall wrench its head back without 9 severing it. He shall sprinkle some of the blood of the victim against the side of the altar, and what is left of the blood shall be drained out at the base of the altar: it is a 10 sin-offering. He shall deal with the second bird as a whole-offering according to custom, and the priest shall make expiation for the sin the man has committed, and it shall be forgiven him.

[a] *So Sept.; Heb. adds* and it is concealed by him, he will become unclean and incur guilt.
[b] which he has ... pardoned: *so Sam.; Heb. om.*
[c] *So Sept.; Heb.* guilt.

If the man cannot afford two turtle-doves or two young 11
pigeons, for his sin he shall bring as his offering a tenth of
an ephah of flour, as a sin-offering. He shall add no oil to
it nor put frankincense on it, because it is a sin-offering.
He shall bring it to the priest, who shall scoop up a 12
handful from it as a token and burn it on the altar on the
food-offerings to the LORD: it is a sin-offering. The priest 13
shall make expiation for the sin the man has committed
in any one of these cases, and it shall be forgiven him. The
remainder[a] belongs to the priest, as with the grain-
offering.

✶ 1. This verse has nothing to do with the sin-offering, since
it is concerned with an offence with which the sacrificial
system could not deal (cp. the comment on 4: 2), but belongs
to the sphere of law. It may have found its way in here because
of the similarity of its introductory formula *if a person* to that
in the section verses 2–5. Its purpose was probably to extend
the force of the commandment against giving 'false evidence'
(cp. Exod. 20: 16) to the case of a man who would not give
evidence at all. In Israel's legal system, which had no police-
force or other means of detecting crime, the testimony of the
witness was of vital importance, and refusal to speak was a
most serious matter. *solemn adjuration*: cp. Prov. 29: 24. This
means that the witness was put on oath in God's name to
speak the truth and called down a curse on himself if he did
not. In such an event, he *must accept responsibility*, a technical
legal expression meaning that it was left to God to punish
him, implicitly by death (contrast 'he shall...incur guilt'
verse 4; 'a man incurs guilt' 5). There is no room here for
sacrificial expiation.

2–3. The animals mentioned and *uncleanness* in human
beings are described later on in Leviticus. *wild or domestic*: cp.

[a] The remainder: so Sept.; Heb. om.

41

11: 27, 39. *unclean reptile:* cp. 11: 29–31. *unclean in a man:* cp.
15: 7, 19. *guilt:* ʾāshām in a general sense (cp. 4: 3), which can
be expiated.

4. *rashly utters an oath:* the case of a man who pledges himself by an oath to do something he does not intend, or is
unable, to perform. In Hebrew thought, a word, especially
when backed by the force of an oath, has a power of its own
to work *evil or good*. It cannot be recalled and an objective
means of expiation (verse 6) is needed to right the matter.

5. *confesses:* the sacrifice is only potent when accompanied
by true penitence.

7. As with the whole-offering, the permission to offer
turtle-doves and *young pigeons* is probably a later addendum
(cp. the comment on 1: 14–17). That this is so is also suggested
by the fact that a whole-offering now accompanies the sin-
offering (compare Lev. 4: 14 with the later Num. 15: 24).

8–9. *wrench its head back:* this is merely to kill the bird.
Since the bird had no fat parts, none of it could be burned on
the altar in the sin-offering (contrast 1: 15). Again, in accordance with the sin-offering ritual, only *some of the blood* is used
for expiation and *what is left* is reverently disposed of, in
contrast to the whole-offering (cp. 1: 15).

11–13. Once more a later development, representing an
adaptation of the grain-offering, as far as possible, to the ritual
of the sin-offering (note verse 13).

11. *a tenth of an ephah:* the precise specification of the
amount (contrast 2: 1) suggests a comparatively late ritual prescription. The size of the ephah is not certain (cp. pp. 227–8)
but the quantity here would be quite small: according to
Num. 28: 5, a tenth of an ephah was the minimum amount that
could be offered on the altar. *add no oil to it nor put frankincense
on it:* the addition of these to the grain-offering made it 'a
food offering of soothing odour' (cp. the comment on 2: 2).
This was not the purpose of the sin-offering and for this
reason oil and frankincense are not employed, as the verse
points out.

12. Instead, the burning of the *token* becomes the equivalent of the application of the blood in the sin-offering: note again the final clause of this verse. ✳

THE GUILT-OFFERING

The LORD spoke to Moses and said: When any person 14, 15 commits an offence by inadvertently defaulting in dues sacred to the LORD, he shall bring as his guilt-offering to the LORD a ram without blemish from the flock, the value to be determined by you in silver shekels according to the sacred standard, for a guilt-offering; he shall make good 16 his default in sacred dues, adding one fifth. He shall give it to the priest, who shall make expiation for his sin with the ram of the guilt-offering, and it shall be forgiven him.

If and when any person sins unwittingly and does what 17 is forbidden by any commandment of the LORD, thereby incurring guilt, he must accept responsibility. He shall 18 bring to the priest as a guilt-offering a ram without blemish from the flock, valued by you, and the priest shall make expiation for the error into which he has un-wittingly fallen, and it shall be forgiven him. It is a guilt- 19 offering; he has been guilty of an offence against the LORD.

The LORD spoke to Moses and said: When any person **6** 1,[a] 2 sins and commits a grievous fault against the LORD, whether he lies to a fellow-countryman about a deposit or contract, or a theft, or wrongs him by extortion, or finds 3 lost property and then lies about it, and swears a false oath in regard to any sin of this sort that he commits – if he 4 does this, thereby incurring guilt, he shall restore what he has stolen or gained by extortion, or the deposit left with

[a] 5: 20 *in Heb.*

43

5 him or the lost property which he found, or anything at all concerning which he swore a false oath. He shall make full restitution, adding one fifth to it, and give it back to the aggrieved party on the day when he offers his guilt-
6 offering. He shall bring to the LORD as his guilt-offering a ram without blemish from the flock, valued by you, as
7 a guilt-offering.[a] The priest shall make expiation for his guilt before the LORD, and he shall be forgiven for any act which has brought guilt upon him.

✲ It is not certain how far the guilt-offering was a sacrifice, in the sense in which the term may be used of the rites described in Lev. 1–5. There is no mention of the animal being presented or of any part of it being burnt on the altar, and, in marked contrast to the sin-offering, nothing is said about any blood-ritual. It is possible that all these acts, having been already described in the account of the sin-offering, are assumed under the phrase to 'make expiation' (cp. 5: 16, 18; 7: 7 and cp. 7: 1–10). In any case it is clear that the central element in the procedure is not an animal for sacrifice, but financial compensation.

15–16. 'dues sacred to the LORD' are listed in Num. 18: 8–32. Note again that the defaulting must be inadvertent: if anyone deliberately withheld what belonged to God, he broke the covenant and his punishment was death (cp. Josh. 7: 1, 10–11, 26). The sacred dues in fact went to the priesthood and the man who withheld them involved the priests in financial loss. So the animal 'to make good his default' had to have a value equivalent to the loss, as this was assessed by the priest. It had to be a ram, a male animal (contrast 4: 28), perhaps so as to have a fairly considerable financial worth.

15. *silver shekels according to the sacred standard:* an example of the conservatism of religious practice. This refers to the

[a] *So Sam.; Heb. adds* to the priest.

older or 'heavy' shekel which, as Israel became a trading nation under the monarchy, was superseded for ordinary purposes by the 'light' shekel, used in international commerce. But only the sacred shekel was accepted in the sanctuary and hence the necessity for money-changers in the temple (cp. Mark 11: 15; John 2: 14). It is impossible to give any value for the shekel in modern terms (cp. p. 228).

16. *adding one fifth:* as well as making good the loss, the guilty person had to pay a fine of one fifth of the value. *make expiation:* when we note that the expression *the ram of the guilt-offering* could equally well be rendered 'the ram for guilt' (similarly, we could translate 'as his guilt-offering' in verse 15 simply by 'for his guilt' and similar considerations apply in verse 18 and in 6: 5–6), we see that there is no evidence that the animal was offered on the altar, for expiation could be made simply by gifts to the sanctuary (cp. Exod. 30: 15–16; Num. 31: 50 where the N.E.B's 'as a ransom' is the same in Hebrew as 'to make expiation').

17. Here there is a generalized statement, typical of the activity of the compilers, intended to conform the guilt-offering as closely as possible to the sin-offering (cp. 4: 13, 22, 27).

18. *valued by you:* the primary idea of financial compensation, however, still remains.

6: 2–3. These verses are concerned with social and legal offences against fellow-Israelites, in contrast to the cultic offences of the immediately preceding section. Yet these, too, are still *a grievous fault against the LORD.*

4–5. Note that the procedure here is not described as a 'guilt-offering'.

5. *when he offers:* these words are not in the Hebrew, and the phrase could equally well be rendered, as in the Revised Version, 'in the day of his being found guilty' (cp. 4: 23, 28). In fact the guilt-offering is never said to be 'offered': the neutral word 'bring' is alone used (cp. 5: 15, 18; 6: 6).

6. Only after restitution has been made to the aggrieved party does the guilt-offering proper appear. A wrong action

involves not only fellow-men, but God also (cp. the comment on verses 2–3). This idea is probably the product of the developed theology of priestly circles and the *ram* originally had no part in the procedure for dealing with the offences listed in verses 2–3. Even so, the animal is still essentially a due for the priests, and the equivalent of a fine, as the phrase *valued by you* (cp. 5: 15) shows. ✳

INSTRUCTIONS FOR THE PRIESTS

✳ Because the regulations in the section 6: 8 – 7: 21 are addressed to 'Aaron and his sons' (6: 8, 24), they are probably later than the material so far considered, from a time when the priestly hierarchy after the exile was definitely organized and established: there are other details in them which point in the same direction. They are, however, loosely linked with what has gone before, since they furnish further prescriptions about the ritual to be followed in the case of the different sacrifices already listed. What is distinctive about them is that they are concerned almost exclusively with the ritual actions of the priests or with detailing the portions of the various sacrifices which went to them as food. The only partial exception is in the case of the shared-offering (7: 11–21): as has been seen, this was the only sacrifice which could be eaten by the ordinary worshipper and so here directions are given as to how he should do this.

8,[a] 9 The LORD spoke to Moses and said, Give this command to Aaron and his sons: This is the law of the whole-offering. The whole-offering shall remain on the altar-hearth all night till morning, and the altar-fire shall be
10 kept burning there. Then the priest, having donned his linen robe and put on linen drawers to cover himself, shall remove the ashes to which the fire reduces the whole-

[a] *6: 1 in Heb.*

offering on the altar and put them beside the altar. He 11
shall then change into other garments and take the ashes
outside the camp to a ritually clean place. The fire shall 12
be kept burning on the altar; it shall never go out. Every
morning the priest shall have fresh wood burning thereon,
arrange the whole-offering on it, and on top burn the fat
from the shared-offerings. Fire shall always be kept burn- 13
ing on the altar; it shall not go out.

This is the law of the grain-offering. The Aaronites 14
shall present it before the LORD in front of the altar. The 15
priest shall set aside a handful of the flour from it, with
the oil of the grain-offering, and all the frankincense on
it. He shall burn this token of it on the altar as a soothing
odour to the LORD. The remainder Aaron and his sons 16
shall eat. It shall be eaten in the form of unleavened cakes
and in a holy place. They shall eat it in the court of the
Tent of the Presence. It shall not be baked with leaven. I 17
have allotted this to them as their share of my food-
offerings. Like the sin-offering and the guilt-offering, it is
most sacred. Any male descendant of Aaron may eat it, 18
as a due from the food-offerings to the LORD, for generation after generation for all time. Whatever touches them
is to be forfeit as sacred.

The LORD spoke to Moses and said: This is the offering 19, 20
which Aaron and his sons shall present to the LORD:[a] one
tenth of an ephah of flour, the usual grain-offering, half
of it in the morning and half in the evening. It shall be 21
cooked with oil on a griddle; you shall bring it well-
mixed, and so present it crumbled[b] in small pieces as a

[a] *Prob. rdg.; Heb. adds* on the day when he is anointed.
[b] *Heb. word of uncertain mng.*

22 grain-offering, a soothing odour to the LORD. The anointed priest in the line of Aaron shall offer it. This is a rule binding for all time. It shall be burnt in sacrifice to

23 the LORD as a complete offering. Every grain-offering of a priest shall be a complete offering; it shall not be eaten.

24, 25   The LORD spoke to Moses and said, Speak to Aaron and his sons in these words: This is the law of the sin-offering. The sin-offering shall be slaughtered before the LORD in the place where the whole-offering is slaughtered; it is

26 most sacred. The priest who officiates shall eat of the flesh; it shall be eaten in a sacred place, in the court of the

27 Tent of the Presence. Whatever touches its flesh is to be forfeit as sacred. If any of the blood is splashed on a

28 garment, that shall be washed[a] in a sacred place. An earthenware vessel in which the sin-offering is boiled shall be smashed. If it has been boiled in a copper vessel,

29 that shall be scoured and rinsed with water. Any male of priestly family may eat of this offering; it is most sacred.

30 If, however, part of the blood is brought to the Tent of the Presence to make expiation in the holy place, the sin-offering shall not be eaten; it shall be destroyed by fire.

9. The section begins with regulations for the *whole-offering. remain on the altar-hearth all night:* a sign of late date. What is in question here is not the whole-offering of the individual worshipper, but the official daily whole-offerings, one in the morning and one in the evening, of the fully-developed ritual of the second temple (cp. Exod. 29: 38–42; Num. 28: 3–8). There was no evening whole-offering in the monarchical period (cp. 2 Kings 16: 15) nor was it envisaged during the exile (cp. Ezek. 46: 13–15) and it is the evening

[a] *So Sept.; Heb.* you shall wash.

whole-offering which is the specific concern here. This is to stay on the altar all night, so that there would always be a sacrificial offering to preserve the bond between God and his people. The altar-hearth was the uppermost ledge on which offerings were placed (cp. Ezek. 43: 15–16, although the Hebrew word is not the same as here) and it indicates a period when the altar had assumed a more elaborate form.

10. In the morning, the ashes must be removed, so that the fire should never go out (verses 12, 13). Since these are *ashes to which the fire reduces the whole-offering*, they share in the holiness of the offering and must be ritually disposed of (cp. 4: 12). So, to do this, the officiating priest must put on the clothes that were only worn in the sanctuary (cp. 16: 4). *linen drawers:* these were worn to avoid exposure of the 'private parts' of the body, as explained in Exod. 28: 42.

11. For the final disposal of the ashes outside the sanctuary, the priest must change into *other garments*. This was so that anyone he might meet on his journey would not be in danger of coming into contact with the 'holiness' of the ritual vestments (cp. Ezek. 44: 19).

12–13. *it shall never go out:* another ancient taboo, the great significance of which is emphasized by the twice-repeated command. But, for the priestly school, the reason why the fire must not be allowed to go out is that it was the same fire which had been sent from the LORD to consume the first offerings ever made on the altar (cp. the comment on 9: 24). That the idea is a later theological development is shown by the contrast with 1: 7. *arrange the whole-offering on it:* the regular morning offering. It was to be presented as soon as the remains of the evening offering had been removed, so that the altar should never be empty.

14–18. This section deals with the grain-offering from the priests' point of view. On the one hand, it adds the ritual direction, not mentioned in the layman's regulations of 2: 2, that the priests 'shall present it before the LORD in front of the altar' (verse 14). On the other hand, it expands the brief statement in 2: 3 with careful details as to how the priests are to eat their particular share (verses 16–18): the object here is to safeguard the holiness of the offering.

16. *unleavened cakes:* cp. the comment on 2: 11. *in a holy place:* what has once entered the sanctuary must not leave it again for the profane sphere. *the court of the Tent of the Presence:* this expansion of the preceding phrase and the whole of verse 17, which repeats what has just been said, together with the odd introduction of the first person in 17*b*, look like additions to the basic material, reflecting a more developed stage of the cultus and the particular interests of the compilers of Leviticus.

17. *Like the sin-offering and the guilt-offering:* the mention of these two sacrifices here shows that they were of particular importance for the author.

18. The point of this regulation is to safeguard the rights of what had become the sole established priesthood *for all time.* *male descendant:* the offerings had to be eaten in the sanctuary (verse 16), which no woman was allowed to enter. *forfeit as sacred:* the N.E.B. translation does not fully bring out the sense, which is made clear in verses 27–9. *Whatever* or 'whoever' – the Hebrew word can mean both (cp. the comment on 11: 24) – touches what is holy becomes holy itself, and must be ritually cleansed from the contagion, before it can be put to ordinary use again.

19. *The LORD spoke:* the fresh introduction, and the absence here of the regular formula used in this and the following section 'this is the law...' (cp. 6: 9, 14, 25; 7: 1, 11), show that verses 19–23 are a still later addendum, but they are a working-over of an older practice.

20. *Aaron and his sons:* these words have replaced, in the course of developments after the exile, the older 'anointed priest' (verse 22 and cp. the comment on 4: 3). This is the reason for the phrase in the singular, found in the Hebrew (cp. the footnote) 'on the day when he is anointed' and so this is probably the correct text: the phrase can simply mean

'as soon as he is anointed', i.e. as soon as he is installed in office. Here we have a twice-daily offering, performed by the leading priest alone (contrast the corresponding daily whole-offering, which could be performed by any priest, verse 12): in course of time, it became a supplement to the regular daily whole-offering (cp. Exod. 29: 40) but in this verse it is a ceremony in its own right.

21. The ritual follows one variant of the ordinary grain-offering (cp. 2: 5–6).

22. *a complete offering:* the major part of the grain-offering went to the priest (cp. 2: 3). This obviously could not apply in the case of a priest's own offering and this must be given entirely to God. *complete offering:* Hebrew *kālīl*, from a root meaning 'completeness'. Here, at any rate, it does not imply a distinct type of offering and the sense is well given in the Revised Version's 'it shall be wholly burnt'.

23. A priestly expansion makes it clear that the rule of verse 22 applies not only to the anointed priest but to the grain-offering of every priest.

24–30. These verses stipulate that the parts of the animal not burnt on the altar in individual sin-offerings were the priestly due: no directions are given about this in 4: 22–35, although they are for the sin-offerings of 4: 3–21 (cp. 4: 11–12, 21), which are explicitly excluded here (verse 30).

27–8. Now follow directions as to what should be done in certain eventualities which might arise in the course of eating the flesh.

27. *forfeit as sacred:* cp. the comment on verse 18. *if any of the blood is splashed on a garment:* this refers to blood which might splash on to the priest's clothes while he was draining it away (cp. 4: 7). *in a sacred place:* cp. verse 16.

28. Since the flesh of the sin-offering was 'most sacred' (verse 29), it conveyed that quality to everything it came into contact with. The smashing of an *earthenware vessel* was not so much to destroy it as to release the dangerous power it had come to contain. A *copper vessel* was difficult to smash – and

perhaps too costly to put out of use – and therefore had to be cleaned as thoroughly as possible.

29. If the officiating priest, to whom the flesh of the sin-offering rightly belonged (verse 26), had more than he could manage, then *Any male of priestly family* could eat it (cp. the comment on verse 18). ✻

RULES FOR PRIESTS AND LAYMEN

7 1,2 This is the law of the guilt-offering: it is most sacred. The guilt-offering shall be slaughtered in the place where the whole-offering is slaughtered, and its blood shall be flung 3 against the altar all round. The priest shall set aside and present all the fat from it: the fat-tail and the fat covering 4 the entrails, the two kidneys with the fat on them beside the haunches, and the long lobe of the liver with the 5 kidneys. The priest shall burn these pieces on the altar as 6 a food-offering to the LORD; it is a guilt-offering. Any male of priestly family may eat it. It shall be eaten in a 7 sacred place; it is most sacred. There is one law for both sin-offering and guilt-offering: they shall belong to the 8 priest who performs the rite of expiation. The skin of any man's whole-offering shall belong to the priest who 9 presents it. Every grain-offering baked in an oven and everything that is cooked in a pan or on a griddle shall 10 belong to the priest who presents it. Every grain-offering, whether mixed with oil or dry, shall be shared equally among all the Aaronites.

11   This is the law of the shared-offering presented to the 12 LORD. If a man presents it as a thank-offering, then, in addition to the thank-offering, he shall present unleavened cakes mixed with oil, wafers of unleavened flour smeared

with oil, and well-mixed flour and flat cakes mixed with
oil. He shall present flat cakes of leavened bread in 13
addition to his shared thank-offering. One part of every 14
offering he shall present as a contribution for the LORD:
it shall belong to the priest who flings the blood of the
shared-offering against the altar. The flesh shall be eaten 15
on the day of its presentation; none of it shall be put aside
till morning.

If a man's sacrifice is a votive offering or a freewill 16
offering, it may be eaten on the day it is presented or on
the next day.*a* Any flesh left over on the third day shall 17
be destroyed by fire. If any flesh of his shared-offering is 18
eaten on the third day, the man who has presented it shall
not be accepted. It will not be counted to his credit, it
shall be reckoned as tainted and the person who eats any
of it shall accept responsibility. No flesh which comes into 19
contact with anything unclean shall be eaten; it shall be
destroyed by fire.

The flesh may be eaten by anyone who is clean, but the 20
person who, while unclean, eats flesh from a shared-
offering presented to the LORD shall be cut off from his
father's kin. When any person is contaminated by contact 21
with anything unclean, be it man, beast, or reptile,*b* and
then eats any of the flesh from the shared-offerings presented to the LORD, that person shall be cut off from his
father's kin.

* 1–7. Here the guilt-offering has become identical with the
sin-offering (verse 7), so that it is impossible to see any
difference between them. This, again, is evidence of a later

[a] *So Sept.; Heb. adds* and the rest of it shall be eaten.
[b] *So some MSS.; others* noxious thing.

development. Hence it was necessary to set out the full ritual details (verses 2–6), not usual elsewhere in 6: 8 – 7: 21, which are in fact those properly belonging to the sin-offering, because these were not given in 5: 14 – 6: 7, where the guilt-offering is viewed very differently from the way it is in this section.

6–7. The passage returns to the primary concern of 6: 8 – 7: 21, the priest's share of the offerings. *Any male of priestly family...the priest who performs the rite:* the same contrast as in the sin-offering (cp. 6: 26, 29).

8–10. Miscellaneous regulations, unconnected with the foregoing and which interrupt the order of the section (cp. the comment on 6: 19), probably taken from a comprehensive list detailing the priest's share of each sacrifice.

8. The *skin* of the *whole-offering* was the perquisite only of the officiating priest.

9. The category of *grain-offering* listed in 2: 4–10 belongs to the officiating priest (contrast 2: 10).

10. On the other hand, the *grain-offering* of untreated flour and the *dry* grain-offering, which refers to 5: 11, belong to all the Aaronite priests. As has been seen, the mention of the *Aaronites* suggests a later development (cp. the comment on 6: 20). Probably the baked or roasted grain-offering is the more original form, since this was the way ordinary food was prepared in Palestine, and thus for it the old regulation that it should go simply to the officiating priest was retained.

11–19. These verses give supplementary directions about the shared-offering according to various purposes for which it could be offered, as an act of thanksgiving (verse 12), in fulfilment of a vow or completely voluntarily (verse 16).

12. *a thank-offering:* although none of the terms just mentioned contains any idea of 'offering' in the Hebrew, it seems likely that the thank-offering at least was originally a distinct rite, which has been subsumed under the shared-offering by the assimilating tendency of Leviticus. Shared-offerings and thank-offerings appear side by side in 2 Chron. 33: 16 and 29:

31 (where the 'sacrifices' of N.E.B. mean 'shared-offerings') and the thank-offering is found on its own in Pss. 107: 22; 116: 17. This view is further supported by the special grain-offerings which accompany the thank-offering and which are quite different from the grain-offering which was associated with the regular shared-offering (cp. Num. 15: 8–9).

13. *flat cakes of leavened bread:* it is not said that these, or the 'cakes' and 'wafers' of verse 12, were burnt on the altar. They were probably treated as the firstfruits of 2: 12 and so there is no contradiction with 2: 11. But *leavened bread* indicates an older practice than the unleavened items of verse 12, since it was the way ordinary bread was prepared.

14. *as a contribution:* a technical term, *terūmāh* (cp. 7: 32), meaning a part that was 'lifted off' the rest of the offering to be ritually presented to God. But it was not conveyed to him by fire and went to the officiant: the rest was eaten by the worshipper.

15. *none of it shall be put aside till morning:* a very old taboo, characteristic of the archaic ritual of the Passover (cp. Exod. 12: 10). It is no doubt demanded by the idea that night is the time when evil powers are abroad, who might themselves eat the holy flesh.

16. By contrast, the so-called *votive offering* and *freewill offering* seem to be not distinctive rites, but simply occasions on which sacrifices could be offered. They always go together as here in Leviticus (cp. 22: 18, 21, 23; 23: 38) and the whole Hebrew expression probably means just 'required or voluntary': it should be noted that they could consist of whole-offerings as well as shared-offerings (cp. 22: 18; Num. 15: 3). *or on the next day:* the requirements for eating the flesh are less strict than with the thank-offering (cp. also, for the freewill offering, 22: 23).

17. *on the third day:* among the Hebrews and many other peoples, decomposition was thought to set in after a corpse had been dead two days (cp. Hos. 6: 2; John 11: 39). So, again, we have a very ancient taboo here.

18. Failure to consume the flesh by the third day would forfeit God's acceptance of the worshipper (cp. 1: 4) and so nullify the whole purpose of the sacrifice. *It will not be counted to his credit:* to bring a sacrifice is pleasing to God because it is what he commands in his law and therefore wins the divine blessing and favour for the offerer. *reckoned as tainted:* a single Hebrew word, a technical term of the developed priestly sacrificial ritual (only here and 19: 7; Isa. 65: 4; Ezek. 4: 14). *shall accept responsibility:* an indication of the seriousness of the offence (cp. the comment on 5: 1).

19. Just as the 'holy' contaminates (cp. the comments on 6: 11, 27, 28), so does the *unclean:* they are two aspects of the same idea.

20. The thought in verse 20 is carried further. Anyone who by his own uncleanness contaminates the holy offering in fact destroys the holiness of the nation which set Israel apart as God's people. Therefore he had to be expelled from the sacred community and punished by death. That this is the meaning of the technical expression, very common in Leviticus, to be *cut off from his father's kin,* is shown by Exod. 31: 14 (cp. also the comment on 17: 4).

21. An addition to the foregoing to make clear that uncleanness in a person was not confined to the sort of cases discussed in ch. 15, but extended to contact with any unclean human or animal. Probably the primary idea is of contact with a human corpse (cp. 21: 1–3) or a dead animal (cp. ch. 11). *

MISCELLANEOUS INSTRUCTIONS FOR THE LAITY

22, 23 The LORD spoke to Moses and said, Speak to the Israelites in these words: You shall not eat the fat of any ox, 24 sheep, or goat. The fat of an animal that has died a natural death or has been mauled by wild beasts may be 25 put to any other use, but you shall not eat it. Every man who eats fat from a beast of which he has presented any part as a food-offering to the LORD shall be cut off from his father's kin.

You shall eat none of the blood, whether of bird 26 or of beast, wherever you may live. Every person who 27 eats any of the blood shall be cut off from his father's kin.

The LORD spoke to Moses and said, Speak to the Israel- 28, 29 ites in these words: Whoever comes to present a shared-offering shall set aside part of it as an offering to the LORD. With his own hands he shall bring the food-offerings to 30 the LORD. He shall also bring the fat together with the breast which is to be presented as a special gift before the LORD; the priest shall burn the fat on the altar, but 31 the breast shall belong to Aaron and his descendants. You 32 shall give the right hind-leg of your shared-offerings as a contribution for the priest; it shall be the perquisite of the 33 Aaronite who presents the blood and the fat of the shared-offering. I have taken from the Israelites the breast of the 34 special gift and the leg of the contribution made out of the shared-offerings, and have given them as a due from the Israelites to Aaron the priest and his descendants for all time. This is the portion prescribed for Aaron and his 35 descendants out of the LORD's food-offerings, appointed on the day when they were presented as priests to the LORD; and on the day when they were anointed,[a] the 36 LORD commanded that these prescribed portions should be given to them by the Israelites. This is a rule binding on their descendants for all time.

[a] *Lit.* he anointed him.

✲ These verses fall into two groups, divided by the new introductory formula at verse 28. Unlike most of the material in 6: 8 — 7: 21, they are addressed not to the priests, but to the ordinary Israelites (verses 22, 28).

23–7. Here are stated the absolute injunctions against eating the fat or the blood (cp. 3: 17 and the comments on 1: 8 and 4: 4): they have been added at this point because the penalty for their transgression was to be 'cut off from his father's kin', as in the two immediately preceding verses.

23. Only the fat of domestic animals was prohibited, because they were also the sacrificial victims (cp. verse 25 and the comment on 1: 9 (i) p. 22). Presumably the fat of wild animals could be eaten.

24. This is an addition to the basic law, dealing with the fat of domestic animals that had not been slaughtered. It goes back to the period when all slaughter was a sacrificial act (cp. the comment on 3: 1): fat that had not been actually offered to God was available for human use, but the ancient taboo against eating it remained in force.

26. By contrast, the blood of every animal could be neither eaten nor used in any way: even in the case of a wild animal, which could not be offered to God, it had to be reverently disposed of (cp. 17: 13).

28–36. This section is an instruction about two priestly dues from the shared-offering, not mentioned in verses 11–15.

30–1. (i) The *breast* is to go to all the priests as a 'special gift', a technical sacrificial term, Hebrew *tenūpāh*.

32–3. (ii) *the right hind-leg* also was a priestly due, but, in contrast to the 'special gift', it was a *contribution*, that is, it went to the officiating priest alone (cp. verse 14). The last clause of verse 33, which repeats what has just been said, is a later addition: note *Aaronite*, instead of *the priest*.

34. The solemn introduction of God's words in the first person (cp. 6: 17) suggests an attempt to authenticate an innovation: the priests were claiming a part of the shared-offering which had not originally belonged to them. There is

no mention of the special treatment of the breast and the right hind-leg in the shared-offering ritual of ch. 3. *

A CONCLUDING FORMULA

This, then, is the law of the whole-offering, the grain- 37 offering, the sin-offering, the guilt-offering, the installa- tion-offerings, and the shared-offerings, with which the 38 LORD charged Moses on Mount Sinai on the day when he commanded the Israelites to present their offerings to the LORD in the wilderness of Sinai.

* This sums up the section 6: 8 — 7: 36, for it enumerates all the sacrifices dealt with there in the same order. A possible exception is the 'installation-offerings' (cp. the comment on 8: 22–8). This may have come in from ch. 8 (cp. 8: 22, 33), which also deals with various offerings: more likely, however, it refers to 7: 35–6 and perhaps 6: 20.

38. *on Mount Sinai:* the change in setting from 1: 1 shows that 6: 8 — 7: 38 forms a self-contained section, with originally a different background from 1: 1 — 6: 7. The verse represents the distinctive theology of the priestly source (cp. p. 7). *

The hallowing and installation
of the priests

Chs. 8–10 clearly resume the main narrative framework of the priestly work from Exod. 29: 35. Exodus 25–31 consist of instructions for making the Tabernacle and inaugurating the cultus and Exodus 35–40 record how these instructions were in fact carried out. But in Exodus there is no account of how the

59

instructions for consecrating the priests in ch. 29 were put into operation: this is supplied by Lev. 8. Chs. 1–7 have been inserted into the narrative to provide the ritual directions for the sacrifices offered on the occasion of the consecration of the priests. Exodus 40 is also an insertion, for it contains elements which seem more properly in place in Leviticus, e.g. the anointing of the Tabernacle and its contents (Exod. 40: 9–11; cp. Lev. 8: 10–11) and the appearance of the glory of God (Exod. 40: 34–5; cp. Lev. 9: 23).

These chapters seem to be later than 1–7 and probably reflect conditions shortly after the end of the exile. On the one hand, there is the enhanced position of Aaron as the chief priest (cp. the comment on 4: 3) and the fact that the priesthood is confined to his descendants (cp. the comment on 1: 5). On the other hand, there is the position of Moses. It is true that in ch. 9, in accordance with the priestly outlook, his sole function is to devolve the responsibility for the sacrificial cultus upon Aaron alone. But in ch. 8 he leads the worship and consecrates the priesthood, and in this he would appear to have the same position as the old Davidic king. The relationship of Moses and Aaron here may therefore reflect the kind of relationship found in the books of Haggai and Zechariah between Joshua the high priest and Zerubbabel who has many of the features of the Davidic monarch (cp. Hag. 2: 23, the N.E.B. footnote on Zech. 6: 11–12 and especially Zech. 6: 13). It should also be noted that the account of the investiture of Joshua in Zech. 3: 1–9 has very close parallels to the consecration of Aaron in the priestly texts. That this ideal of the perfect union of royal and priestly authority was long cherished in Israel is suggested by the belief in the anointed one of Aaron and the anointed one of Israel found in some of the Dead Sea documents. *

THE INVESTITURE OF AARON AND THE PRIESTS

THE LORD SPOKE to Moses and said, 'Take Aaron and **8** 1, 2 his sons with him, the vestments, the anointing oil, the ox for a sin-offering, the two rams, and the basket of unleavened cakes, and assemble all the community at the 3 entrance to the Tent of the Presence.' Moses did as the 4 LORD had commanded him, and the community assembled at the entrance to the Tent of the Presence. He told 5 the community that this was what the LORD had commanded. He presented Aaron and his sons and washed 6 them in water. He invested Aaron with the tunic, girded 7 him with the sash, robed him with the mantle, put the ephod on him, tied it with its waist-band and fastened the ephod to him with the band. He put the breast-piece[a] on 8 him and set the Urim and Thummim in it. He then put 9 the turban upon his head and set the gold rosette as a symbol of holy dedication on the front of the turban, as the LORD had commanded him. Moses then took the 10 anointing oil, anointed the Tabernacle and all that was within it and consecrated them. He sprinkled some of the 11 oil seven times on the altar, anointing the altar, all its vessels, the basin and its stand, to consecrate them. He 12 poured some of the anointing oil on Aaron's head and so consecrated him. Moses then brought the sons of Aaron 13 forward, invested them with tunics, girded them with sashes[b] and tied their tall head-dresses on them, as the LORD had commanded him.

[a] *Or* pouch.
[b] *So Sam.; Heb.* sash.

✲ This chapter contains an account of the installation of the priesthood. In the priestly narrative, this is represented as the beginning of priesthood in Israel, but the ceremonial followed is no doubt derived from contemporary practice and would be used whenever occasion arose. It consists of at least eight distinct actions: presenting (verse 6), washing (verse 6), clothing (verses 7–13), hallowing the sanctuary (verses 10–11), three separate sacrifices (verses 14–28), a purificatory rite (verse 30), a sacred meal (verse 31), and a period of seclusion (verse 33), together with anointing in the case of Aaron (verse 12). Such collections of rites, designed to secure that nothing was omitted for the proper efficacy of the ceremony, are typical of similar occasions in the ancient Near East, especially at coronations such as those of the Egyptian Pharaohs. Thus the whole had to be performed as a unity: there is no central moment of 'consecration', beside which the other rituals can be viewed as of secondary importance.

1–3. *The LORD spoke:* this phrase indicates the beginning of a new section (cp. the comment on 6: 19). Detailed directions for the careful preparation of the objects to be used in the ceremonies are a regular feature of ancient Near Eastern ritual texts, such as that containing the ceremonial for the Babylonian New Year festival. *assemble all the community:* the presence of the people is not mentioned in either Exod. 29 or 40 and these chapters may indicate a period when they were not allowed to approach as near to the altar as is envisaged here.

6. *presented:* the priests are regarded as a sacrificial offering (cp. 1: 3 and, for a similar idea with regard to the Levites, Num. 3: 12; 8: 16). *washed them in water:* this is the first of a number of purificatory rites in this section. The heaping up of ceremonies to ensure complete ritual purity is again characteristic of ancient Near Eastern texts but also reflects the concerns of the priestly theology. As an indication of the significance of such practices, it should be noted that several of them are also found in the ritual for cleansing 'a man

suffering from a malignant skin disease' in ch. 14; for the washing, cp. 14: 8–9.

7–9. For a detailed description of the high-priestly insignia, cp. Exod. 28: 1–38. Two general points may be made:

(1) The various garments are probably those worn by the kings before the exile: such seems to be certainly the case with *the breast-piece* (or 'pouch', cp. the footnote), *the turban* and *the gold rosette*. Here is further evidence of how the high priest after the exile increasingly occupied the place of the king (cp. the comment on 4: 3). However, the priestly theology gives a distinctively Israelite and religious purpose to the clothing. Thus the *ephod* is to bring the twelve tribes before God (cp. Exod. 28: 9–10, 29) and the *rosette* preserves the holiness of the officiant (cp. Exod. 28: 36 and below).

(2) The insignia had a profound symbolic and cosmic meaning and hence great significance was attached to them in Jewish thought (cp. Wisd. of Sol. 18: 24; Ecclus. 45: 6–14): although these passages are late, they only develop much older ideas. Nor must we under-rate the tremendous impression which the wearing of splendid clothes made on the populace of the ancient world, as is shown by the description of the high priest Simeon II (cp. Ecclus. 50: 1–21 and cp. Acts 12: 21–2). *Urim and Thummim:* these were probably originally two stones for casting lots to obtain an oracle, but the expression 'the breast-piece of judgement' in Exod. 28: 30, suggests that by this time they had come to symbolize the divine justice which the high priest dispensed. *the gold rosette:* the Hebrew word means a 'flower' and seems to derive from the practices of the Egyptian monarchy, where it expressed the idea of the eternal life of the king. Here it is understood as a symbol of the high priest's consecration to his office.

10–11. *consecrated:* this means to 'make holy', that is, to create a special relationship with God, by setting the person or thing apart from the ordinary human world and by removing any contamination which would hinder such a relationship. The maintenance of holiness in the worship and the community of Israel is the dominant practical purpose of the priestly theology. Were Aaron to be consecrated in a setting that was not itself holy, such contamination would occur and so *the Tabernacle and all that was within it* had to be consecrated first. *seven times:* cp. the comment on 4: 5–7. *Tabernacle:* apparently this indicates the entire sanctuary area, including 'the court of the Tent of the Presence' (cp. 8: 16).

12. The high priest is only anointed on the head, because the head was regarded as the chief part of the body and so symbolized the entire man.

13. Aaron is the chief concern of this chapter and so the installation of *the sons of Aaron* is much more briefly described. They are consecrated simply by clothing and there is no mention of anointing: contrast the later practice in Exod. 40: 14–15.

THE SACRIFICES

14 He then brought up the ox for the sin-offering; Aaron
15 and his sons laid their hands on its head, and he slaughtered it. Moses took some of[a] the blood and put it with his finger on the horns round the altar. Thus he purified the altar, and when he had poured out the rest of the blood at the base of the altar, he consecrated it by making
16 expiation for it. He took all the fat upon the entrails, the long lobe of the liver, and the two kidneys with their fat,
17 and burnt them on the altar, but the ox, its skin, its flesh, and its offal, he destroyed by fire outside the camp, as the LORD had commanded him.

18   Moses[b] then brought forward the ram of the whole-offering; Aaron and his sons laid their hands on the ram's
19 head, and he slaughtered it. Moses flung its blood against

[a] some of: so Sept.; Heb. om.
[b] So Sept.; Heb. om.

the altar all round. He cut the ram up and burnt the head, 20
the pieces, and the suet. He washed the entrails and the 21
shins in water and burnt the whole on the altar. This was
a whole-offering, a food-offering of soothing odour to
the Lord, as the Lord had commanded Moses.

Moses then brought forward the second ram, the ram 22
for the installation of priests. Aaron and his sons laid their
hands upon its head, and he slaughtered it. Moses took 23
some of its blood and put it on the lobe of Aaron's
right ear, on his right thumb, and on the big toe of
his right foot. He then brought forward the sons of 24
Aaron, put some of the blood on the lobes of their right
ears, on their right thumbs, and on the big toes of
their right feet. He flung the rest of the blood against the
altar all round; he took the fat, the fat-tail, the fat cover- 25
ing the entrails, the long lobe of the liver, the two kidneys
with their fat, and the right leg. Then from the basket of 26
unleavened cakes before the Lord he took one unleavened
cake, one cake of bread made with oil, and one wafer, and
laid them on the fatty parts and the right leg. He put the 27
whole on the hands of Aaron and of his sons, and he[a]
presented it as a special gift before the Lord. He took it 28
from their hands and burnt it on the altar on top of the
whole-offering. This was an installation-offering, it was
a food-offering of soothing odour to the Lord.

✻ 14. The ritual for the sin-offering on this occasion broadly
follows that prescribed for the layman (cp. 4: 22–35), presumably because Aaron and his sons were not yet fully priests
since the installation ceremonies had not been completed. *he*

[a] Or, with Vulg., they.

slaughtered it: it is not clear to whom the pronoun refers. Normally, it would be expected to mean Aaron, as the principal offerer, but perhaps it indicates Moses, acting as did the kings before the exile (cp. 2 Sam. 6: 13).

15. *making expiation for it:* at first sight, it is curious that the blood makes expiation for the altar and not for the offerers. But both ideas are probably present, as is suggested by the Day of Atonement ritual in ch. 16. There the blood makes expiation for the whole community and for the sanctuary (cp. 16: 15–19) because the holy place has been defiled by 'the uncleanness of the Israelites' (16: 19). So here expiation is made both for the priests and for the altar, which was their special sphere of operation and so might be in danger of defilement by any uncleanness of theirs. The whole section thus represents another purificatory rite.

16. Cp. the comment on 3: 3–4.

17. Cp. the comment on 4: 4.

18–21. The object of *the whole-offering* is to secure the divine approval for the installation ceremony. It closely follows the directions of ch. 1, but there an ox is the usual victim (cp. 1: 3). The *ram*, and the fact that two rams are prominent in the ritual, again recalls the Day of Atonement, with its two 'he-goats' (cp. 16: 5).

22–8. This sacrifice is basically the 'shared-offering' as it had come to be combined with the 'grain-offering' (cp. p. 55). But it has two exceptional features:

(i) The sacrifice is for *the installation of priests*. The word *installation* is a technical term, *millū'īm*, meaning 'filling (i.e. of the hand)'. It enshrines the oldest Israelite idea of how a priest assumes office (cp. Judg. 17: 5, 12) where 'installed' is literally 'filled the hand of' and it simply signified his right to receive the priestly share of sacrificial offerings. The way in which this right was conveyed is shown in verses 26–7: all the offerings, except for the *fatty parts*, listed there formed the special perquisites of the priests (cp. 2: 10; 7: 32–4), and they are placed in their hands to indicate possession (cp. 7: 35–6). But because the Aaronites were not yet fully priests (cp. the comment on verse 14), they were not able to eat them on this occasion. They were, therefore, given over to God, because they primarily belonged to him and were only secondarily given by him to his priests (cp. 7: 14). No doubt this explains the anomaly of the *fatty parts* here: the burning of the fat was the distinctive task of the priest (cp. the comment on 1: 8), so it was appropriate that this should be placed in his hands at his installation to signify what he would do in the future, although, of course, on this occasion Moses does the burning since he alone has priestly functions in this chapter. *presented it as a special gift:* it has often been noted that only the breast was properly speaking *a special gift* (cp. verse 29), while the 'cakes' and the *right leg* were a 'contribution' (see the comment on 7: 28–36), and so, if it is Aaron or his sons (cp. the footnote on verse 27) who do the presenting, the correct sacrificial ritual is not observed. Another concept may thus lie behind the words and the pronoun may refer to Moses. The Hebrew is literally 'presented them' and could refer to the Aaronites, for the Levites, whose installation ceremony has much in common with that of the priests, and is perhaps derived from it, were presented to God 'as a special gift' when they were admitted to office (cp. Num. 8: 11–13).

(ii) Some of the sacrificial blood is used for another purificatory rite, which again recurs in the cleansing of 'a man suffering from a malignant skin disease' (cp. 14: 14): the rest of the blood is disposed of as in the normal 'shared-offering' (cp. 3: 8). Organs on the right side of the body are purified because, in the Old Testament, this is the side of good fortune, and *ear*, *thumb* and *big toe*, the top, middle and bottom of the human frame, symbolize that the entire person is cleansed when the purifying blood is applied to them. ✳

FURTHER INSTALLATION RITES

29 Moses then took the breast and presented it as a special gift before the LORD; it was his portion of the ram of
30 installation, as the LORD had commanded him. He took some of the anointing oil and some of the blood on the altar and sprinkled it on Aaron and his vestments, and on his sons and their vestments with him. Thus he consecrated Aaron and his vestments, and with him his sons and their vestments.

31 Moses said to Aaron and his sons, 'Boil the flesh of the ram at the entrance to the Tent of the Presence, and eat it there, together with the bread in the installation-basket, in accordance with the command: "Aaron and his sons
32 shall eat it." The remainder of the flesh and bread you
33 shall destroy by fire. You shall not leave the entrance to the Tent of the Presence for seven days, until the day which completes the period of your installation, for it
34 lasts seven days. What was done this day followed the
35 LORD's command to make expiation for you. You shall stay at the entrance to the Tent of the Presence day and night for seven days, keeping vigil to the LORD, so that you do not die, for so I was commanded.'

36 Aaron his sons did everything that the LORD had commanded through Moses.

☆ 29. An incidental note, in which Moses appears as the officiating priest and the correct ritual is performed (cp. 7: 31). If, however, as suggested above, a civil leader is envisaged, the purpose may be to indicate that he retained something of the priestly character of the kings before the exile and that, in this special case of the *ram of installation*, the priest's share properly belonged to him.

30. A further purificatory rite, with special emphasis on the consecration of the *vestments*. These too are made cultically pure and brought into the sphere of the holy. According to Exod. 29: 29–30, the vestments retained their sanctity and were to be used by successive high priests.

31. The shared-offering concluded with a sacred meal (cp. the comment on ch. 2). *in accordance with the command:* this is added to make clear that in this instance the meal consisted of the portions reserved for the priesthood, as in the case of the sin-offering (cp. 6: 29).

32. Cp. 7: 17; 19: 6.

33–5. This is the final purificatory rite. *seven days:* a probationary period of this length to make sure that all was well is a common feature in laws dealing with the removal of ritual uncleanness and again the closest parallel is with the case of 'a man suffering from a malignant skin-disease' (cp. 14: 8 and also 15: 13, 19, 28). *to make expiation:* here is a good example of the tendency of the compilers of Leviticus to subsume all rites involving sacrifice under the idea of expiation (cp. pp. 11f.). *You shall stay at the entrance to the Tent of the Presence:* 10: 7 might suggest that, as persons in a state of ritual seclusion, the Aaronites must not enter the sphere of ordinary profane life, but, in view of 14: 8, the words would seem to mean that the Aaronites must not enter the Tent of the Presence, which only priests could do, until they were ritually clean and their installation was completed. *keeping vigil to the LORD:* the translation suggests that the priests would be occupied in some kind of divine service during the seven-day period and indeed Exod. 29: 36–7 implies that the whole sacrificial complex just described was repeated on each of the seven days. But the Exodus passage is a later expansion and the Hebrew here need mean no more than 'observe the LORD's charge', that is, not to enter the holy place (cp. 18: 30; 22: 9, where the same Hebrew phrase occurs). *so that you do not die:* a frequent solemn warning in Leviticus (cp. 10: 6, 9; 15: 31; 16: 2, 13; 22: 9), generally used to stress the great

danger incurred by anyone who came into contact with the
sanctuary when in a state of ritual impurity. ✶

THE FIRST SACRIFICES FOR THE PRIESTHOOD

9 On the eighth day Moses summoned Aaron and his sons
2 and the Israelite elders. He said to Aaron, 'Take for yourself a bull-calf for a sin-offering and a ram for a whole-
offering, both without blemish, and present them before
3 the LORD. Then bid the Israelites take a he-goat for a
sin-offering, a calf and a lamb, both yearlings without
4 blemish, for a whole-offering, and a bull and a ram for
shared-offerings to be sacrificed before the LORD, together with a grain-offering mixed with oil. This day the
LORD will appear to you.'

5   They brought what Moses had commanded to the
front of the Tent of the Presence, and all the community
6 approached and stood before the LORD. Moses said, 'This
is what the LORD has commanded you to do, so that the
7 glory of the LORD may appear to you. Come near to the
altar,' he said to Aaron; 'prepare your sin-offering and
your whole-offering and make expiation for yourself and
for your household.*a* Then prepare the offering of the
people and make expiation for them, as the LORD has
commanded.'

8   So Aaron came near to the altar and slaughtered the
9 calf, which was his sin-offering. The sons of Aaron presented the blood to him, and he dipped his finger in the
blood and put it on the horns of the altar. The rest of
10 the blood he poured out at the base of the altar. Part of

[a] *So Sept.; Heb.* for the people.

the sin-offering, the fat, the kidneys, and the long lobe of the liver, he burnt on the altar as the LORD had commanded Moses, but the flesh and the skin he destroyed by fire 11 outside the camp. Then he slaughtered the whole-offering; 12 his sons handed him the blood, and he flung it against the altar all round. They handed him the pieces of the 13 whole-offering and the head, and he burnt them on the altar. He washed the entrails and the shins and burnt them 14 on the altar, on top of the whole-offering.

* After the narrative of the beginning of the priesthood in Israel, there naturally follows an account of the beginning of sacrifice. The description of the sacrifices in this chapter broadly corresponds with what is said in chs. 1–7, but there are slight differences in the terminology and ritual, some of which will be noted in the commentary, which show that the two sections were originally independent of one another. What is striking is that Aaron is virtually the sole actor in all that takes place and this is a further indication that both chs. 8 and 9 are really concerned with him (cp. the comment on 8: 13). All the authority of Moses in the cultic sphere is now transferred entirely to him. As has been seen, this represents the annexation by the high priest of the former religious role of the king (cp. the comments on verses 15 and 22). Thus this chapter is probably based on what actually occurred at the installation of each new high priest (cp. the comment on verse 17).

1–2. The sacrifices take place in the setting of a great public festival. *On the eighth day:* this, of course, was the earliest possible occasion after the end of the priestly installation, but it is perhaps significant that, in Israel's great autumn festival, the eighth day was marked by a specially important public assembly for worship (cp. 23: 36 and also 23: 16). *the Israelite elders:* cp. the comment on 4: 15. *a bull-calf:* this is a different

Hebrew word from the one used for the sin-offering of 'the anointed priest' in 4: 3. It may seem strange that Aaron has again to offer *a sin-offering* and *a whole-offering*, when he has already done so in ch. 8, but in fact such offerings to ensure the officiant's ritual holiness had to be made on every occasion of particular solemnity, cp. e.g. the Day of Atonement ritual, 16: 3.

3. *a he-goat:* according to 4: 14, the animal for the community's *sin-offering* should be a 'bull', but again it was a he-goat on the Day of Atonement (cp. 16: 15). The doubling of the victim in the case of the *whole-offering* and the *shared-offerings* is probably because these were sacrifices of the whole community, as opposed to the individual ones of chs. 1 and 3.

4. *a grain-offering mixed with oil:* since 'frankincense', is not mentioned, presumably the variety of grain-offering described in 2: 4–10 is intended. *the LORD will appear to you:* these words enshrine an ancient religious concept. The Hebrew is literally 'be seen' and the deity was thought to be present in the sanctuary to his worshippers in visible form (cp. Exod. 23: 16–17 and the N.E.B. footnote; Pss. 63: 2; 68: 24). Originally the idea was of seeing the god's statue or some similar representation of him but the concept is refined in different ways in different writings in the Old Testament: the specifically priestly concept is now introduced.

6. *the glory of the LORD:* this is what the worshippers see according to the thought of the priestly writers. In the Old Testament, the word *glory* almost always means the visible appearance of wealth and splendour which indicated a man's importance. For the priestly school, *the glory of the LORD* took the form of a fiery cloud, symbolizing the divine essence in contrast to human substance. Perhaps the clearest description of it is in Exod. 24: 15–17 (cp. also Exod. 16: 10). Most typically, it was, as here, a cultic manifestation at the entrance to the sanctuary (cp. Exod. 32:9; 40: 34–5; Num. 16: 42). The

appearance of the glory of the LORD is the real purpose and climax of the whole ceremony described in this chapter.

7. Once more, *expiation* appears here as the dominant sacrificial notion.

9. *The sons of Aaron* are merely Aaron's assistants in the ritual (cp. verses 12, 13, 18). *put it on the horns of the altar:* the reference here is to 'the altar of whole-offering' outside the Tent. Thus there is a divergence from the prescriptions for the sin-offering of 'the anointed priest' in 4: 5–7, but the reason is probably because Aaron only enters the Tent for the first time in verse 23. ✳

THE FIRST SACRIFICES FOR THE COMMUNITY

He then brought forward the offering of the people. He 15 took the he-goat, the people's sin-offering, slaughtered it and performed the rite of the sin-offering as he had previously done for himself. He presented the whole- 16 offering and prepared it in the manner prescribed. He 17 brought forward the grain-offering, took a handful of it and burnt it on the altar, in addition to the morning whole-offering. He slaughtered the bull and the ram, the 18 shared-offerings of the people. His sons handed him the blood, and he flung it against the altar all round. But 19 the fatty parts of the bull, the fat-tail of the ram, the fat covering the entrails, and the two kidneys with the fat upon them,[a] and the long lobe of the liver, all this fat they 20 first put on the breasts of the animals and then burnt it on the altar. Aaron presented the breasts and the right leg as 21 a special gift before the LORD, as Moses had commanded.

Then Aaron lifted up his hands towards the people and 22

[a] the fat covering . . . upon them: *so Sept.; Heb.* and the covering and the kidneys.

pronounced the blessing over them. He came down from
performing the rites of the sin-offering, the whole-
23 offering, and the shared-offerings. Moses and Aaron
entered the Tent of the Presence, and when they came
out, they blessed the people, and the glory of the LORD
24 appeared to all the people. Fire came out from before the
LORD and consumed the whole-offering and the fatty
parts on the altar. All the people saw, and they shouted
and fell on their faces.

* 15. *slaughtered it:* 4: 15 does not make it clear exactly who
killed the victim in the community's sin-offering, but we
should expect it to be 'the elders'. In this passage, Aaron performs the whole sacrificial action on behalf of the people,
following what had been the practice of the Israelite king on
similar important occasions (cp. 1 Sam. 13: 9–10; 1 Kings 3:
4, 15; 8: 5, 62–4; 9: 25).

17. *in addition to the morning whole-offering:* cp. the comment
on 6: 9. The words could mean one of three things:

(i) Aaron instituted the daily morning whole-offering at
the same time as the other sacrifices mentioned.

(ii) The 'whole-offering' of verse 16 is taken by the compiler of the chapter to be the morning whole-offering.

(iii) The narrative is drawn from what actually happened
at the installation of a high priest, which took place in the
morning when the regular daily sacrifice was being offered.

21. *a special gift:* cp. the comment on 8: 22–8.

22. *pronounced the blessing:* the priestly formula of blessing
is given in Num. 6: 22–7. Although this rite was reserved to
the priests after the exile, it was earlier the prerogative of the
king (cp. 2 Sam. 6: 18).

23. Aaron's installation is now complete and so he is able to
enter *the Tent of the Presence* for the first time. *they blessed the
people:* it has been claimed that this is superfluous after the

'blessing' of verse 22 and is therefore a later addition. However, it may be noted that in another inauguration ceremony,
the dedication of the temple, there was a double royal blessing
(cp. 1 Kings 8: 14, 55), and a manifestation of *the glory of the
Lord* (cp. 1 Kings 8: 10–11).

24. *Fire came out from before the LORD:* that is, *came out*
from the cloud in which was manifested 'the glory of the
LORD', which itself had the character of fire (cp. the comment
on verse 6). *consumed the whole-offering:* again this has been
said to be a secondary addition, because the sacrifices had
already been burned on the altar. But this is to be too literal
minded and what we have here is a legend of the origin of the
perpetual altar fire (cp. the comment on 6: 12–13). God's own
nature could be thought of as 'fire' (cp. Deut. 4: 24), so the
consumption of the sacrificial elements indicated his approval
and acceptance of what had been offered. By this means, the
sanctuary was inaugurated and so the priestly writers after the
exile attached a similar legend to the dedication of the temple
(cp. 1 Chron. 21: 26; 2 Chron. 7: 1; 2 Macc. 2: 10–11). But
the basic idea is a very old one (cp. Judg. 6: 21; 13: 19–20;
1 Kings 18: 38). ✳

THE SIN OF NADAB AND ABIHU

Now Nadab and Abihu, sons of Aaron, took their fire- **10**
pans, put fire in them, threw incense on the fire and
presented before the LORD illicit fire which he had not
commanded. Fire came out from before the LORD and **2**
destroyed them; and so they died in the presence of the
LORD. Then Moses said to Aaron, 'This is what the LORD **3**
meant when he said: Among those who approach me, I
must be treated as holy; in the presence of all the people
I must be given honour.' Aaron was dumbfounded.
Moses sent for Mishael and Elzaphan, the sons of Aaron's **4**

uncle Uzziel, and said to them, 'Come and carry your cousins outside the camp away from the holy place.' 5 They came and carried them away in their tunics outside 6 the camp, as Moses had told them. Moses then said to Aaron and to his sons Eleazar and Ithamar, 'You shall not leave your hair dishevelled or tear your clothes in mourning, lest you die and the LORD be angry with the whole community. Your kinsmen, all the house of Israel, shall weep for the destruction by fire which the LORD has 7 kindled. You shall not leave the entrance to the Tent of the Presence lest you die, because the LORD's anointing oil is on you.' They did as Moses had said.

* On p. 16, it was pointed out that during the exile priestly groups from various Israelite sanctuaries congregated at Jerusalem and became united by being given a common descent from Aaron. The present passage, although its date and background cannot be precisely determined, shows, however, that this situation was not reached without bitter controversy and that not all priests who claimed Aaronite descent were ultimately admitted into the priesthood. After the exile, the priesthood came to be thought of as confined to the descendants of the two younger sons of Aaron, Eleazar and Ithamar, while his two elder sons, Nadab and Abihu, were punished for a cultic sin and died leaving no issue (cp. Num. 3: 2–4; 26: 60–1; 1 Chron. 24: 1–2, all of which depend on this passage in Leviticus). The verses here, then, constitute what is known as an aetiological tale, that is, a narrative which gives the reason why and how a contemporary situation has come about. As the very similar story in Num. 16 shows, there was an existing tale of the dire punishment of a group within the temple ministry, which was adapted to fit various situations of conflict; compare Num. 16: 7, 17–18 with Lev. 10: 1 and Num. 16: 35 with Lev. 10: 2.

The actual situation behind the passage, therefore, is that of the exile or shortly after. But these verses owe their present position in the setting of the first priestly installation ceremony to two factors. On the one hand, there is an obvious link between the identical phrase 'Fire came out from before the LORD' in verse 2 and 9: 24. On the other hand, the compilers of Leviticus wished to stress that the constitution of the priesthood as they knew it in their day had been the same from its first beginning and that only one particular group had ever in fact belonged to it.

1. *presented before the LORD illicit fire:* in Num. 16, the offering of incense indicates the pretensions of a non-priestly group to the priesthood (cp. Num. 16: 8–10). The point is different here, because Nadab and Abihu are priests (cp. the comment on verse 5). What was wrong was that their offering was *illicit*. As the words *which he had not commanded* show, the meaning is of something not legally correct, with special reference to the command in Exod. 30: 9, where the N.E.B's 'unauthorized' translates the same Hebrew word. However, the basic meaning of the term seems to be 'foreign', cp. the N.E.B's 'alien' in Isa. 43: 12 for the same Hebrew word, and so perhaps Nadab and Abihu are pictured as guilty of introducing a ritual characteristic of a non-Israelite religion: we may compare how, according to Ezek. 44: 9–14, the Levites were demoted from the priesthood for their idolatry. The offering of incense was an important element in Israel's worship and detailed directions for its preparation are given in Exod. 30: 34–8.

3. Into the mouth of Moses is put a piece of priestly teaching to instruct the people in the purpose of sanctuary worship (cp. the comment on 9: 4, on the presence of God in the sanctuary). It is in rhythmical form, perhaps to make it easy to remember. The immediate reference here is to the divine appearance in verse 2 (cp. the comment on 9: 24).

dumbfounded: the word probably means 'rooted to the spot' from terror at what he had witnessed.

4. *Mishael and Elzaphan:* according to 21: 1–4, a priest was only permitted to prepare for burial the corpse of 'a near blood-relation', but the high-priest could not come into contact with any dead body at all (21: 10–12). Presumably Eleazar and Ithamar (verse 6), as Aaron's successors, are considered to belong to the high-priestly circle. Mishael and Elzaphan were not sufficiently closely related to the deceased to be covered by the exemption in 21: 2–3, so no doubt they were thought of as young men, not yet old enough to be installed as priests. *outside the camp away from the holy place:* a corpse was a potent source of defilement, so it must be removed both from the sanctuary and from the holy community.

5. *in their tunics:* in the light of 8: 13, this phrase indicates that Nadab and Abihu had been invested as priests.

6–7. For the prohibitions in these verses, cp. 21: 10, 12. *the LORD be angry with the whole community:* cp. the comment on 4: 3. *You shall not leave the entrance to the Tent of the Presence:* in 21: 12 there is a general prohibition on the high priest's leaving the sanctuary to participate in a funeral. The changed wording here refers back to 8: 33–5, and so places the whole episode on the occasion of the installation of the first priests. ✲

MISCELLANEOUS COMMANDS FOR THE PRIESTS

8, 9 The LORD spoke to Aaron and said: You and your sons with you shall not drink wine or strong drink when you are to enter the Tent of the Presence, lest you die. This is
10 a rule binding on your descendants for all time, to make a distinction between sacred and profane, between clean
11 and unclean, and to teach the Israelites all the decrees which the LORD has spoken to them through Moses.

12 Moses said to Aaron and his surviving sons Eleazar and Ithamar, 'Take what is left over of the grain-offering out of the food-offerings of the LORD, and eat it without

leaven beside the altar; it is most sacred. You shall eat it 13 in a sacred place; it is your due and that of your sons out of the LORD's food-offerings, for so I was commanded. You shall eat the breast of the special gift and the leg of 14 the contribution in a clean place, you and your sons and daughters; for they have been given to you and your children as your due out of the shared-offerings of the Israelites. The leg of the contribution and the breast of 15 the special gift shall be brought, along with the food-offerings of fat, to be presented as a special gift before the LORD, and it shall belong to you and your children together, a due for all time; for so the LORD has commanded.'

Moses made searching inquiry about the goat of the 16 sin-offering and found that it had been burnt. He was angry with Eleazar and Ithamar, Aaron's surviving sons, and said, 'Why did you not eat the sin-offering in the 17 sacred place? It is most sacred. It was given to you to take away the guilt of the community by making expiation for them before the LORD. If the blood is not brought 18 within the sacred precincts, you shall eat the sin-offering there as I was commanded.' But Aaron replied to Moses, 19 'See, they have today presented their sin-offering and their whole-offering before the LORD, and this is what has befallen me; if I eat a sin-offering today, will it be right in the eyes of the LORD?' When Moses heard this, he 20 deemed it right.

✶ This passage falls into three sections, each originally quite independent, which have been loosely attached to the narrative of the installation of the priests.

8–11. A connection is made with the immediately pre-ceding section by the link-words *Tent of the Presence* and *lest you die*, verse 9. *wine or strong drink:* that is, the produce of the vine and beer made from grain. The original purpose of this prohibition was because of the use of such intoxicating drinks in Canaanite religion (cp. Judg. 9: 27): we may compare the similar abstension of the 'Rechabites', a group that deliber-ately rejected the civilization of Canaan (cp. Jer. 35: 5–8). But, in the priestly theology, it has become a mark of someone who is set apart as holy, as in the case of the 'Nazirite' (cp. Num. 6: 1–8) or John the Baptist (cp. Luke 1: 15). Priests are always in this condition, so for them the command is *a rule binding on your descendants for all time*. It is a sign of the *dis-tinction between sacred and profane*, a distinction which, in priestly thought, is built into the whole structure of nature and society, as will be seen in later chapters. Because this is so, the priests have a duty to instruct the whole nation about the *decrees* which ensure that this vital distinction is properly observed. We see here that the priest was not only a cultic officiant but that he always had an important teaching office as well (cp. Deut. 33: 10).

12–15. The present context of this section may be deter-mined by verses 12–13: in the account of the first grain-offering in 9: 17, nothing is said about what should happen to *what is left over of the grain-offering* and so the lack is now supplied on the basis of the directions in 6: 16–17. Verses 14–15 are probably additional priestly directions, in answer to the question: 'what are the priests to do with their special perquisite of the shared-offerings?' (cp. the comment on 7: 28–36). *daughters: the special gift* and the *contribution* did not have the same degree of sanctity as the *grain-offering*, which was *most sacred* (cp. the comment on 2: 10), and could be eaten only by males.

16–20. This passage probably owes its position here to the mention of the somewhat unusual 'he-goat' in 9: 3, 15 (cp. the comment on 9: 3). In fact, we have here an example of a common way in which law was transmitted in Israel. This was by means of a story, telling how some knotty problem had been resolved by a great figure in the past, whose decision thereafter became a precedent when similar difficulties arose on later occasions (cp. 24: 10–23; Num. 9: 6–14; 1 Sam. 30: 21–5). Unfortunately, what really is meant by the existing narrative is not wholly clear. Perhaps the underlying problem is this: how should *the goat of the sin-offering* be treated on special occasions such as the installation of priests or the Day of Atonement (cp. the comment on 9: 3), when it was a community offering, but otherwise an individual offering? Moses appears to hold that it should always be regarded as an individual offering: in this case, it should have been eaten by the priests, because *the blood is not brought within the sacred precincts* (cp. 4: 22–6; 6: 30). Aaron may be saying that it should be regarded as a community sin-offering, in which case some of the blood was brought into the Tent of the Presence (cp. 4: 16–18), and so the animal could not be eaten by the priests. The obscure statement in verse 19 may originally have meant that the high priest, on these special occasions, acted as the community's representative and therefore shared in their sin-offering: so he could not himself eat it. But, as the text stands, *this is what has befallen me* is probably to be understood to refer to 10: 1–7: Aaron is saying that, after the disaster that had befallen his family because of an incorrect ritual, to perform further cultic actions at this time would be too dangerous. If the interpretation suggested above is correct, verse 20 would imply that Aaron's interpretation was *deemed right* by Moses and thus would become the rule for the future. *

Laws of purification and atonement

* Following upon the installation of the priests, chs. 11–16 are largely made up of examples of directions to the people on how to preserve that 'distinction between sacred and profane', which was the specific priestly concern (cp. the comment on 10: 8–11). In these chapters, it is constantly stressed that the matter at issue is 'ritual' cleanness or uncleanness: the object of the priestly teaching is to ensure that men are in the right condition to take part in the cultic worship which maintained the bond between the holy God and his holy community (cp. particularly 15: 31). Hence we have here different collections of originally oral instructions, a kind of preaching in fact, given by priests at various sanctuaries. But, in line with the systematizing tendency of the compilers of Leviticus, all this diverse material has been unified and ordered and given a common theological interpretation: we can also trace a continuing process of expansion and definition in the course of the priestly transmission of this body of teaching, which leads up to the great elaboration of the purity laws characteristic of later Rabbinical writings. Thus ch. 11 deals with the basic pattern of clean and unclean running through all creation, ch. 12 is concerned with the same question at childbirth, the beginning of human life, chs. 13–15 list various situations which cause impurity for individuals and society, while ch. 16 describes the all-embracing ceremony which annually removed every trace of uncleanness from the entire nation and so renewed its right relationship with God. The whole is made into a legal code by a succession of summaries which provide the basic framework (cp. 11: 46–7; 12: 7*b*; 13: 59; 14: 54–7; 15: 32–3; 16: 29–34).

The original material of these chapters is very old and expresses ancient religious concepts which it is very difficult for us either to recover or to understand. Nor is it easy to say how far these concepts were still alive for those who compiled Leviticus. In later Judaism, the purity laws were thought of as binding merely because they had been commanded by God. But in Leviticus uncleanness is certainly a concrete and dangerous reality, indicating the presence of something fundamentally wrong, which is why the priestly writers do not draw the clear distinction between ritual impurity and moral sin which comes so naturally to us. *

CLEAN AND UNCLEAN BEASTS

THE LORD SPOKE to Moses and Aaron and said, Speak **11** 1, 2 to the Israelites in these words: Of all animals on land these are the creatures you may eat: you may eat any animal which has a parted foot or a cloven hoof and also chews the cud; those which have only a cloven hoof or 4 only chew the cud you may not eat. These are: the camel, because it chews the cud but has not a cloven hoof; you shall regard it as unclean; the rock-badger,[a] because it 5 chews the cud but has not a parted foot; you shall regard it as unclean; the hare, because it chews the cud but has 6 not a parted foot; you shall regard it as unclean; the pig, 7 because it has a parted foot and a cloven hoof but does not chew the cud; you shall regard it as unclean. You 8 shall not eat their flesh or even touch their dead bodies; you shall regard them as unclean.

* As has been seen, ch. 11 is made up of different units, and thus there is some degree of repetition and inconsistency. Nevertheless, a single clear idea can be traced behind all the regulations. The division between clean and unclean creatures is not made on hygienic grounds or because certain animals

[a] *Or* rock-rabbit.

were considered to have peculiarly repulsive habits. Nor does it seem likely that the creatures regarded as impure were sacred animals in non-Israelite cults, for while this is true of some of them (e.g. the 'pig', verse 7), it does not seem to be so of others (e.g. the 'small creatures in shoals', verse 10, or the reptiles of verses 29–30). Rather, ritual purity, as will be seen, involves completeness or perfection. This in turn means being a perfect specimen of the category of being to which one belongs: if the characteristics of another category are taken on, this brings imperfection and confusion and the proper order of the world is destroyed. The infringement of the proper order of being seems to be the reason for the difference between clean and unclean creatures here: the unclean animals are those which display the characteristics of a species other than their own. Behind this idea is the priestly doctrine of creation as found in Gen. 1. There God creates by making a distinction or separation between the different parts of the universe, 'the vault of heaven', 'the waters of the seas' and 'the earth', and by assigning creatures with appropriate characteristics to each part, birds, fish and animals. Any creature which seems to diverge from its proper nature or proper sphere is therefore lacking in perfection and so 'unclean'.

In verses 1–22, the criterion of cleanness and uncleanness is whether or not a particular animal may be eaten. Hence the norm is the domestic animals which were bred for food in the semi-nomadic society of ancient Israel and so these are mentioned first.

3. *any animal which has a parted foot or a cloven hoof and also chews the cud:* this description characterizes the beasts normally kept by the Israelites, and such animals were thought of as in a sense part of the community. They alone provided the sacrificial victims (cp. the general direction in 1: 2), their 'first-born' were treated in the same ways as those of men (cp. Exod. 22: 29–30) and, in the priestly expansion of the sabbath commandment, the same prohibition applies equally to human beings and domestic animals (cp. Exod. 20: 10). Wild animals,

of course, are also presupposed in this verse (cp. Deut. 14: 4–5), but only those which had the same characteristics as domestic animals and so were fit for eating. *or a cloven hoof:* a better translation would be 'and a cloven hoof'. Verses 7 and 26 show that all three features must be present.

4–7. This section is an expansion of the foregoing regulation, developed in the course of priestly teaching, to answer the question: 'what about animals which have one or more of the characteristics prescribed but not all?' Such creatures are not complete, from the standpoint of suitability for eating and so, in this context, are *unclean*. The *rock-badger* and the *hare* do not in fact 'chew the cud' but the constant grinding of their teeth made it appear that they did so.

8. *touch their dead bodies:* a further expansion, which really belongs to the section beginning with verse 24. Its introduction here is the work of the compilers. ✶

CLEAN AND UNCLEAN WATER CREATURES, BIRDS AND INSECTS

Of creatures that live in water these you may eat: all those 9 that have fins and scales, whether in salt water or fresh; but all that have neither fins nor scales, whether in salt or 10 fresh water, including both small creatures in shoals and larger creatures, you shall regard as vermin. They shall 11 be vermin to you; you shall not eat their flesh, and their dead bodies you shall treat as those of vermin. Every 12 creature in the water that has neither fins nor scales shall be vermin to you.

These are the birds you shall regard as vermin, and for 13 this reason they shall not be eaten: the griffon-vulture,[a] the black vulture, and the bearded vulture;[b] the kite and 14 every kind of falcon; every kind of crow,[c] the desert-owl, 15 16

[a] *Or* eagle.   [b] *Or* ossifrage.   [c] *Or* raven.

the short-eared owl, the long-eared owl, and every kind
17 of hawk; the tawny owl, the fisher-owl, and the screech-
18, 19 owl; the little owl, the horned owl, the osprey, the stork,[a]
every kind of cormorant, the hoopoe, and the bat.

20 All teeming winged creatures that go on four legs shall
21 be vermin to you, except those which have legs jointed
22 above their feet for leaping on the ground. Of these you
may eat every kind of great locust, every kind of long-
headed locust, every kind of green locust, and every kind
23 of desert locust. Every other teeming winged creature
24 that has four legs you shall regard as vermin; you would
make yourselves unclean with them: whoever[b] touches
25 their dead bodies shall be unclean till evening. Whoever
picks up their dead bodies shall wash his clothes but
remain unclean till evening.

* 9–12. These verses deal with water creatures.

9. *fins and scales:* these are the proper characteristics for
living and moving in aquatic conditions. Creatures that do not
possess them are therefore imperfect.

10. *small creatures in shoals and larger creatures:* the distinction
corresponds to that between 'all living creatures that move
and swarm in the waters' and 'the great sea-monsters' of
Gen. 1: 21. *vermin:* a different term is used here and in the
following verses for animals that may not be eaten from that
employed in verses 1–8, where the word is 'unclean'. This
suggests that verses 9–23 originally formed an independent
block of material.

13–19. The reason for the distinction between birds is more
difficult to discover. Partly this is because it is not easy to
identify all of them, as the N.E.B. footnotes indicate: about
half of the names occur only here in the Old Testament. But

[a] Or heron. [b] Or whatever.

also, in contrast to verses 3 and 9, there are no clear physical characteristics given to separate the birds that may be eaten from those which may not. It may be observed, however, that all of the latter seem to be birds of prey or eaters of carrion. Perhaps it was considered that birds should feed only in their proper sphere, 'the vault of heaven' (cp. the comment on II: 1–8): those that ate creatures of the land or, as with e.g. the cormorant, of the waters, went outside their true element and so must be classed as 'vermin'.

19. *the bat:* the inclusion of the bat among the birds shows that the lists of creatures do not rest on any 'scientific' knowledge.

20–5. These verses deal with insects.

20. *teeming:* this word includes all creatures that are not clearly animals, birds or fishes, whether on land or in water: in verse 10, 'in shoals' translates this same Hebrew term. They are characterized by their small size and indeterminate movement. *winged creatures that go on four legs:* the standard is the 'animals on land' of verse 2. Any creature that has four legs ought to walk on the ground as they do: if it also has wings and flies it is trespassing on another sphere of existence.

21. Some such creatures, however, have *legs jointed,* so that they can hop along the ground and this allows them to qualify.

22. Locusts are of this kind and thus may be eaten. In fact, locusts, like all other insects, have six legs. But the Hebrews regarded the two hind legs, which are longer and stronger than the others, as separate limbs and did not include them in the number of legs.

24–5. The second half of verse 24 introduces a fresh section which continues to verse 40. It is concerned not with the prohibition of eating certain creatures but with the uncleanness that results from contact with them. Here touching the *dead bodies* of *vermin* makes a person *unclean* and the concept of impurity is given a further dimension. Death destroys the proper order of things, which, for the Hebrew, is life (cp. Gen. 2: 7): so a corpse brings physical defilement, in just the same way as the diseases dealt with in chs. 13–15 (cp. Num. 5: 2). Contact with a human corpse meant being unclean for a week (cp. Num. 19: 11, 16), but with an animal the case was less serious and the uncleanness lasted only until the beginning of the succeeding day, since the Hebrews began their day at sundown. *whoever:* the fact that the case of a person touching the dead bodies of unclean creatures is dealt with in the following verses suggests that the N.E.B. footnote is to be preferred here (cp. verses 26, 27, 31–2, 36). *wash his clothes:* a regular purificatory ritual that occurs frequently in the following chapters (cp. the comment on 8: 6). In Hebrew thought a man's *clothes* were considered to be virtually part of his person (cp. 2 Kings 2: 13–15). ✳

FURTHER LISTS OF UNCLEAN CREATURES
AND MISCELLANEOUS REGULATIONS

26 You shall regard as unclean every animal which has a parted foot but has not a cloven hoof and does not chew
27 the cud: whoever[a] touches them shall be unclean. You shall regard as unclean all four-footed wild animals that go on flat paws; whoever[a] touches their dead bodies shall
28 be unclean till evening. Whoever takes up their dead bodies shall wash his clothes but remain unclean till evening. You shall regard them as unclean.

29   You shall regard these as unclean among creatures that teem on the ground: the mole-rat,[b] the jerboa, and every
30 kind of thorn-tailed lizard; the gecko, the sand-gecko, the
31 wall-gecko, the great lizard, and the chameleon. You shall regard these as unclean among teeming creatures; whoever[a] touches them when they are dead shall be un-
32 clean till evening. Anything on which any of them falls

[a] *Or* whatever.   [b] *Or* weasel.

when they are dead shall be unclean, any article of wood or garment or skin or sacking, any article in regular use; it shall be plunged into water but shall remain unclean till evening, when it shall be clean. If any of these falls into 33 an earthenware vessel, its contents shall be unclean and it shall be smashed. Any food on which water from such a 34 vessel is poured shall be unclean, and any drink in such a vessel shall be unclean. Anything on which the dead body 35 of such a creature falls shall be unclean; an oven or a stove shall be broken, for they are unclean and you shall treat them as such; but a spring or a cistern where water 36 collects shall remain clean, though whatever*a* touches the dead body shall be unclean. When any of their dead 37 bodies falls on seed intended for sowing, it remains clean; but if the seed has been soaked in water and any dead 38 body falls on it, you shall treat it as unclean.

When any animal allowed as food dies, all that touch 39 the carcass shall be unclean till evening. Whoever eats any 40 of the carcass shall wash his clothes but remain unclean till evening; whoever takes up the carcass shall wash his clothes and be unclean till evening. All creatures that 41 teem on the ground are vermin; they shall not be eaten. All creatures that teem on the ground, crawl on their 42 bellies, go on all fours or have many legs, you shall not eat, because they are vermin which contaminate. You 43 shall not contaminate yourselves through any teeming creature. You shall not defile yourselves with them and make yourselves unclean by them. For I am the LORD 44 your God; you shall make yourselves holy and keep yourselves holy, because I am holy. You shall not defile

[a] *Or* whoever.

yourselves with any teeming creature that creeps on the
45 ground. I am the LORD who brought you up from Egypt
to become your God. You shall keep yourselves holy,
because I am holy.

46   This, then, is the law concerning beast and bird, every
living creature that swims in the water and every living
47 creature that teems on the land. It is to make a distinction
between the unclean and the clean, between living
creatures that may be eaten and living creatures that may
not be eaten.

✻ 26. The fact that this verse repeats, but in a negative form
and with reference to touching, the provisions of verse 3,
indicates that it comes from an originally separate collection.
whoever touches them: this might seem to imply 'touches them,
whether they are dead or not' and so be stricter than similar prohibitions elsewhere in the chapter. But perhaps the compiler is
summarizing and presupposes the fuller regulations in verse 24.

27. *that go on flat paws:* on this translation, presumably
animals are meant which do not have 'a parted foot or a cloven
hoof', and so the phrase would be repeating what has just been
said in different language (the word *wild* is not in the Hebrew).
Possibly, however, a distinct class of animals is intended. The
Hebrew word rendered by *flat paws* means literally 'the palm
of the hand': it is used of animals only here in the Old Testament. Perhaps, then, the idea is of animals such as monkeys,
whose front feet appeared to have the form of hands but who
used them for walking and not for their proper purpose. Thus
they would be acting unnaturally and so be *unclean*.

29–30. The precise significance of this list is difficult to
determine because it is again far from clear which particular
creatures are being mentioned. But it may be intended to
amplify verse 27: these animals and reptiles all seemed to have
hands in place of forefeet.

There follows a typical series of casuistic expansions of the basic regulations to deal with cases of special difficulty. Basically, the aim seems to be to distinguish between those objects which were impregnated with uncleanness and those which were not, but there is also the aim of ensuring that uncleanness did not unduly affect what was necessary for the maintenance of life.

32. So *any article in regular use* is only temporarily unclean and eventually becomes clean if it is *plunged into water* (cp. verse 25).

33. By contrast, a porous *earthenware vessel* was considered to become impregnated with uncleanness and so must be destroyed (cp. the comment on 6: 28).

34. For obvious reasons, liquids in particular would be considered to soak up uncleanness and thus be especially dangerous.

35. *an oven or a stove:* these were made of burnt clay, so the principle of verse 33 applies.

36. *a spring or a cistern:* two considerations seem to be present here:

(i) with a spring, the water is always flowing or fresh and cistern can also be translated as 'well', where too the water is continually renewed (cp. Jer. 6: 7, where the same Hebrew word as here is used). So the taint of uncleanness would rapidly be removed.

(ii) an adequate water supply was essential for life in Palestine: this must not be endangered and so the operation of uncleanness is restricted (cp. the comment above).

whatever: probably we should prefer the N.E.B. footnote. The man who removed *the dead body* from the water was unclean, following the provisions of verse 28.

37. *seed intended for sowing:* again, the need to preserve the essentials of life limits the application of the principle of uncleanness.

38. *soaked in water:* cp. the comment on verse 34.

39–40. These verses deal with a domestic animal which has not been slaughtered but 'has died a natural death' (cp. the comment on 7: 24). The bringing together of the prohibitions of 'touching', 'eating' and 'taking up', which originally had separate backgrounds (cp. the comment on verses 24–5), betrays the work of the compilers.

41–2. It would seem that this is a continuation of verses 20–3, as is shown by the prohibition *they shall not be eaten* and the term *vermin*. It deals with a further category of 'teeming' creatures (cp. the comment on verses 20–5), those that have no wings but go *on the ground* and again the criterion is the behaviour of the domestic animals of verse 3: creatures which do not conform to this norm are unclean. *crawl on their bellies:* walking is the proper motion for land creatures, so a reptile that 'crawls', such as the snake (cp. Gen. 3: 14), is unclean. *go on all fours:* cp. the comment on verse 27. *have many legs:* the norm is four legs (cp. verses 20 and 23), so creatures, like centipedes, which have many legs are unclean.

43–5. Again, this seems to be a distinct section, which is important because its language expresses the theological ideas of the so-called 'law of holiness', chs. 17–26. It is primarily concerned with every *teeming creature*, presumably because they were thought to have the highest degree of uncleanness, but it shows us the profound religious significance with which the priestly writers, as the guardians of the nation's life, came to invest the ancient taboos, so that they saw in them the guarantee of Israel's entire distinctive relationship with its God. *I am the LORD your God:* Israel's God is unique, standing apart from all other religious beings or powers, and this is what is meant by describing him as *holy*. *you shall make yourselves holy and keep yourselves holy, because I am holy:* the nation which acknowledges the one true God must have the same characteristics as he has. *You shall not defile yourselves:* Israel maintains its holiness by avoiding completely any impurity which destroys its unity with its God and its distinctiveness from all other peoples, who have not the knowledge of the divine demands. *who brought you up from Egypt:* the nation's unique character rests on the divine choice, and so there is introduced a reference to the saving history by which Israel became the people of God. Here Leviticus is in line with the basic faith of the Old Testament (cp. Exod. 20: 2–3).

46–7. A systematizing summary to round off the legislation about impurity in animals. We may note again the centrality of the priestly concept of *distinction* as the fundamental structure of religion and society. ✶

PURIFICATION AFTER CHILDBIRTH

The LORD spoke to Moses and said, Speak to the Israelites **12** 1, 2 in these words: When a woman conceives and bears a male child, she shall be unclean for seven days, as in the period of her impurity through menstruation. On the 3 eighth day, the child shall have the flesh of his foreskin circumcised. The woman shall wait for thirty-three days 4 because her blood requires purification; she shall touch nothing that is holy, and shall not enter the sanctuary till her days of purification are completed. If she bears a 5 female child, she shall be unclean for fourteen days as for her menstruation and shall wait for sixty-six days because her blood requires purification. When her days of purifi- 6 cation are completed for a son or a daughter, she shall bring a yearling ram for a whole-offering and a young pigeon or a turtle-dove for a sin-offering to the priest at the entrance to the Tent of the Presence. He shall present 7 it before the LORD and make expiation for her, and she shall be clean from the issue of her blood. This is the law for the woman who bears a child, whether male or female. If she cannot afford a ram, she shall bring two 8 turtle-doves or two young pigeons, one for a whole-offering and the other for a sin-offering. The priest shall make expiation for her and she shall be clean.

* Numerous taboos are associated with child-bearing among many different peoples but the concern of this particular chapter is very clearly limited. It deals solely with impurity caused by the emission of blood in childbirth (cp. verses 4, 5, 7). The predominant idea of purity here is that it implies physical perfection or completeness: any bodily discharge brings imperfection and so uncleanness, and hence the case of 'the woman who bears a child' is no different from those dealt with in ch. 15. It is not suggested that there is anything inherently wrong or evil in the sexual act or in childbirth.

2. *impurity through menstruation:* cp. 15: 19–24. There is nothing exceptional in the impurity caused by childbirth, although the Hebrews understood the connection between menstruation and conception (cp. Gen. 18: 11, where the real meaning of the Hebrew is given by the Jerusalem Bible translation, 'Sarah had ceased to have her monthly periods').

3. *circumcised:* according to the priestly theology, circumcision is the effectual sign of the covenant between God and his people (cp. Gen. 17: 9–14). Only a male who was circumcised could belong to the holy community and therefore the ceremony had to be performed *On the eighth day*, that is, at the earliest possible moment after the main seven-day period of the mother's uncleanness was over. In earlier days, circumcision was probably an initiatory rite, marking the change from childhood to adolescence (cp. Gen. 17: 25) and fitting the recipient for marriage (cp. Exod. 4: 24–6, and the commentary in Ronald E. Clements, *Exodus* in this series).

4. *thirty-three days:* a further period of waiting is necessary to make sure that the discharge was fully cleared up (cp. 15: 25). The figure thirty-three is to bring the total period up to forty days, forty being one of the chief sacred numbers before the exile. *shall not enter the sanctuary:* this is a further indication of how the temple was seen as the centre of holiness in Israel and how all the purity regulations are framed with the object of securing entrance to it (cp. p. 82).

5. *a female child:* in this case, the period of impurity is

doubled. A female was considered potentially more unclean than a male because of her liability to the impurity of menstruation and childbirth.

6. *When her days of purification are completed:* as in all the regulations in chs. 12–15, it should be noted that sacrifices can only be made when the offerer is already in a state of purity. They are not 'magical', but restore the right relationship of the woman to God and the community which had been temporarily broken by the fact of childbirth.

7. *present it:* the singular pronoun may suggest that the 'whole-offering' of verse 6 is a later elaboration of the ritual (cp. the comment on 5: 7).

This is the law: the systematizing summary of the compilers.

8. This verse too is a later addition (cp. the comment on 1: 14–17). ✻

THE MALIGNANT SKIN-DISEASE

The LORD spoke to Moses and Aaron and said: When any **13** 1, 2 man has a discoloration on the skin of his body, a pustule or inflammation, and it may develop into the sores of a malignant skin-disease, he shall be brought to the priest, either to Aaron or to one of his sons. The priest shall 3 examine the sore on the skin; if the hairs on the sore have turned white and it appears to be deeper than the skin, it shall be considered the sore of a malignant skin-disease, and the priest, after examination, shall pronounce him ritually unclean. But if the inflammation on his skin is 4 white and seems no deeper than the skin, and the hairs have not turned white, the priest shall isolate the affected person for seven days. If, when he examines him on the 5 seventh day, the sore remains as it was and has not spread in the skin, he shall keep him in isolation for another seven days. When the priest examines him again on the seventh 6

day, if the sore has faded and has not spread in the skin, the priest shall pronounce him ritually clean. It is only a
7 scab; the man shall wash his clothes and so be clean. But if the scab spreads on the skin after he has been to the priest to be pronounced ritually clean, the man shall show
8 himself a second time to the priest. The priest shall examine him again, and if it continues to spread, he shall pronounce him ritually unclean; it is a malignant skin-disease.

9 When anyone has the sores of a malignant skin-disease,
10 he shall be brought to the priest, and the priest shall examine him. If there is a white mark on the skin, turning
11 the hairs white, and an ulceration appears in the mark, it is a chronic skin-disease on the body, and the priest shall pronounce him ritually unclean; there is no need for
12 isolation because he is unclean already. If the skin-disease breaks out and covers the affected person from head to
13 foot as far as the priest can see, the priest shall examine him, and if he finds the condition spread all over the body, he shall pronounce him ritually clean. It has all gone
14 white; he is clean. But from the moment when raw flesh
15 appears, the man shall be considered unclean. When the priest sees it, he shall pronounce him unclean. Raw flesh is to be considered unclean; it is a malignant skin-disease.
16 On the other hand, when the raw flesh heals and turns
17 white, the man shall go to the priest, who shall examine him, and if the sores have gone white, he shall pronounce him clean. He is ritually clean.

* As with ch. 11, chs. 13–14 consist of a number of originally separate collections of priestly case law, which have been

brought together and given a common theme by the compilers of Leviticus. The general theme is the diagnosis and the ritual treatment of 'a malignant skin-disease', a term which clearly covers a number of different types of skin-disease. In view of the way in which the material in these chapters has originated, it is impossible to expect complete logic or consistency in the arrangement. But, broadly speaking, ch. 13 consists of instructions to the priest as to how he is to determine whether a particular deformation is or is not 'a malignant skin-disease', while ch. 14 describes the expiatory rites to be performed by the individual who is cured of this particular disease. However, in each chapter an originally quite separate section has been incorporated dealing with stains or infections in inanimate objects, which appeared to be analogous to skin-diseases in humans: one, 13: 47–58, concerns garments, the other, 14: 33–53, concerns houses. This fact alone shows that the regulations are not based on medical knowledge or hygienic considerations, neither of which the Hebrews really understood. Again, the point is one of ritual uncleanness (cp. 13: 3): as was seen in discussing ch. 12, the 'malignant skin-disease' made a man imperfect and so unable to come into contact with the holy place and the holy community which would be in turn rendered unclean by him. It is impossible to say precisely what the various diseases referred to actually were nor do we know why one was ritually unclean and the others not, and no doubt the authors of Leviticus did not know either. But none of the conditions described can possibly be identified as leprosy, which was unknown in the ancient Near East. That we have here very old material is shown by the fact that, apart from the obvious addition at the end of 13: 2, only 'the priest' is mentioned in these chapters (cp. the comment on 1: 5).

2–8. These verses are concerned with a disease that looks as though it 'may develop into the sores of a malignant skin-disease'.

3. The priest is carefully instructed in the criteria for deter-

mining whether or not this is so. In this section, the evidence for the presence of *a malignant skin-disease* is a sore on which *the hairs...have turned white* and which goes *deeper than the skin*.

4–5. If these symptoms are not present, the priest shall shut off *the affected person* from all human contact for the regular *seven days*. Here can be seen the overriding concern of the chapters to protect the sacral community from defilement. At the end of this period, a further examination takes place and, if *the sore remains as it was*, a further seven days' *isolation* is imposed.

6–7. If at the end of this time, the sore is clearing up, the priest is to declare that the sufferer is *ritually clean*. But his disease has had at least the elements of great danger in it: so, to make sure, he must perform the regular purificatory rite for a minor defilement (cp. the comment on 11: 24–5).

7–8. If, however, the disease breaks out again, a further examination takes place, and, if the disease *continues to spread*, it must be diagnosed as *a malignant skin-disease*.

9. Verse 8 naturally leads on to the case where *the sores of a malignant skin-disease* can be recognized as such from the first. But the criteria for the diagnosis of this disease are different from those in verses 2–8, indicating that verses 9–17 are an originally separate body of instruction.

10–11. The signs are *a white mark on the skin*, the *turning the hairs white* and *an ulceration. there is no need for isolation*: the case is obvious and there is no necessity for the testing procedure of verses 4–6.

12–15. This is a further development of the foregoing rule, in answer to the question: 'must all these symptoms be present?' It is now made clear that the essential criterion for uncleanness is *when raw flesh appears*: the words *raw flesh* translate the same Hebrew expression as 'an ulceration' in verse 10. Even if 'white marks' have spread all over the sufferer's body, provided the skin is not broken he is *clean*. This probably indicates a relaxation of an older viewpoint,

according to which a white skin-disease was a special mark of
God's disfavour (cp. Exod. 4: 6; Num. 12: 10; 2 Kings 5: 27)..

16–17. A further elaboration in the course of actual practice, in answer to the question: 'what happens, however, if
the raw flesh heals and turns white?' If this occurs, all is well. ✷

VARIOUS OTHER SKIN-DISEASES

When a fester appears on the skin and heals up, but is 18, 19
followed by a white mark or reddish-white inflammation
on the site of the fester, the man shall show himself to the
priest. The priest shall examine him; if it seems to be 20
beneath the skin and the hairs have turned white, the
priest shall pronounce him ritually unclean. It is a malignant skin-disease which has broken out on the site of the
fester. But if the priest on examination finds that it has no 21
white hairs, is not beneath the skin and has faded, he shall
isolate him for seven days. If the affection has spread at all 22
in the skin, then the priest shall pronounce him unclean;
for it is a malignant skin-disease.[a] But if the inflammation 23
is no worse and has not spread, it is only the scar of the
fester, and the priest shall pronounce him ritually clean.

Again, in the case of a burn on the skin, if the raw spot 24
left by the burn becomes a reddish-white or white inflammation, the priest shall examine it. If the hairs on the 25
inflammation have turned white and it is deeper than the
skin, it is a malignant skin-disease which has broken out
at the site of the burn. The priest shall pronounce the man
ritually unclean; it is a malignant skin-disease. But if the 26
priest on examination finds that there is no white hair on
the inflammation and it is not beneath the skin and has

[a] malignant skin-disease: *so one MS.; others* sore.

27 faded, he shall keep him in isolation for seven days. When the priest examines him on the seventh day, if the inflammation has spread at all in the skin, the priest shall pro-

28 nounce him unclean; it is a malignant skin-disease. But if the inflammation is no worse, has not spread and has faded, it is only a mark from the burn. The priest shall pronounce him ritually clean because it is the scar of the burn.

29 When a man, or woman, has a sore on the head or chin,

30 the priest shall examine it; and if it seems deeper than the skin and the hair is yellow and sparse, the priest shall pronounce him ritually unclean; it is a scurf, a malignant skin-disease of the head or chin. But when the priest sees

31 skin-disease of the head or chin. But when the priest sees the sore, if it appears to be no deeper than the skin and yet there is no yellow[a] hair on the place, the priest shall

32 isolate the affected person for seven days. He shall examine the sore on the seventh day: if the scurf has not spread and there are no yellow hairs on it and it seems no deeper than

33 the skin, the man shall get himself shaved except for the scurfy part, and the priest shall keep him in isolation for

34 another seven days. The priest shall examine it again on the seventh day, and if the scurf has not spread on the skin and appears to be no deeper than the skin, the priest shall pronounce him clean. The man shall wash his clothes and

35 so be ritually clean. But if the scurf spreads at all in the

36 skin after the man has been pronounced clean, the priest shall examine him again. If it has spread in the skin, the priest need not even look for yellow hair; the man is

37 unclean. If, however, the scurf remains as it was but black hair has begun to grow on it, it has healed. The man is ritually clean and the priest shall pronounce him so.

[a] *So Sept.; Heb.* black.

When a man, or woman, has inflamed patches on the 38
skin and they are white, the priest shall examine them. If 39
they are white and fading, it is dull-white leprosy that
has broken out on the skin. The man is ritually
clean.

When a man's hair falls out from his head, he is bald 40
behind but not ritually unclean. If the hair falls out from 41
the front of the scalp, he is bald on the forehead but clean.
But if on the bald patch behind or on the forehead there 42
is a reddish-white sore, it is a malignant skin-disease
breaking out on those parts. The priest shall examine him, 43
and if the discoloured sore on the bald patch behind or on
the forehead is reddish-white, similar in appearance to a
malignant skin-disease on the body, the man is suffering 44
from such a disease; he is ritually unclean and the priest
must not fail to pronounce him so. The symptoms are in
this case on his head.

One who suffers from a malignant skin-disease shall 45
wear his clothes torn, leave his hair dishevelled, conceal
his upper lip, and cry, 'Unclean, unclean.' So long as the 46
sore persists, he shall be considered ritually unclean. The
man is unclean: he shall live apart and must stay outside
the settlement.

* 18–23. This section is closely linked with verses 2–8, but
refers to a different and potentially less serious situation where
a *fester* has healed up but then develops secondary symptoms.
The criteria for the recognition of uncleanness are the same
(compare verse 20 with verse 3), but, in a case of doubt, the
isolation period is only seven days and if, at the end of this, all
is well, no rite of purification need be performed (contrast
verse 6).

24–8. Here another type of disease is discussed: the procedure to be followed is identical with that in verses 18–23.

29–37. The particular case of *a sore on the head or chin* follows verses 2–8 even more closely (although the reference to a *man, or woman* shows it to be from another collection), except that the sign of the *malignant skin-disease* is the *yellow and sparse* appearance of the hair; perhaps the point is to differentiate from the naturally white hair of an elderly person. *get himself shaved:* letting the hair grow was one mark of ritual seclusion (cp. Num. 6: 5) and thus shaving it off was in this instance the sign of a partial return to normal life (cp. 14: 8–9; Num. 6: 18). *except for the scurfy part:* this could not be shaved since it was still under suspicion and the evidence could not be destroyed. The disease is again a more serious one, so there is a two-week *isolation* period and a ritual washing. Verses 35–6 correspond to verses 7–8. Verse 37 is a further explanation to make it plain that the hair must grow *black* again before the sufferer could be pronounced fully clean.

38–9. This passage, from the same collection since it refers to a *man, or a woman*, is concerned with a disease which looked like the unclean one, but was not so in fact (cp. the comment on verses 12–15). *dull-white leprosy:* the expression translates a single Hebrew word, occurring only here in the Old Testament. It seems to mean only some sort of skin eruption and certainly not leprosy as the term is understood today.

40–4. If part of a man's hair falls out, although he could be held to be imperfect, he is not for this alone to be considered unclean. But if the loss of hair is accompanied by a *discoloured sore* which is *similar in appearance to a malignant skin-disease* elsewhere *on the body*, then the man has this disease.

45–6. The *One who suffers from a malignant skin-disease* has to perform the regular rites of mourning: he is symbolically dead to the holy community. *wear his clothes torn:* cp. 10: 6; 21: 10. *leave his hair dishevelled:* cp. 10: 6; 21: 10; Num. 5: 18. *conceal his upper lip:* cp. Ezek. 24: 17, 22. *cry 'Unclean, unclean':* in order that everyone should avoid the unclean person and not be defiled by coming into contact with him. *he shall live apart:* this is not the temporary 'isolation' of verses 4, 5, 21, 26, 31, 33, but an indefinite separation, only to be ended when the symptoms of the disease had disappeared. *settlement:* this is the word translated elsewhere in Leviticus as 'camp' (cp. 14: 3). In priestly thought, it denotes not just the area where people live but rather the sphere of the holy community. *

UNCLEANNESS IN CLOTHES AND SKINS

When there is a stain of mould, whether in a garment of 47
wool or linen, or in the warp or weft of linen or wool, or 48
in a skin or anything made of skin; if the stain is greenish 49
or reddish in the garment or skin, or in the warp or weft,
or in anything made of skin, it is a stain of mould which
must be shown to the priest. The priest shall examine it 50
and put the stained material aside for seven days. On the 51
seventh day he shall examine it again. If the stain has
spread in the garment, warp, weft, or skin, whatever the
use of the skin, the stain is a rotting mould: it is ritually
unclean. He shall burn the garment or the warp or weft, 52
whether wool or linen, or anything of skin which is
stained; because it is a rotting mould, it must be destroyed
by fire. But if the priest sees that the stain has not spread 53
in the garment, warp or weft, or anything made of skin,
he shall give orders for the stained material to be washed, 54
and then he shall put it aside for another seven days. After 55
it has been washed the priest shall examine the stain; if it
has not changed its appearance, although it has not spread,
it is unclean and you shall destroy it by fire, whether the
rot is on the right side or the wrong. If the priest examines 56
it and finds the stain faded after being washed, he shall

57 tear it out of the garment, skin, warp, or weft. If, however, the stain reappears in the garment, warp or weft, or
in anything of skin, it is breaking out afresh and you shall
58 destroy by fire whatever is stained. If you wash the
garment, warp, weft, or anything of skin and the stain
disappears, it shall be washed a second time and then it
shall be ritually clean.

59 This is the law concerning stain of mould in a garment
of wool or linen, in warp or weft, or in anything made
of skin; by it they shall be pronounced clean or unclean.

✲ As already noted, this is a distinct section which views decay in garments or skins in the same way as discolorations on the human body, because of a general similarity in appearance. The problem, therefore, is approached in a broadly similar way. Regulations are given for five different situations:

47–52. (i) When a *stain of mould* appears, the *garment or skin* must be put aside for *seven days*. If at the end of this period, the stain has spread, it must be judged *a rotting mould:* it is irremediable and must be destroyed by burning. It must be totally removed from contact with anyone, just as the 'unclean man' had to be.

53–5. (ii) The introduction of the second person singular in verse 55, and also verses 57 and 58, indicates a number of expansions of the basic regulations to deal with various problematic cases. Here we have the answer to the question: 'what happens if, after seven days, the stain has not spread and is only affecting part of the garment?' Then, so to speak, a second chance is allowed: the priest has the garment washed, waits for *another seven days* and then re-examines it. If the stain has still *not changed its appearance*, the garment must be burned. *on the right side or the wrong:* the Hebrew could equally well mean 'on the front or on the back' and this gives the required sense: even if the object is only partially stained, yet it must all be destroyed.

56. (iii) But if the stain has *faded* after washing, the priest need only tear out the infected part and the rest is available for ordinary use.

57. (iv) But if, even after this, *the stain reappears*, thus proving that it is in fact 'a rotting mould', what remains of the garment must be burned.

58. (v) But if, after the washing mentioned in verse 54, the stain seems to have disappeared, the garment is to be washed again, to make sure, and then it is ritually clean and can be used normally.

59. The summary mentions only the problem of *clean or unclean* garments and skins, thus showing that verses 47–58 had assumed their existing form before being incorporated into a larger unit. ✱

THE CLEANSING RITES FOR A MALIGNANT SKIN-DISEASE

The LORD spoke to Moses and said: This is the law concerning a man suffering from a malignant skin-disease. On the day when he is to be cleansed he shall be brought to the priest. The priest shall go outside the camp and examine him. If the man is healed of his disease, then the priest shall order two clean small birds to be brought alive for the man who is to be cleansed, together with cedar-wood, scarlet thread, and marjoram.[a] He shall order one of the birds to be killed over an earthenware bowl containing fresh water. He shall then take the living bird and the cedar-wood, scarlet thread, and marjoram and dip them and the living bird in the blood of the bird that has been killed over the fresh water. He shall sprinkle the

14 1, 2

3

4

5

6

7

[a] *Or* hyssop.

blood seven times on the man who is to be cleansed from his skin-disease and so cleanse him; the living bird he

8 shall release to fly away over the open country. The man to be cleansed shall wash his clothes, shave off all his hair, bathe in water and so be ritually clean. He may then enter

9 the camp but must stay outside his tent for seven days. On the seventh day he shall shave off all the hair on his head, his beard, and his eyebrows, and then shave the rest of his hair, wash his clothes and bathe in water; then he shall be ritually clean.

✶ After the insertion 13: 47–58, we return to the situation of 13: 45–6 and there now follow the rules as to how the sufferer from a malignant skin-disease is to be restored to the community and its worship, after the signs of his affliction have disappeared (cp. the comment on 12: 6). Because of the great danger for the entire national life caused by uncleanness, the man can only return to ordinary life in a series of carefully controlled stages, each marked by appropriate rituals.

As now presented in Leviticus, there are two main steps in the process, various cleansing rites, verses 1–9, by which the man is brought back to civil and family life, and a sacrificial procedure, verses 10–32, by which he is enabled again to take his place as a worshipper. We thus have another example of the multiplication of purificatory ceremonies characteristic of the cultus after the exile (cp. the comment on 8: 6). It seems likely, however, that the rites of verses 1–9 are older and more original than the sacrificial procedure: they reflect very ancient religious ideas which are no longer those of the developed priestly theology. In them, the underlying concept appears to be that disease is a sign that a man is possessed by evil forces or spirits. Even when the outward symptoms have disappeared, these forces still have to be expelled from the individual, in case they resume their malignant activity, and this is the object of the rites here prescribed.

2–3. *he shall be brought to the priest. The priest shall go outside the camp:* perhaps there are two originally distinct directions here. In the one case, when the man appears to have recovered, someone brings him to the place where the priest is living (cp. Mark 1: 44; Luke 17: 14): in the other, the priest goes and examines him, having presumably been told that there is *a priori* evidence for the man's recovery, *outside the camp* (cp. the comment on 13: 45–6). In either case, the ceremonies then performed are not sacrifices, for they have no connection with the altar or the sanctuary. *If the man is healed of his disease:* nor do they effect the actual healing of the disease, which must have occurred before they can begin.

4. *two clean small birds:* this presupposes the regulations of 11: 13–19. The birds have to be small for easy ritual manipulation. The other articles mentioned in this verse are found in a similar purificatory rite at Num. 19: 6: they were all believed to have apotropaic force, that is, to have a power in them able to drive away evil spirits. *cedar-wood:* this has a strong scent and a powerful odour was considered to be able to drive away demons (cp. Tobit 6: 16–17; 8: 2–3). The 'cedar-boards' used so extensively in Solomon's temple (cp. 1 Kings 6: 14–18) may have had more than a merely aesthetic purpose. *scarlet thread:* two passages in the Old Testament, in what is probably their original significance, suggest that a 'scarlet thread' was used to ward off evil powers at childbirth (cp. Gen. 38: 28, 30) or from a house (cp. Josh. 2: 18, 21). Scarlet is similar in colour to blood and, as will be seen, blood was considered to have great apotropaic force. *marjoram:* whatever its precise botanical definition (cp. the footnote), this was a herb used in seasoning, whose pungency was believed to drive away evil influences. It was sprinkled on the house to ward off evil on Passover night (cp. Exod. 12: 22) and on an individual to make him ritually clean (cp. Ps. 51: 7).

5–6. *one of the birds to be killed:* each of the birds removes evil in a different way. In this instance, it is done through its blood. Blood was the seat of life (cp. 17: 11) and so the positive life-force of the blood was considered to be able to defeat the negative force of evil (cp. Exod. 12: 7, 13, 22–3). *an earthenware bowl:* the reason why this is specified is explained in the comments on 6: 28 and 11: 33. *containing fresh water:* the Hebrew is literally 'living', i.e. 'running' water. Running water appeared to have a life of its own and so also to be a positive force to combat evil (cp. too the comment on 11: 36).

7. *He shall sprinkle the blood seven times:* the blood is ritually sprinkled on the man and so he is made ritually clean (cp. the comment on 4: 5–7). *the living bird he shall release:* this is the second way of removing evil. It can best be understood from the close parallel of the treatment of the 'live goat' on the Day of Atonement, ch. 16. There the priest 'lays' all the nation's sins on the goat's head and it is sent away 'into the wilderness' (cp. 16: 21). So here the sufferer's uncleanness is transferred to the living bird, which then removes it from human habitation (cp. verse 53), by flying away to a place where it can do no harm. *the open country:* a further idea may be contained in these words. Just as 16: 8–10 may suggest that the goat on the Day of Atonement was destined for some evil power, so 17: 5, 7 make it clear that the open country was the realm of 'demons'. We would then have in this verse the common idea that evil spirits can be neutralized by sending them back to where they properly belong (cp. Mark 5: 11–13) or perhaps the ritual was originally designed to propitiate demons living in the open country. Similar rites which transfer uncleanness to live animals are common in the religions of the ancient Near East.

8. *shave off all his hair:* cp. the comment on 13: 29–37. *must stay outside his tent:* the purification was not complete, so, although the man *may . . . enter the camp*, he must not come into contact with his family and possessions. To do so would be to run the risk of bringing uncleanness on them, as Achan's uncleanness, incurred by the theft of holy objects, infected his

entire household and led to their destruction (cp. Josh. 7: 1, 24–6). Anyone in a state of separation from ordinary life, whether because of impurity or purity, such as a soldier on active service, had to abstain from family life (cp. 2 Sam. 11: 9–11).

9. A further probationary period follows, after which there is another very thorough shaving off of all the man's hair. Because of its continual growth, even after death, the hair was viewed, like the blood, as the seat of life: Samson's bodily vigour resided in his hair (cp. Judg. 16: 17). Thus its infection by uncleanness would be particularly dangerous and very careful precautions must be taken. ✳

THE SACRIFICIAL PROCEDURE

On the eighth day he shall bring two yearling[a] rams and 10 one yearling ewe, all three without blemish, a grain-offering of three tenths of an ephah of flour mixed with oil, and one log of oil. The officiating priest shall place the 11 man to be cleansed and his offerings before the LORD at the entrance to the Tent of the Presence. He shall then 12 take one of the rams and offer it with the log of oil as a guilt-offering, presenting them as a special gift before the LORD. The ram shall be slaughtered where the sin- 13 offerings and the whole-offerings are slaughtered, within the sacred precincts, because the guilt-offering, like the sin-offering, belongs to the priest. It is most sacred. The 14 priest shall then take some of the blood of the guilt-offering and put it on the lobe of the right ear of the man to be cleansed, and on his right thumb and the big toe of his right foot. He shall next take the log of oil and pour 15 some of it on the palm of his own left hand, dip his right 16

[a] yearling: *so Sam.; Heb. om.*

109

forefinger into the oil on his left palm and sprinkle some
17 of it with his finger seven times before the LORD. He shall
then put some of the oil remaining on his palm on the
lobe of the right ear of the man to be cleansed, on his right
thumb and on the big toe of his right foot, on top of the
18 blood of the guilt-offering The remainder of the oil on
the priest's palm shall be put upon the head of the man to
be cleansed, and thus the priest shall make expiation for
19 him before the LORD. The priest shall then perform the
sin-offering and make expiation for the uncleanness of the
man who is to be cleansed. After this he shall slaughter
20 the whole-offering and offer it and the grain-offering on
the altar. Thus the priest shall make expiation for him,
and then he shall be clean.

21   If the man is poor and cannot afford these offerings, he
shall bring one young ram as a guilt-offering to be a
special gift making expiation for him, and a grain-offering
of a tenth of an ephah of flour mixed with oil, and a log
22 of oil, also two turtle-doves or two young pigeons,
whichever he can afford, one for a sin-offering and the
23 other for a whole-offering. He shall bring them to the
priest for his cleansing on the eighth day, at the entrance
24 to the Tent of the Presence before the LORD. The priest
shall take the ram for the guilt-offering and the log of oil,
and shall present them as a special gift before the LORD.
25 The ram for the guilt-offering shall then be slaughtered,
and the priest shall take some of the blood of the guilt-
offering, and put it on the lobe of the right ear of the man
to be cleansed and on his right thumb and on the big toe
26 of his right foot. He shall pour some of the oil on the palm
27 of his own left hand and sprinkle some of it with his right

forefinger seven times before the LORD. He shall then put 28
some of the oil remaining on his palm on the lobe of the
right ear of the man to be cleansed, and on his right
thumb and on the big toe of his right foot exactly where
the blood of the guilt-offering was put. The remainder of 29
the oil on the priest's palm shall be put upon the head
of the man to be cleansed to make expiation for him before
the LORD. Of the birds which the man has been able to 30
afford, turtle-doves or young pigeons, whichever it may
be, the priest shall deal with one as a sin-offering and with 31
the other as a whole-offering and shall make the grain-
offering with them. Thus the priest shall make expiation
before the LORD for the man who is to be cleansed. This 32
is the law for the man with a malignant skin-disease who
cannot afford the regular offering for his cleansing.

* As seen by the compilers of Leviticus, the purpose of these
sacrifices was the usual one of making 'expiation', verses
18–20. Probably, however, the most original element is the
'guilt-offering', which is described in much greater detail
than the other sacrifices, and was specially efficacious in cases
of uncleanness (cp. 5: 2–3 and the comment on 4: 2). The
important part of it was the manipulation of the blood and
we are not in fact told that this 'guilt-offering' was burnt on
the altar, although this may be presupposed (cp. the comment
on verse 12 and on 5: 14 – 6: 7). Essentially then, we have
here a final cleansing ceremony: the other sacrifices have been
added to conform to what had become the regular practice of
the developed priestly ritual.

10. Cp. the comment on 8: 1–3. *three tenths of an ephah:* for
the ephah, cp. the comment on 5: 11. Here the reference is to
the regular grain-offering (cp. the comment on 2: 1) and the
quantity specified is considerable (contrast verse 21). *one log of*

oil: the term only occurs in the Old Testament in this chapter. It is quite distinct from the oil mixed with the grain-offering. For the amount, cp. p. 228.

11. *place:* this is the ordinary word for 'station', to be distinguished from the sacrificial term which is 'present' (cp. verse 12 and contrast 8: 6. Note also the careful distinction in this respect between the goat to be offered and sacrificed and the goat that is not, in the Day of Atonement ceremony; 16: 7–10).

12. *as a guilt-offering:* this need mean no more than 'for guilt', i.e. to remove guilt (cp. the comment on 5: 16) and that this is correct is suggested by the inclusion of *the log of oil* which did not form part of the regular guilt-offering. *special gift:* cp. the comment on 7: 30–1, and note again how the guilt-offering is regarded primarily as something paid as a due (cp. p. 44).

13. *where the sin-offerings and the whole-offerings are slaughtered:* this careful direction perhaps represents an assimilation of the originally different *guilt-offering* to the sacrifices proper (cp. the comment on 7: 1–7). *most sacred:* cp. the comment on 2: 10.

14. The rite is the same, and with the same purpose, as that found in the installation of priests (cp. the comment on 8: 22–8). Presumably the remainder of the blood was disposed of as in 8: 24.

16. *seven times before the LORD:* this may have been to consecrate the oil, but more probably it was to convey it to God, since a part of anything 'presented' had to go to him (cp. the comment on 4: 5–7).

17. Unlike the installation of priests, a second purificatory ceremony follows with the oil. In the Old Testament, oil is a symbol of vigour and prosperity or wholeness (cp. Pss. 92: 10; 104: 15). Probably the original purpose of Jacob's pouring oil on the pillar at Bethel was to convey life to the deity residing in it (cp. Gen. 28: 18–19 and also Judg. 9: 9) and such is no doubt the intention here (cp. the comment on verses 5–6).

18. *the head of the man:* the action here must be distinguished from the rite of 8: 12 where the technical expression 'anointing oil' is used. Oil was poured on the head of a guest (cp. Ps. 23: 5) and to have oil on one's head was the right and normal thing (cp. Eccles. 9: 8). So what is now done indicates full acceptance once more into the life of society.

19–20. The three sacrifices in these verses are only mentioned briefly (cp. p. 111) and we are not told how the animals of verse 10 were divided between *the sin-offering* and *the whole-offering:* probably, in view of 4: 32, the 'yearling ewe' was for the former. *and the grain-offering:* this probably reflects a fairly late stage in the development of sacrificial practice when the grain-offering had become the regular accompaniment of the whole-offering (cp. the comment on 2: 1–16).

21–32. This section, to meet the case of a man who could not afford the considerable outlay involved in the requirements of verse 10, is a separate and later addition (cp. the comments on 1: 14–17; 12: 8), as is shown by the fact that the summary in verse 32 only mentions *the law* for one *who cannot afford the regular offering.* Otherwise, the ritual is identical. ✳

INFECTION IN HOUSES

The LORD spoke to Moses and Aaron and said: When you 33, 34 have entered the land of Canaan which I give you to occupy, if I inflict a fungous infection upon a house in the land you have occupied, its owner shall come and report 35 to the priest that there appears to him to be a patch of infection in his house. The priest shall order the house to 36 be cleared before he goes in to examine the infection, or everything in it will become unclean. After this the priest shall go in to inspect the house. If on inspection he finds 37 the patch on the walls consists of greenish or reddish depressions, apparently going deeper than the surface, he 38

shall go out of the house and, standing at the entrance,
39 shall put it in quarantine for seven days. On the seventh
day he shall come back and inspect the house, and if the
40 patch has spread in the walls, he shall order the infected
stones to be pulled out and thrown away outside the city
41 in an unclean place. He shall then have the house scraped
inside throughout, and all the daub*ᵃ* they have scraped
off*ᵇ* shall be tipped outside the city in an unclean place.
42 They shall take fresh stones to replace the others and
replaster the house with fresh daub.

43 If the infection reappears in the house and spreads after
the stones have been pulled out and the house scraped*ᶜ*
44 and redaubed, the priest shall come and inspect it. If the
infection has spread in the house, it is a corrosive growth;
45 the house is unclean. The house shall be demolished,
stones, timber, and daub, and it shall all be taken away
46 outside the city to an unclean place. Anyone who has
entered the house during the time it has been in quaran-
47 tine shall be unclean till evening. Anyone who has slept
48 or eaten a meal in the house shall wash his clothes. But if,
when the priest goes into the house and inspects it, he
finds that the infection has not spread after the redaubing,
then he shall pronounce the house ritually clean, because
the infection has been cured.

49 In order to rid the house of impurity, he shall take two
small birds, cedar-wood, scarlet thread, and marjoram.
50 He shall kill one of the birds over an earthenware bowl
51 containing fresh water. He shall then take the cedar-wood,

[a] *Or* mud.
[b] *So Pesh.; Heb.* have brought to an end.
[c] *So Sept.; Heb.* brought to an end.

marjoram, and scarlet thread, together with the living
bird, dip them in the blood of the bird that has been killed
and in the fresh water, and sprinkle the house seven times.
Thus he shall purify the house, using the blood of the 52
bird, the fresh water, the living bird, the cedar-wood, the
marjoram, and the scarlet thread. He shall set the living 53
bird free outside the city to fly away over the open
country, and make expiation for the house; and then it
shall be clean.

This is the law for all malignant skin-diseases, and for 54
scurf, for mould in clothes and fungus in houses, for a 55, 56
discoloration of the skin, scab, and inflammation, to 57
declare when these are pronounced unclean and when
clean. This is the law for skin-disease, mould, and fungus.

---

* The procedure for dealing with 'a fungous infection' in a
house is actually a combination of what is prescribed in 13:
47–58 and 14: 1–7. Perhaps originally only what is laid down
in verses 33–48 was necessary and the subsequent ritual in
verses 49–53 is an addition, reflecting the increasing priestly
concern with impurity and uncleanness. It is also noteworthy
that, although verses 49–53 are identical with the regulations
for 'a man suffering from a malignant skin-disease', there is
nothing corresponding to the sacrificial procedure for the
latter case, which again suggests that the sacrificial procedure
represents a further development in ritual procedure (cp. the
comment on 14: 1–9).

34. *When you have entered the land of Canaan:* this section
presupposes settled conditions in Palestine, where the
Israelites are living in houses (contrast verse 8) and in cities,
verses 40, 45, 53 (contrast again verse 8), although the word
need mean no more than a quite small village. It is thus concerned with an actual situation, but God's words to Moses and

Aaron have been added by the compilers, who saw all these laws as being given in the wilderness period: hence the regulations here are made to refer to the future. *if I inflict:* in the Old Testament, God is the source of all that happens, so even 'disasters' can be attributed directly to him (cp. Amos 3: 6).

36. *order the house to be cleared:* only when the priest has given his decision does uncleanness begin and this shows again that impurity is not so much a physical fact as a ritual concept (cp. the comment on 13: 1–17). So, if the essential articles of daily life are removed from the house before the priestly verdict is given, they will not *become unclean* and may continue in use.

37. *greenish or reddish depressions:* cp. 13: 49. *going deeper than the surface:* the evidence is similar to that for 'a malignant skin-disease', the presence of which was shown by sores that went below the skin (cp. the comment on 13: 10–15).

38. *seven days:* cp. the comment on 13: 47–52.

39–42. The directions here are parallel to those of 13: 56 and have the similar purpose of enabling the house to continue in use if at all possible. *in an unclean place:* the *infected stones* and the *daub* or 'mud' (cp. the footnote) could not be burned, so they must be taken to a place where they can do no harm (cp. verse 45 and the comment on verse 7).

43–5. Again the procedure here corresponds to that in 13: 51–2, and the expression *corrosive growth* is parallel to the 'rotting mould' there.

46–7. The directions here indicate the careful priestly concept of degrees of impurity. Anyone who has *slept or eaten a meal* in the infected house is more unclean than someone who has merely *entered* it and so must perform an actual purificatory rite (cp. the similar distinction in 11: 24–5).

49–53. It is noteworthy that the procedure here is exactly the same as in the case of skin-disease in human beings (cp. the comment on 13: 47–59).

54–7. The final summary covers all the material in chs. 13–14 and shows how all the originally diverse regulations in them have now been systematized in a single large collection. ✶

MALE SEXUAL IMPURITIES

The LORD spoke to Moses and Aaron and said, Speak to **15**1, 2 the Israelites and say to them: When any man has a discharge from his body, the discharge is ritually unclean. This is the law concerning[a] the uncleanness due to his 3 discharge whether it continues or has been stopped; in either case he is unclean.

Every bed on which the man with a discharge lies down 4 shall be ritually unclean, and everything on which he sits shall be unclean. Any man who touches the bed shall 5 wash his clothes, bathe in water and remain unclean till evening. Whoever sits on anything on which the man 6 with a discharge has sat shall wash his clothes, bathe in water and remain unclean till evening. Whoever touches 7 the body of the man with a discharge shall wash his clothes, bathe in water and remain unclean till evening. If the man spits on one who is ritually clean, the latter 8 shall wash his clothes, bathe in water and remain unclean till evening. Everything on which the man sits when 9 riding shall be unclean. Whoever touches anything that 10 has been under him shall be unclean till evening, and whoever handles such things shall wash his clothes, bathe in water and remain unclean till evening. Anyone whom 11 the man with a discharge touches without having rinsed his hands in water shall wash his clothes, bathe in water and remain unclean till evening. Any earthenware bowl 12

[a] the law concerning: *so Sept.; Heb. om.*

touched by the man shall be smashed, and every wooden bowl shall be rinsed with water.

13   When the man is cleansed from his discharge, he shall reckon seven days to his cleansing, wash his clothes, bathe
14 his body in fresh water and be ritually clean. On the eighth day he shall obtain two turtle-doves or two young pigeons and, coming before the LORD at the entrance to the Tent of the Presence, shall give them to the priest.
15 The priest shall deal with one as a sin-offering and the other as a whole-offering, and shall make for him before the LORD the expiation required by the discharge.

16   When a man has emitted semen, he shall bathe his
17 whole body in water and be unclean till evening. Every piece of clothing or skin on which there is any semen
18 shall be washed and remain unclean till evening. This applies also to the woman with whom a man has had intercourse; they shall both bathe themselves in water and remain unclean till evening.

* In this chapter, there is a further series of priestly instructions but clearly intended for ordinary people: unlike the cases in the two preceding chapters, the priest plays no part, except in the purificatory ceremony of verses 14–15, 29–30, which is probably a later addition (cp. the comment on 14: 1–9). In the cases dealt with, it was up to the individual to see to the restoration of his own state of uncleanness, and clearly they were regarded less seriously than the 'malignant skin-disease' of chs. 13–14. This corresponds to the conditions of ordinary life, for the 'discharges' described in this chapter would occur more frequently and be less easily visible than the 'malignant skin-disease'. The legislation is concerned with emissions from the sexual organs (cp. the comment on verse 2), but it is not suggested that they or the sexual act are in any

way themselves 'unclean' (cp. the comment on verses 16–18).
It is only something abnormal in connection with them that is
so regarded. But the processes of human reproduction are
mysterious to early peoples and therefore surrounded by
various taboos.

2. The general rule is first stated and then followed by
detailed regulations to cover various cases of its application,
which are not arranged in any very clear order. *from his body:*
the word *body* is a euphemism for the sexual organ (cp. Ezek.
23: 20, where 'members' translates the same Hebrew word,
and the comment on 6: 10).

3. *whether it continues or has been stopped:* a ruling to answer
the question: 'is it only a persistent discharge which need be
regarded as unclean?'.

4. It is striking that, in contrast to verse 12, nothing is said
about how the uncleanness acquired by the objects mentioned
in this verse, and by the saddle in verse 9, is to be dealt with.
Presumably they were too valuable to be destroyed and too
cumbersome to wash. Probably they were reckoned *unclean*
for the rest of the day (cp. 11: 24).

5–6. These verses deal with the secondary infection that a
person suffers if he comes into contact with anything used by
the man with a discharge. He had to perform a comparatively
minor purificatory rite (cp. the comment on 11: 24–5).

8. *spits:* among many peoples, spittle is considered to contain the life-force of a man. Hence it has magical properties
and is surrounded by strong taboos (cp. e.g. Mark
7: 33).

9–10. *anything that has been under him:* this refers to *Everything on which the man sits when riding*. Anyone who just
brushes against it is unclean for a limited period but if he
actually *handles* the unclean objects, the infection is greater and
he must perform the usual purificatory rite. Perhaps the same
distinction is found in 11: 24–5, 27–8.

11. An unclean man may touch another person, without
defiling him, provided he has first *rinsed his hands*. Again, the

taboo is limited, so that it does not interfere too much with ordinary relationships.

12. Cp. the comment on 6: 28; 11: 33.

13. The man with the primary infection has to remain unclean for a longer period than the one who has only a secondary infection (cp. the comment on verses 5–6).

14–15. As already noted, the final sacrificial ceremony of *expiation* is a later addition. Nor is there anything corresponding to the ceremony of 14: 12–18.

16–18. This is a distinct section, dealing with the particular case of the emission of *semen*. If any of this falls on anything, including the body of a woman *with whom a man has had intercourse*, it becomes unclean and must be purified. ✻

FEMALE SEXUAL IMPURITIES

19 When a woman has a discharge of blood, her impurity shall last for seven days; anyone who touches her shall be 20 unclean till evening. Everything on which she lies or sits 21 during her impurity shall be unclean. Anyone who touches her bed shall wash his clothes, bathe in water and 22 remain unclean till evening. Whoever touches anything on which she sits shall wash his clothes, bathe in water and 23 remain unclean till evening. If he is on the bed or seat where she is sitting, by touching it he shall become un- 24 clean till evening. If a man goes so far as to have intercourse with her and any of her discharge gets on to him, then he shall be unclean for seven days, and every bed on which he lies down shall be unclean.

25 When a woman has a prolonged discharge of blood not at the time of her menstruation, or when her discharge continues beyond the period of menstruation, her impurity shall last all the time of her discharge; she shall be

unclean as during the period of her menstruation. Any 26
bed on which she lies during the time of her discharge
shall be like that which she used during menstruation, and
everything on which she sits shall be unclean as in her
menstrual uncleanness. Every person who touches them 27
shall be unclean; he shall wash his clothes, bathe in water
and remain unclean till evening. If she is cleansed from 28
her discharge, she shall reckon seven days and after that
she shall be ritually clean. On the eighth day she shall 29
obtain two turtle-doves or two young pigeons and bring
them to the priest at the entrance to the Tent of the
Presence. The priest shall deal with one as a sin-offering 30
and with the other as a whole-offering, and make for her
before the LORD the expiation required by her unclean
discharge.

In this way you shall warn the Israelites against un- 31
cleanness, in order that they may not bring uncleanness
upon the Tabernacle where I dwell among them, and so
die.

This is the law for the man who has a discharge, or who 32
has an emission of semen and is thereby unclean, and for 33
the woman who is suffering her menstruation – for everyone, male or female, who has a discharge, and for the
man who has intercourse with a woman who is unclean.

* 19–24. As verse 25 shows, these verses are concerned with
the ordinary menstrual period, again something that was very
mysterious to early peoples. Although the woman's *impurity*
lasted seven days, no purificatory rite is prescribed: presumably this was because menstruation was a regular, normal
occurrence. The regulations are basically the same as those for
'the man with a discharge'. *If he is on the bed or seat:* a better

translation would be 'it'. This is an expansion of the regulation of verse 22, in response to the question: 'what is the situation if a man touches, not the piece of furniture on which the menstruating woman has sat, but just an object lying on it?' The answer is that he incurs a lesser degree of impurity. *goes so far as to have intercourse with her:* because the menstrual period was so heavily taboo, intercourse was originally strictly forbidden during it, on pain of death (cp. 18: 19; 20: 18). Here the development of Israel's legal practice has brought a relaxation of the old prohibition, but the man still incurs the same full seven-day period of uncleanness as the woman.

25–30. By contrast, any unusual or exceptional *discharge of blood*, by that very fact requires a special purificatory rite (verses 29–30; cp. the comment on verses 14–15). As long as the discharge continues, the same taboos operate as during the menstrual period.

31. *you shall warn the Israelites:* this shows the object and method of the priests' teaching office for the laity (cp. p. 80). *uncleanness upon the Tabernacle where I dwell:* again we see that the whole purpose of the rules about purity and impurity is to preserve the holiness of the sanctuary and the nation's communion with the God who dwells there. *and so die:* if the nation's holiness were destroyed by the people's uncleanness, Israel would cease to exist.

32–3. The final summary, fitting the various laws of this chapter into a single pattern. ✷

THE DAY OF ATONEMENT: THE PREPARATION

16 The LORD spoke to Moses after the death of Aaron's two sons, who died when they offered illicit fire before the
2 LORD.[a] He said to him: Tell your brother Aaron that he must not enter the sanctuary within the Veil, in front of the cover over the Ark, except at the appointed time, on

[a] when. . .LORD: *so Sept.; Heb.* when they came near before the LORD.

pain of death; for I appear in the cloud above the cover.
When Aaron enters the sanctuary, this is what he shall do. 3
He shall bring a young bull for a sin-offering and a ram
for a whole-offering. He shall wear a sacred linen tunic 4
and linen drawers to cover himself, and he shall put a
linen sash round his waist and wind a linen turban round
his head; all these are sacred vestments, and he shall bathe
in water before putting them on. He shall take from the 5
community of the Israelites two he-goats for a sin-offering
and a ram for a whole-offering. He shall present the bull 6
as a sin-offering and make expiation for himself and his
household. Then he shall take the two he-goats and set 7
them before the LORD at the entrance to the Tent of the
Presence. He shall cast lots over the two goats, one to be 8
for the LORD and the other for the Precipice.[a] He shall 9
present the goat on which the lot for the LORD has fallen
and deal with it as a sin-offering; but the goat on which 10
the lot for the Precipice has fallen shall be made to stand
alive before the LORD, for expiation to be made over it
before it is driven away into the wilderness to the
Precipice.

✻ The expression 'the Day of Atonement' does not occur in
this chapter but only, in the entire Old Testament, at 23: 27,
28, where 'day of expiation' translates the same Hebrew
expression, and 25: 9: however, verse 29 shows that at least
the compilers of Leviticus identified the celebration of ch. 16
with the Day of Atonement mentioned elsewhere. The
Hebrew term means literally 'day of expiations' and this well
describes its character, for what we have in this chapter is a
combination of a number of separate rites designed to secure

[a] Or for Azazel.

the complete purity of the sanctuary and the nation (cp. the comment on 8: 1–13). From the literary point of view, it is possible to separate out three sections, the first concerned with the preliminaries to the celebration, verses 1–10, the second describing the principal ceremonies of the day, verses 11–28, and a final systematizing summary in the usual manner of the priestly compilers, verses 29–34. But one can also see three distinct ritual concerns, each of which originally had its own background and significance:

(i) the rules to be observed by the high priest whenever he penetrated 'the sanctuary within the Veil' (verses 2–4, 12–13).

(ii) various purificatory sacrifices and rites, which follow the general pattern of the sacrificial legislation in Leviticus and reflect the preoccupation of the priestly theology with 'expiation' (verses 5–6, 11, 14–19, 23–5).

(iii) the particular rite of the goat that carries away the 'sins' of the Israelites (verses 8–10, 20–2), which rests on ancient ideas different from the dominant ones of priestly outlook after the exile (cp. the comment on 14: 7).

In the existing text of ch. 16, these various elements are all combined together in a way which does not always allow them to be easily distinguished and this indicates that the regulations here for the Day of Atonement are the result of a long period of evolution and development. No doubt the celebration as it appears in this chapter has the form it took in the Jerusalem temple after the exile but it has a much longer history than that. In 23: 23–36, there are three distinct celebrations in 'the seventh month' of which the Day of Atonement is one (cp. verse 29), but before the exile these were all parts of a great autumnal festival complex. This marked the turn of the year (cp. Exod. 23: 16 and the N.E.B. footnote, and 25: 9 which associates the Day of Atonement with the New Year). Thus one element in this festival was concerned with ensuring a prosperous new year and the ceremonies that came to be associated specifically with the Day of Atonement had as their object to provide the nation with a fresh start, so that it could enter on the ensuing twelve months freed from any uncleannesses with which it had become infected during the preceding year. The great autumnal feast was therefore the Israelite version of a New Year Festival common to many of the peoples of the ancient Near East: the closest parallel to the Day of Atonement is provided by the Babylonian New Year Festival, which had a preparatory period of several days, during which a whole series of purificatory and expiatory rites were carried out in the temple, several of which closely resemble some of the rituals of the Day of Atonement. Since the ceremonies involved the whole people, a leading part was played by the king, as the embodiment of the nation: so, on the Day of Atonement, all the rites were performed by the high priest, who, as has been seen, increasingly assumed the religious role of the former Davidic king after the exile.

The 'Day of Atonement', then, is essentially ancient, as representing the purifying and expiatory aspect of the central New Year Festival before the exile. But it has been picked out and given a special emphasis by the compilers of Leviticus because for them 'expiation' was the main concern of the whole cultus. Thus they recount its celebration as the first public occasion on which Aaron officiated after his installation at the very beginning of Israel's existence as a holy community and they present it as the climax and culmination of all the practices to maintain purity which, for them, could alone preserve the nation's holiness and life (cp. the comment on verse 1).

1. *after the death of Aaron's two sons:* ch. 16 is the last section of the priestly narrative framework in Leviticus. It completes the account of the arrangements for the cultus made at Sinai. Hence it originally followed directly on the narrative in ch. 10 (cp. p. 2). The various laws about ritual uncleanness in chs. 11-15 were inserted because the Day of Atonement ritual was seen as the supreme expression and realization of the ideal lying behind them.

2. *the sanctuary within the Veil:* this was the most sacred part

of the temple, where God was thought to dwell (cp. the comment on verses 11–14), divided from the rest by the Veil (cp. the comment on 4: 6). *the cover over the Ark:* in priestly thought after the exile, the Ark is merely a container for the two tablets of the law (cp. Exod. 25: 16; Deut. 10: 2; 1 Kings 8: 9). Real religious significance was only given to the cover, a large golden plate on top of the Ark, to which two 'cherubim' were attached (cp. Exod. 25: 17–21). Two closely connected ideas are associated with it:

(i) the cover was viewed as a kind of throne on which God was believed to appear, enveloped in a *cloud*, with the 'cherubim' as his attendants. Hence this was the place where the high priest would actually 'meet' God in person (cp. Exod. 25: 22; 30: 6). It was the divine presence which made the inner *sanctuary* so holy and so dangerous to enter.

(ii) the Hebrew word for *cover* is related to the verb 'to expiate'. Since 'expiation' was made by transmitting the sacrificial blood to God, when it was brought into his immediate presence it would be particularly efficacious, and so the cover was the place of expiation *par excellence. except at the appointed time:* this translation suggests that the high priest went behind the Veil only once a year, as seems to have been the later practice (cp. Heb. 9: 6–7). However, the Hebrew means 'not at all times': since the regulations dealing with the high priest's entry into the sanctuary were originally separate from the Day of Atonement rituals (cp. p. 124), he was at this date probably able to enter the holy place at other times also. *on pain of death:* cp. the comment on verses 11–14.

3. The *young bull* and the *ram* belong to the priestly expiatory rites in this chapter (cp. p. 124): their purpose is explained in verses 6, 11 and 24.

4. The *sacred vestments* here are not the specifically high-priestly ones (cp. 8: 7–9) but those worn by the ordinary priest (cp. 8: 13; Exod. 28: 40–3). This probably indicates an old regulation, reflecting the situation before the exile, when the high priest had not yet gained the unique status he later

enjoyed (cp. the comment on 4: 3). On the other hand, the vestments used on this occasion would run a special risk of becoming infected with holiness and perhaps of having to be destroyed: the high-priestly garments, which in any case were preserved for successive generations (cp. the comment on 8: 30), were too costly to be exposed to this danger. *bathe in water:* it is noteworthy that the priest who officiated each day in the Babylonian New Year Festival had to don a special dress and wash himself before he entered the temple.

5. *for a sin-offering:* this shows the priestly tendency to give a single interpretation to what are actually distinct rituals. In fact, only one of the *he-goats* was used as a sin-offering (cp. verse 9).

8. *cast lots:* this, too, was an ancient custom, the object of which was to put the responsibility for the choice on God. Probably 'the Urim and Thummim' were used (cp. 1 Sam. 14: 41–2 and the comment on 8: 7–9). *for the Precipice:* two possible meanings for this obscure word are given in the N.E.B. text and footnote:

(i) it may be a place-name, indicating where the goat met its fate. There is a similar Arabic word meaning 'rough ground' and, in later times, the goat was in fact pushed over a cliff a few miles from Jerusalem to its death.

(ii) it may be the name of some wilderness deity or spirit, whom Jewish monotheism came to regard as evil (cp. the comment on 14: 7). The first goat is said to be *for the LORD*, so another divine name might be expected here, and in the later book of Enoch *Azazel* is an evil demon. Perhaps the two translations need not be sharply distinguished: examples occur of names which are both those of places or natural objects and also of deities, e.g. 'Bethel' (compare Gen. 28: 18–19 with Jer. 48: 13).

9–10. *for expiation to be made over it:* the goat which was *driven away into the wilderness* did not itself 'make expiation', as did the goat *for the LORD*, because it was not treated as a *sin-offering*. This not very clear expression is an attempt to assimilate an alien rite to the dominant priestly sacrificial practice and theology of expiation. ✳

THE CEREMONIES OF THE DAY OF ATONEMENT

11 Aaron shall present his bull as a sin-offering, making expiation for himself and his household, and then
12 slaughter the bull as a sin-offering. He shall take a firepan full of glowing embers from the altar before the LORD, and two handfuls of powdered fragrant incense, and bring
13 them within the Veil. He shall put the incense on the fire before the LORD, and the cloud of incense will hide the
14 cover over the Tokens so that he shall not die. He shall take some of the bull's blood and sprinkle it with his finger both on the surface of the cover, eastwards, and seven times in front of the cover.

15 He shall then slaughter the people's goat as a sin-offering, bring its blood within the Veil and do with its blood as he did with the bull's blood, sprinkling it on the
16 cover and in front of it. He shall make for the sanctuary the expiation required by the ritual uncleanness of the Israelites and their acts of rebellion, that is by all their sins; and he shall do the same for the Tent of the Presence, which dwells among them in the midst of all their un-
17 cleanness. No other man shall be within the Tent of the Presence from the time when he enters the sanctuary to make expiation until he comes out, and he shall make expiation for himself, his household, and the whole assembly of Israel.

18 He shall then come out to the altar which is before the LORD and make expiation for it. He shall take some of the

bull's blood and some of the goat's blood and put it all over the horns of the altar; he shall sprinkle some of the 19 blood on the altar with his finger seven times. So he shall purify it from all the uncleanness of the Israelites and hallow it.

When Aaron has finished making expiation for the 20 sanctuary, for the Tent of the Presence, and for the altar, he shall bring forward the live goat. He shall lay both his 21 hands on its head and confess over it all the iniquities of the Israelites and all their acts of rebellion, that is all their sins; he shall lay them on the head of the goat and send it away into the wilderness in charge of a man who is waiting ready. The goat shall carry all their iniquities 22 upon itself into some barren waste and the man shall let it go, there in the wilderness.

Aaron shall then enter the Tent of the Presence, take off 23 the linen clothes which he had put on when he entered the sanctuary, and leave them there. He shall bathe in 24 water in a consecrated place and put on his vestments; then he shall go out and perform his own whole-offering and that of the people, thus making expiation for himself and for the people. He shall burn the fat of the sin-offering 25 upon the altar. The man who drove the goat away to the 26 Precipice shall wash his clothes and bathe in water, and not till then may he enter the camp. The two sin-offerings, 27 the bull and the goat, the blood of which was brought within the Veil to make expiation in the sanctuary, shall be taken outside the camp and destroyed by fire – skin, flesh, and offal. The man who burns them shall wash his 28 clothes and bathe in water, and not till then may he enter the camp.

✲ 11–14. These verses are a combination of an expiatory rite with the regulations for the high priest's entry *within the Veil*. First, Aaron offers a *sin-offering...for himself* and the entire priesthood. Normally, the manipulation of the blood, which was the distinctive feature of the sin-offering, was done 'in front of the sacred Veil' (cp. 4: 6), but, on this special occasion, to gain the maximum effect, it was done in the very presence of God himself. Aaron must go within the Veil and a special precaution had to be taken. This consisted of producing a *cloud of incense* which hid the *cover*, so that Aaron was protected from seeing the divine presence there (cp. the comment on verse 2), because normally no man could see God and live (cp. Exod. 33: 20). *over the Tokens:* as verse 2 shows, 'the Ark' is meant. It often has this title in priestly material because it was believed to contain the tablets of the law which were the guarantees of God's covenant with his people (cp. the comment on verse 2 and Exod. 25: 16, 22). Protected by the cloud of incense, Aaron is now able to carry out the expiatory blood-ritual. *on the surface of the cover:* this corresponds to the rite of 4: 7 and in later times the 'altar of incense' also figured in the ceremonial of the Day of Atonement (cp. Exod. 30: 10). *eastwards:* that is, 'on the front', because the Hebrews faced eastwards when taking directions. *in front of the cover:* this sprinkling was in the air and corresponds to the rite in 4: 6.

15–17. *the people's goat* makes *expiation* for the Tent of the Presence and all its parts because this has been defiled by the sins of the Israelites. *all their sins* covers two classes of offences, *ritual uncleanness* and *acts of rebellion*, that is, the deliberate defiance of the will of a personal God. *the Tent of the Presence, which dwells among them:* an elliptical expression with the same meaning as 15: 31. *No other man shall be within the Tent of the Presence:* while Aaron is engaged in the highly dangerous proceedings 'within the Veil' (cp. the comment on verses 11–14), everybody must keep well away from the dangerous area.

18–19. This section concerns 'the altar of whole-offering', which was outside the Tent of the Presence. Basically, the rite corresponds to 4: 25. *some of the bull's blood and some of the goat's blood:* the area 'within the Veil' was purified in two stages, with *the bull's blood* on behalf of the priesthood (verse 14) and *the goat's blood* on behalf of the people (verse 15). Probably the idea is that the area which only the high priest could enter needed a special purification by him. For the altar, which was much more widely accessible, the two lots of blood are used together. *he shall sprinkle some of the blood on the altar:* possibly this represents a further ceremonial development, influenced by what was done in the case of the 'cover' (cp. verses 14–15).

20–2. For the significance of this distinctive rite, cp. the comment on 14: 7. *a man who is waiting ready:* this man has not been mentioned before but his role is explained in verse 26.

23–6. Strictly speaking, the purifying process for the nation was now completed and hence the emergence of the high priest, arrayed once more in his proper *vestments*, was an occasion for intense joy (cp. Ecclus. 50: 5ff.). *and leave them there:* the clothes which Aaron had worn to enter the inner-most sanctuary were infected with holiness. They had to remain in a holy place so that no-one would be in danger of coming into contact with them. *bathe in water in a consecrated place:* not until he has washed off the 'holiness' can the high priest leave the sacred sphere. *his own whole-offering and that of the people:* cp. verses 3 and 5. The whole-offering is said to 'make expiation': as has been noted, this was not its real purpose but for the compilers of Leviticus every sacrifice 'made expiation' whatever the occasion.

26. *the goat* on which Aaron laid his hands had transferred to it by this act 'all the iniquities of the Israelites' (verse 21), and so became unclean. *The man who drove the goat away* was therefore also unclean and had to purify himself.

27. Cp. the comment on 4: 4.

28. This verse suggests that the pronoun 'he' in 4: 12, 21 refers not to the priest, as would appear at first sight, but to a layman. ✷

A SUMMARIZING CONCLUSION

29 This[a] shall become a rule binding on you for all time. On the tenth day of the seventh month you shall mortify yourselves; you shall do no work, whether native Israelite

30 or alien settler, because on this day expiation shall be made on your behalf to cleanse you, and so make you

31 clean before the LORD from all your sins. This is a sabbath of sacred rest for you, and you shall mortify yourselves;

32 it is a rule binding for all time. Expiation shall be made by the priest duly anointed and installed to serve in succession

33 to his father; he shall put on the sacred linen clothes and shall make expiation for the holy sanctuary, the Tent of the Presence, and the altar, on behalf of the priests and the

34 whole assembly of the people. This shall become a rule binding on you for all time, to make for the Israelites once a year the expiation required by all their sins.

And Moses carried out the LORD's commands.

✷ The purpose of this section is to integrate the ancient feast of the Day of Atonement into the festival calendar as it developed after the exile, which is preserved in ch. 23 and will be discussed more fully there. The compilers assimilated the Day of Atonement into the pattern and outlook of that calendar in four ways:

(i) it is made clear that the ceremonies of the Day of Atonement did not constitute a once-for-all event at the beginning of Israel's history but were to be repeated annually,

[a] So Sept.; Heb. om.

as 'a rule binding on you for all time', verse 29 (cp. verses 31, 34).

(ii) in pursuance of this object, the date for the annual observance is carefully specified, verse 29. 'the seventh month' represents the Babylonian scheme of reckoning, which the Israelites adopted after the exile. It was called *Tishri* and ran roughly from mid-September to mid-October.

(iii) following the regulations of 23: 27–9, the command is given that, on the Day of Atonement, 'you shall mortify yourselves'. This entailed primarily fasting and wearing sack-cloth (cp. Ps. 35: 13; Isa. 58: 3–5). It is typical of the outlook of Judaism after the exile, which, with its enhanced awareness of sin, attached increasing importance to fasting as a sign of repentance and as a means of pleading for God's mercy in the face of national disasters (cp. Ezra 8: 21–3; Joel 1: 14; 2: 12, 15). Fixed days of fasting came to be listed in a regular calendar during this period (cp. Neh. 9: 1; Zech. 8: 19), but the Day of Atonement was soon considered as the most prominent of these and this is the situation presupposed here.

(iv) in the view of the priestly theologians, the fundamental observance in the calendar was the 'sabbath' (cp. the comment on 23: 3; Gen. 2: 3; Exod. 20: 11). So the basic sabbath taboo 'you shall do no work', verse 29, was extended to all the 'seasons' appointed in the calendar and thus here the Day of Atonement is described as 'a sabbath of sacred rest', verse 31.

32. *the priest duly anointed and installed to serve in succession to his father:* here, too, is evidence of a situation comparatively late after the exile. There is a regular succession of high priests, with son following father (cp. Neh. 12: 10–11), as was the case with the Davidic kings. Clearly the high priest is now regarded as the sole head of the nation and every real trace of the organization of Israel before the exile has disappeared. ✳

133

The law of holiness

✴ It has long been recognized that chs. 17–26 largely comprise an independent collection, which, like chs. 1–7, was incorporated into the narrative of the priestly source. The name given to it, 'the law of holiness', derives from the exhortation, which frequently recurs in these chapters in more less similar words, 'you shall be holy, because I, the LORD your God, am holy' (cp. 19: 2; 20: 7, 8, 26; 21: 6, 8, 15, 23; 22: 9, 16, 32). Thus there is an over-riding theme in this block of material, that Israel is to be set apart from all other peoples, just as its God is set apart from all other beings (cp. 20: 24, 26), and that this holiness is maintained by the strict observance of the divine laws which ensure purity and cleanness: the repeated exhortation to keep God's commandments is a second clear characteristic of these particular chapters (cp. 18: 4–5; 19: 19a, 37; 20: 8, 22; 22: 31; 26: 3, 14). Hence the basic purpose of 'the law of holiness' is not fundamentally different from that in chs. 11–16 and it is not difficult to see why the two should have been united together. But there are differences between them. First, the characteristic expressions already noted, together with others, do not occur in the distinctively priestly material, except in sections which look like additions (cp. the opening of the comment on 11: 43–5): again, the dominant priestly concern 'to make expiation' is only referred to four times in chs. 17–26 and once more there are good grounds for believing that some of these are additions (cp. the comments on 19: 20–2). Secondly, the outlook that the nation's holiness depends on the purity of the temple, the priesthood and the cult, although certainly present in these chapters, is not so prominent as it is in much of the other material we have surveyed, while an interest in the social and ethical duties of the ordinary Israelite is much more to the fore (cp. e.g. 19: 1–18). Thirdly, chs. 17–26 are distinguished by their notes of exhortation and stringent warning. Their most characteristic sections read like strongly emotive sermons, where the aim is not so much to instruct the hearers about the law, which is well known to them already, as to win them to obey it. So the divine commandments are presented as absolutely binding and their form is usually apodictic (see p. 14) because it was unthinkable that they could be disregarded. Noteworthy, also, is the frequency with which the death penalty is prescribed for infringements (cp. 17: 9, 14; 18: 29; 19: 8; 20: 2–21, 27; 21: 9; 24: 16) and it is likely that this was intended to bring home to the hearers the real seriousness of law-breaking rather than being regularly carried out in actual practice.

Although chs. 17–26 display a common linguistic usage and a common theme, like all the collections in Leviticus they are not a complete unity and a long period of historical development lies behind them. On the one hand, it is possible to see how an earlier form of this section has been expanded and modified to make it conform more closely to the distinctive outlook of priestly theology after the exile: this seems particularly clear in the case of ch. 23. On the other hand, the existing 'law of holiness' has been built up from a number of smaller units and originally independent collections of laws dealing with particular topics. As in chs. 11–15, the rough extent of some of these collections can be traced from concluding summaries, taking the form of general exhortations to observe the divine commandments, which appear to have been appended at their close when they were brought together (cp. 18: 24–30; 19: 37; 20: 22–4; 22: 31–3). But there are other conclusions which seem to suggest a variant arrangement (cp. 21: 24; 23: 44) and blocks of material, notably the narrative in 24: 10–14, 23, which seem to be quite independent. Probably the most that can be said is that we have here various pieces of teaching, representing the traditions of priestly instruction at different Israelite shrines. Thus much of the material is of very early date, going back well before the exile, before Jerusalem emerged as the sole national sanctuary.

This fact, taken in conjunction with the later working-over after the exile, makes it possible to suggest a date and a setting for the compilation of the original 'law of holiness'. The curses of 26: 14–39 seem to reflect the circumstances of the Babylonian invasion and the exile. We may therefore think of chs. 17–26 as coming into existence in the same way and in the same situation as chs. 1–7 and as forming a counterpart to the latter. When the priests of other sanctuaries took refuge at Jerusalem at the time of the exile, they would need to codify their different traditions of teaching as well as their traditions of cultic practice. So 'the law of holiness' may have been created in this circle as a kind of manual for preaching: we might say that chs. 17–26 and 1–7 together show the way in which 'the ministry of the word and sacraments' was exercised at Jerusalem during the exile. The aim of this preaching was to prepare the people to become a new holy community, when the exile had ended, and to warn them against a repetition of those sins which, in the view of the priests, had brought disaster on the Israel of the past.

Two further considerations support this view. First, another keynote of chs. 17–26 is the phrase 'I am the LORD' or 'I am the LORD your God' (18: 2 and some 37 times elsewhere in the section). This expression is a profession of faith in the uniqueness of Israel's God, in contrast to other divine beings (cp. the comment on 11: 43–5). So it is frequently linked with warnings against apostasy in favour of foreign, and more specifically Canaanite, cults (cp. 18: 3, 21, 24–30; 19: 26–8, 31; 20: 22–4; 26: 1). These warnings are not found elsewhere in Leviticus, but there is evidence to suggest that precisely around the time of the exile there was a recrudesence of such cults in Palestine, because Israel's God appeared to be powerless to protect his own people (cp. Jer. 44: 2–3, 16–19; Ezek. 8: 6–18; Isa. 57: 3–10; 65: 3–5, 11). So it was specially necessary for the preachers behind 'the law of holiness' to call their hearers back to the true God and to warn them of the ever-present danger of backsliding.

Secondly, there is the universally recognized relationship between 'the law of holiness' and the book of Ezekiel. This relationship raises many problems but it may be noted that perhaps the chief point of contact is the emphasis on holiness in both works and, as has been seen, it is the concept of holiness which is the principal factor unifying the diverse elements in chs. 17–26. Ezekiel was active during the time of the exile and he was also of priestly descent (cp. Ezek. 1: 3): thus he belonged to the same environment and shared the same outlook as the compilers of 'the law of holiness'. Perhaps we should see the book of Ezekiel and Lev. 17–26 as two forms of preaching, both based on the same materials now incorporated in 'the law of holiness', and both having as their object to explain to the nation the reason for the calamities that had befallen it and to build up a new sacral community for the future. Here, again, can be seen the fundamental identity of what have often been too sharply distinguished as 'priestly' and 'prophetic' theologies (cp. p. 9). *

THE PROPER PLACE OF SACRIFICE

THE LORD SPOKE to Moses and said, Speak to Aaron, **17** 1, 2 his sons, and all the Israelites in these words: This is what the LORD has commanded. Any Israelite who 3 slaughters an ox, a sheep, or a goat, either inside or outside the camp, and does not bring it to the entrance of the 4 Tent of the Presence to present it as an offering to the LORD before the Tabernacle of the LORD shall be held guilty of bloodshed: that man has shed blood and shall be cut off from his people. The purpose is that the Israelites 5 should bring to the LORD the animals which they slaughter in the open country; they shall bring them to the priest

at the entrance to the Tent of the Presence and sacrifice
6 them as shared-offerings to the LORD. The priest shall
fling the blood against the altar of the LORD at the entrance
to the Tent of the Presence, and burn the fat as a soothing
7 odour to the LORD. They shall no longer sacrifice their
slaughtered beasts to the demons[a] whom they wantonly
follow. This shall be a rule binding on them and their
descendants for all time.

8   You shall say to them. Any Israelite or alien settled in
9 Israel who offers a whole-offering or a sacrifice and does
not bring it to the entrance of the Tent of the Presence to
sacrifice it to the LORD shall be cut off from his father's kin.

* This section illustrates very clearly how 'the law of holiness' was formed by the reinterpretation of older material.
Here the main purpose is to warn the Israelites against heathen
cults (verse 7), and this is the reason for including this passage
in 'the law of holiness' (cp. p. 136); but this particular piece of
teaching is presented as the interpretation (verse 5), of an
ancient regulation in casuistic form (verses 3-4). Even the
regulation, however, has undergone development and two
stages in particular may be distinguished:

(i) as verse 4*b* suggests, its original purpose was in relation
to the taboo on blood. It was to prevent any improper use of
the blood whenever an animal was slaughtered for food and
to make sure that the blood was conveyed to God to whom it
belonged (cp. 1 Sam. 14: 32-4). It presupposes a time when
there was no distinction between 'sacrificial' slaughter and
'ordinary' slaughter (contrast Deut. 12: 15-16) and when
there was always a shrine available in the vicinity, to which a
man could easily come on the comparatively rare occasions
when domestic animals were killed for food.

(ii) however, as it now stands, the regulation obviously

[a] Or satyrs.

implies only one sanctuary. This is partly because of its present setting in the context of Sinai, where only a single place of worship could be envisaged (cp. 'the Tabernacle of the LORD' (verse 4) which is the regular priestly term in Exodus for the sanctuary at the time of Moses). But it may also correspond to the situation of a small community living around Jerusalem during the exile, when all other shrines had been destroyed.

3. *an ox, a sheep or a goat:* only domestic animals are considered, because only these could be offered in sacrifice and so brought to the sanctuary (cp. the comment on verses 13–14).

4. *guilty of bloodshed:* this is a technical legal term which elsewhere in the Old Testament is only used with reference to the killing of one human being by another. Here, however, the killing an animal makes a person guilty of bloodshed and this probably represents a very ancient concept. Early man was highly conscious of his kinship with the animals (cp. the comment on 11: 3): he looked back to an ideal time when men did not eat them (cp. Gen. 1: 29) and when therefore the killing of them was equivalent to murder. When men began to kill and eat animals, the guilt incurred could be expiated by giving the blood to God – that is, the life of the animal was transferred to him – although an animal still incurred blood-guilt if it killed a human being (cp. Gen. 9: 3–6). *shall be cut off from his people:* this is a characteristic expression of chs. 17–26 (cp. verse 10 and 18: 29. It appears also several times in ch. 20 and elsewhere: cp. also 7: 20). The meaning is that the offender will be punished by death but the method of execution is not specified. Perhaps the phrase implies that God himself will take vengeance (cp. the comment on 20: 4–5).

5–6. In these verses, 'the law of holiness' reinterprets the old regulation. All animals that are killed must be brought to *the Tent of the Presence* and there treated as *shared-offerings.* When the blood has been disposed of (cp. 3: 2) and the fat, the LORD's share, burnt on the altar (cp. 3: 3–5), the rest of the animal is available for human consumption. *the open country:* this may simply mean 'away from the sanctuary', but it perhaps has the overtones of 14: 7 (cp. the comment on p. 108).

7. *to the demons:* quite otherwise than the intention of the old regulation, the slaughtering of an animal away from the sanctuary is viewed here as a sacrifice to the demons who were thought to inhabit 'the open country'. The footnote suggests that they took the form of 'satyrs' – that is, goat-footed demons or he-goats – which infested waste places (cp. Isa. 13: 21; 34: 14). *whom they wantonly follow:* shrines for such demons existed at the very gates of Jerusalem and, although they had been suppressed in Josiah's reformation (cp. 2 Kings 23: 8), they had probably come into use again after the fall of Judah (cp. p. 136).

8–9. This is a supplementary expansion to clarify two points:

(i) the regulation covered not only 'shared-offerings', which alone are specified in verses 3–7, but also the *whole-offering* and any other animal *sacrifice* as well.

(ii) it covered not only *Any Israelite* but also the *alien settled in Israel*. The alien had a clearly defined status in Israelite society and so he was bound to observe its basic cultic regulations (cp. e.g. Exod. 12: 48–9; 20: 10). 'The law of holiness' evinces a particular concern for the alien: this is probably a reflection of the situation resulting from the Babylonian invasions, when the disturbed conditions in the area caused many inhabitants from the surrounding countries to settle in Palestine. ✳

THE PROHIBITION OF EATING BLOOD

10 If any Israelite or alien settled in Israel eats any blood, I will set my face against the eater and cut him off from his
11 people, because the life of a creature is the blood, and I appoint it to make expiation on the altar for yourselves: it is the blood, that is the life, that makes expiation.

Therefore I have told the Israelites that neither you, nor 12
any alien settled among you, shall eat blood.

Any Israelite or alien settled in Israel who hunts beasts 13
or birds that may lawfully be eaten shall drain out the
blood and cover it with earth, because the life of every 14
living creature is the blood,[a] and I have forbidden the
Israelites to eat the blood of any creature, because the life
of every creature is its blood: every man who eats it shall
be cut off.

Every person, native or alien, who eats that which has 15
died a natural death or has been mauled by wild beasts
shall wash his clothes and bathe in water, and remain
ritually unclean till evening; then he shall be clean. If he 16
does not wash his clothes and bathe his body, he must
accept responsibility.

☆ 10–12. These verses are linked with the preceding section
by the catch-phrase *any Israelite or alien* but also because they
too deal with blood, but here the question concerns eating the
blood, which is strictly prohibited. *because the life of a creature
is the blood:* the reason for the prohibition is a very old one.
Originally, the meaning was that the blood belonged only to
God, because it contained the life which belonged to the
source of life. But, according to the dominant priestly viewpoint, God has 'appointed' or 'given' the blood to the
Israelites *to make expiation* for them. It must go *on the altar* and
this is why it cannot be eaten.

13–14. A further development of the foregoing to deal
with the question: 'what is to be done with the blood of game
or wild *birds*, since they cannot be offered in sacrifice (cp. the
comment on verse 3) and so the procedure in verses 5–6 cannot apply?' *that may lawfully be eaten:* that is, in accordance

[a] *So Sept.; Heb. adds* within it.

141

with the rules of 11: 1–8, 13–19. It is assumed that hunting would only be for food. *drain out the blood:* cp. Deut. 12: 24. *cover it with earth:* because the blood is the life, it retains all its mysterious and dangerous power (cp. Gen. 4: 10) and hence every trace of it must be obliterated.

15–16. A section which is loosely linked to verses 13–14 by the theme of eating. It deals with dead domestic animals which have not been killed by man and lays down the same rule as 11: 40. It is of course assumed that the blood of such animals will have been drained out before they are eaten. ✳

AN INTRODUCTORY EXHORTATION

18₁,₂ The LORD spoke to Moses and said, Speak to the Israelites
³ in these words: I am the LORD your God. You shall not do as they do in Egypt where you once dwelt, nor shall you do as they do in the land of Canaan to which I am bringing you; you shall not conform to their institutions.
⁴ You must keep my laws and conform to my institutions
⁵ without fail: I am the LORD your God. You shall observe my institutions and my laws: the man who keeps them shall have life through them. I am the LORD.

✳ Again, ch. 18 shows the use of old legal collections in the context of preaching. It consists of an ancient list (verses 6–18) and appended miscellaneous laws (verses 19–23) all dealing with sexual offences: but this material is introduced (verses 1–5) and concluded (verses 24–30), by exhortatory passages of a quite different kind, which warn the Israelites against these sins and explain why they are to avoid them.

2. *I am the LORD your God:* this formula has its origin in the cultic address at a regular act of worship in Israel before the exile, when the Sinai covenant was repeated and renewed. On

this occasion, God was believed to appear in the sanctuary (cp. Ps. 50: 2–3), to announce himself (cp. Ps. 50: 7) and then to utter warnings and commandments to the worshippers (cp. Ps. 50: 8–15). In actual practice, the divine words would be given through the officiating priest, who, like the prophet, spoke in God's name.

3. The sexual offences of the following sections were understood by the preacher as being characteristic of Egyptian and Canaanite religion and society and for him this is the reason for avoiding them. In Israelite eyes, Canaan was particularly characterized by sexual licence (cp. Gen. 9: 20–5). *Egypt:* the Israelites were considered to have worshipped the gods of Egypt during their stay there and never subsequently to have entirely cast off their influence (cp. Ezek. 20: 7–8, 24). But, in the context of 'the law of holiness', the mention of Egypt has a contemporary reference. In the years immediately before the exile, the influence of Egypt and its cults was very marked in Judah and, after the fall of Jerusalem, a number of Jews had migrated there and adopted the worship of the country: this may be the point made in Jer. 44: 8.

4. There is a complete distinction between the 'institutions' of Egypt and Canaan and the *laws* and *institutions* of the God of Israel, which must be kept *without fail*.

5. *shall have life through them:* keeping the divine commandments brings prosperity and success, which is what the Hebrews primarily understood by *life*. The phrase recurs in a similar sermon on the same theme in Ezek. 20: 11, 13, 21. ✻

SEXUAL OFFENCES WITHIN THE FAMILY

No man shall approach a blood-relation for intercourse. 6
I am the LORD. You shall not bring shame on your father 7
by intercourse with your mother: she is your mother;
you shall not bring shame upon her. You shall not have 8
intercourse with your father's wife: that is to bring shame

9 upon your father. You shall not have intercourse with your sister, your father's daughter, or your mother's daughter, whether brought up in the family or in another

10 home; you shall not bring shame upon them. You shall not have intercourse with your son's daughter or your daughter's daughter: that is to bring shame upon yourself.

11 You shall not have intercourse with a daughter of your father's wife, begotten by your father: she is your sister,

12 and you shall not bring shame upon her. You shall not have intercourse with your father's sister: she is a blood-

13 relation of your father. You shall not have intercourse with your mother's sister: she is a blood-relation of your

14 mother. You shall not bring shame upon your father's

15 brother by approaching his wife: she is your aunt. You shall not have intercourse with your daughter-in-law: she is your son's wife; you shall not bring shame upon her.

16 You shall not have intercourse with your brother's wife:

17 that is to bring shame upon him. You shall not have intercourse with both a woman and her daughter, nor shall you take her son's daughter or her daughter's daughter to have intercourse with them: they are her blood-relations, and such conduct is lewdness.

* Apart from verse 6, which, as will be seen, is an addition made in the course of preaching, the regulations of this section go back probably to the very earliest days of Israelite settlement in Palestine. They show a society organized on the basis of the large family group living together. The explanations of why the rules must be observed do not invoke any divine law, but are based solely on the fact of existing relationships within the family group. They suggest a period in Israel's history before the national religion had made its influence dominant in every department of moral and social practice and when there was no 'nation', but the groups which were later to comprise it were living together as large families in a semi-nomadic state in Palestine. The regulations here enable us to see precisely who were then considered to belong to the Hebrew large family group. Their purpose is not to prohibit certain kinds of marriages, as has commonly been supposed, e.g. in the Table of Kindred and Affinity at the end of the Book of Common Prayer, nor even simply to prevent sexual intercourse with females of close blood-relationship. Rather, the primary concern is with those who are living together in close proximity to one another in a tent encampment, although, of course, the real kernel of those so living was formed of people closely related by blood. The rules aim to regulate sexual relationships and to forbid all promiscuity within the group, with the object of preserving peace and harmony among those living together. Comparable rules for sexual relationships are to be found in many communities throughout the world.

6. The phrase *I am the LORD* is a sermonic addition (cp. the comment on verse 2) to a general regulation condemning incest, not originally connected with verses 7–17.

7. *You shall not: You* is singular in the Hebrew, and the prohibitions are in apodictic form. Nothing is said of any penalty for their infringement, because to break them would be virtually inconceivable, since they are concerned with the fundamentals of the group's life that allow it to exist at all. Throughout, the person addressed is the head of the group, with reference to whom all the relationships are viewed. He would be a man in the prime of life, which explains why he and not his father is the head of the family. *bring shame on your father:* in the N.E.B., *bring shame* and 'have intercourse' represent the same Hebrew expression, which is literally 'uncover the nakedness of'. The mention of the father here is very awkward in the Hebrew text and is almost certainly an addition. Originally, the verse referred only to the mother,

and the reason for not having intercourse with her is simply that *she is your mother*, a close kinswoman.

8. The reference is to a wife of the father who is not the mother of the head of the family. In ancient Hebrew society, there was no objection to a man having more than one wife (cp. Gen. 26: 34). Here the ground of the prohibition is that intercourse with such a wife would bring *shame upon your father:* it would be an invasion of his rights and thus an obvious cause of dissension within the group.

9. *your father's daughter, or your mother's daughter:* these terms define what is meant by *sister*. At first sight, this verse seems to overlap with verse 11, but it is concerned with a woman *brought up* (the Hebrew is literally 'born') *in the family or in another home.* The prohibition is the same whether the woman in question was the offspring of two members both of whom belonged to the same family group or of two persons, either or both of whom did not belong to it. The regulation applies to all such persons who were now living together in one unit, an indication that, as already noted, proximity as much as kinship is the concern of this section. In view of verse 10, a prohibition of intercourse by the head of the family with his daughter probably once followed here: it has accidentally dropped out in the course of literary transmission.

10. *that is to bring shame on yourself:* we might expect it to be said to bring shame on the head of the family's son or daughter, rather than on himself: but grandchildren were considered to belong to the grandfather at least as much as to their own parents (cp. Gen. 31: 43).

11. This verse refers to a daughter of the father by a wife other than the mother of the person addressed (cp. the comment on verse 8) and thus a half-sister.

12–13. The relationship to the father's sister and the mother's sister is constituted by the head of the family's prior relationship to his father and mother.

14. The paternal uncle was an important figure in the family (cp. 1 Sam. 10: 14; 2 Kings 24: 17; Amos 6: 10) and it

is because she belongs to him that intercourse is forbidden with the aunt (cp. the comment on verse 8).

15. Forbidding intercourse with the daughter-in-law provides the clearest indication that these regulations do not rest on a basis of close blood-relationship, for the son's wife could very often come from another family group and so not be nearly related to her father-in-law. The point is that she belongs to the son, whose rights must be respected.

16. The same considerations apply as in verse 14, for the brother stood in the same relation to the existing head of the family as the uncle stood to his father.

17. *with both a woman and her daughter:* probably the aim of this verse is to forbid to the head of the family intercourse with the mother of the woman he has married. Intercourse with a mother-in-law was strictly prohibited (cp. Deut. 27: 23) and she is not otherwise referred to in the list here. *nor shall you take her son's daughter:* the latter part of this verse does not belong to the original set of regulations, as is shown by the quite different reason given, *such conduct is lewdness.* ✵

VARIOUS SEXUAL OFFENCES

You shall not take a woman who is your wife's sister to 18 make her a rival-wife, and to have intercourse with her during her sister's lifetime.

You shall not approach a woman to have intercourse 19 with her during her period of menstruation. You shall not 20 have sexual intercourse with the wife of your fellow-countryman and so make yourself unclean with her. You 21 shall not surrender any of your children to Molech and thus profane the name of your God: I am the LORD. You 22 shall not lie with a man as with a woman: that is an abomination. You shall not have sexual intercourse with 23 any beast to make yourself unclean with it, nor shall a woman submit herself to intercourse with a beast: that is a violation of nature.

✻ A number of miscellaneous, and later, prohibitions are now added, because they too mostly dealt with sexual crimes. They have the effect of transforming the ancient family code into a general condemnation of all forms of sexual immorality.

18. Unlike verses 7–17, it is marriage that is in question here. In early Israel, there was no objection to a man marrying two sisters simultaneously (cp. Gen. 29: 21–9). Clearly this is a later rule, probably made because a second wife always tended to become a 'rival' to the first (cp. Gen. 21: 10; 30: 1) and this would be specially the case where her own sister was involved.

19. Cp. the comment on 15: 19–24.

20. This is a general prohibition of adultery. *make yourself unclean:* as verses 24–30 show, the uncleanness produced by adultery is here intended to be punished with death (cp. the comment on 17: 4 and 20: 10).

21. Strictly speaking, this verse has nothing to do with sexual offences, but it has come in because it refers to a foreign cult, and in this section such offences are viewed as characteristic of non-Israelite worship (cp. the comment on verse 3). *Molech:* cp. the comment on 20: 2.

22–3. Homosexuality and bestiality bring about uncleanness because they are a *violation of nature* (cp. p. 84): men should only have intercourse with women and human beings with human beings. ✻

THE CONCLUDING EXHORTATION

24 You shall not make yourselves unclean in any of these ways; for in these ways the heathen, whom I am driving
25 out before you, made themselves unclean. This is how the land became unclean, and I punished it for its iniquity so

that it spewed out its inhabitants. You, unlike them, shall 26
keep my laws and my rules: none of you, whether natives
or aliens settled among you, shall do any of these abominable things. The people who were there before you did 27
these abominable things and the land became unclean. So 28
the land will not spew you out for making it unclean as
it spewed them out; for anyone who does any of these 29
abominable things shall be cut off from his people.
Observe my charge, therefore, and follow none of the 30
abominable institutions customary before your time; do
not make yourselves unclean with them. I am the LORD
your God.

✶ 24–5. *You shall not make yourselves unclean in any of these
ways:* this might be described as the 'text' for the whole
sermon. Next, a reason for keeping the command is given.
The *heathen* who had once inhabited Palestine *made themselves
unclean* by these practices: in turn, *the land became unclean*
through them, and it reacted by spewing them out. Thus an
appeal is made to history: it was because of the sins of the
former inhabitants that Israel was able to take possession of the
promised land. Notice how the land is personified here (cp.
19: 29; 26: 43), an old religious concept which underlies the
language of Hos. 2.

26–9. The sequence of thought is not very clear, perhaps
because the verses consist of originally independent sayings,
but there are two possibilities:

(i) The first is that preferred by the N.E.B. All the
Canaanites did 'these abominable things' but only some individual Israelites perhaps do and, if anyone does, he will be
exterminated, verse 29, so that the land will not become unclean and 'spew out' Israel.

(ii) Verse 27 can be treated as a parenthesis, as in the
Revised Standard Version, and the beginning of verse 28

translated 'lest the land spew you out' (cp. 20: 22). Israel would therefore be warned that it could meet the same fate as the Canaanites (cp. Ezek. 36: 17–19).

28. *as it spewed them out:* clearly Israel is regarded as already being in Palestine and the artificiality of the Sinai setting is plain (contrast verse 3).

30. The final word that brings together everything that has previously been said. ✳

DUTIES TO GOD AND NEIGHBOUR

19 1,2 The LORD spoke to Moses and said, Speak to all the community of the Israelites in these words: You shall be 3 holy, because I, the LORD your God, am holy. You shall revere, every man of you, his mother and his father. You 4 shall keep my sabbaths. I am the LORD your God. Do not resort to idols; you shall not make gods of cast metal for yourselves. I am the LORD your God.

5   When you sacrifice a shared-offering to the LORD, you shall slaughter it so as to win acceptance for yourselves. 6 It must be eaten on the day of your sacrifice or the next day. Whatever is left over till the third day shall be 7 destroyed by fire; it is tainted, and if any of it is eaten on 8 the third day, it will not be acceptable. He who eats it must accept responsibility, because he has profaned the holy-gift to the LORD: that person shall be cut off from his father's kin.

9   When you reap the harvest of your land, you shall not reap right into the edges of your field; neither shall you 10 glean the loose ears of your crop; you shall not completely strip your vineyard nor glean the fallen grapes. You shall leave them for the poor and the alien. I am the LORD your God.

You shall not steal; you shall not cheat or deceive a 11
fellow-countryman. You shall not swear in my name 12
with intent to deceive and thus profane the name of your
God. I am the LORD. You shall not oppress your neigh- 13
bour, nor rob him. You shall not keep back a hired man's
wages till next morning. You shall not treat the deaf with 14
contempt, nor put an obstruction in the way of the blind.
You shall fear your God. I am the LORD.

You shall not pervert justice, either by favouring the 15
poor or by subservience to the great. You shall judge your
fellow-countryman with strict justice. You shall not go 16
about spreading slander among your father's kin, nor take
sides against your neighbour on a capital charge. I am the
LORD. You shall not nurse hatred against your brother. 17
You shall reprove your fellow-countryman frankly and
so you will have no share in his guilt.[a] You shall not seek 18
revenge, or cherish anger towards your kinsfolk; you
shall love your neighbour as a man like yourself. I am the
LORD.

✴ Ch. 19 has been described as 'the priestly Decalogue', and
not without justification, for the brief, apodictic and predominantly negative form of the thirty or so separate regulations is very similar to that of the Ten Commandments.
Probably the purpose is similar too: as the Decalogue represents an early summary of the basic law which formed the
content of God's covenant with his people, so the aim of this
chapter is to produce a similar summary for the period of the
exile and this accounts, in contrast to the two preceding chapters, for the wide range of topics which it covers. Two further
points may be noted. There appear to be some direct contacts
with the Decalogue of Exod. 20 and the whole list is clearly

[a] *Or* and for that you will incur no blame.

made up of a number of separate collections, each generally, though not invariably, concluded by the typical explanation of 'the law of holiness', 'I am the LORD.' Probably, then, we see here the way in which the fundamental covenant law was understood in different Israelite sanctuaries, as their priests taught, expounded and so developed it over the years. It is not surprising, therefore, that in ch. 19 there are reminiscences, not only of the Decalogue, but of a very wide area of Old Testament material, notably the early legal code in Exod. 21–3, Deuteronomy and the great prophets, such as Isaiah, Jeremiah and Micah. This does not mean that the author of the chapter is quoting from actual books, but that the teaching of Deuteronomy and the prophets rests, like his, on the demands of the covenant law and indeed on the way that law was taught and transmitted at the sanctuaries.

This chapter consists of material that was given in priestly instruction, as the opening verses 1–2 and the closing verses 36b–37 clearly show; but unlike so much of the rest of Leviticus, it contains no specific regulations for the priests. It deals exclusively with the religious and social duties of the ordinary Israelite towards God and his fellow-countrymen. It reflects the legal and economic conditions of the period of the Israelite monarchy and so of a later stage of the nation's development than that represented in 18: 7–17. Like most ancient collections of laws, there is no clear or logical order in the way the commands are set out – or none, at least, that we can discover – but the compiler simply strings together loosely what was available to him. His object was to preserve what he could of the old legal traditions from the wreck of the national life, that they might once more provide the structure for the revived Israel he hoped to see.

2. *all the community of the Israelites:* it is emphasized that what follows provides for everyone in the nation. *You shall be holy:* here is the regular preaching formula of the compilers of 'the law of holiness'.

3. *You shall revere . . . his mother and his father:* cp. Exod. 20:

12; Deut. 27: 16. The placing of this command at the head of the series is significant. More than anything else, family life had been disrupted by the Babylonian deportations (cp. Lam. 4: 2–4, 10; 5: 2–3) and had to be maintained. Significant also may be the mention of the mother before the father. 'The law of holiness' shows a particular concern for the mother (cp. 20: 19; 21: 2 and note that, together with the present verse, these are the only occurrences of the order *mother–father* in the whole Old Testament): since her sphere was essentially the home, the break-up of the family would especially endanger her position (cp. Mal. 2: 14–16). *keep my sabbaths:* cp. Exod. 20: 8 and the comments on 16: 29–34 and 23: 3.

4. Cp. Exod. 34: 14, 17, from another collection of covenant law; Deut. 27: 15. *Do not resort to idols:* this refers to the worship of deities other than the LORD. *gods of cast metal:* by contrast, this prohibition forbids the introduction of metal images into the cult of Israel's God (cp. Exod. 32: 4–5; 1 Kings 12: 28–30).

5–8. Cp. 7: 16–18. The *shared-offering* is picked out because this was the sacrifice in which the layman, in the communal meal, had the greatest share. *cut off from his father's kin:* cp. the comment on 17: 4. The words are a preaching addition to the basic statement, *He who eats it must accept responsibility*, which alone occurs in 7: 18, to bring home the gravity of the offence.

9. First is given a series of ancient harvest regulations, the original purpose of which was to leave part of the crop for the spirits of the soil, a custom found among many early peoples.

10. But this is reinterpreted as a charitable gift for *the poor and the alien* (cp. the comment on 17: 8–9), two classes who would be particularly vulnerable in the harsh conditions during the exile (cp. 23: 22; Deut. 24: 19–21; Ruth 2: 15–16).

11. *you shall not cheat:* again, an interpretation of the basic law, as found in Exod. 20: 15, to make it cover not only open

robbery but also any action that deprived a man of what was rightfully his.

12. This is to make clear that what the basic law meant by 'the wrong use of the name of the LORD' (cp. Exod. 20: 7) was an oath taken *with intent to deceive*. In Hebrew thought, a man's name enshrined his personality (cp. 1 Sam. 25: 25) and thus to invoke *the name of your God* in such a case involved the deity himself in the deception.

13. *You shall not keep back a hired man's wages:* a further explanation of what is implied in the law of Exod. 20: 15, in favour of a class peculiarly liable to exploitation. If a hired man's wages were not paid as soon as he had finished his work, he would not be able to eat until the next day (cp. Matt. 20:8). A fairly advanced economic system is reflected in this verse.

14. *treat the deaf with contempt:* the Hebrew really means 'to utter a curse'. In the thought of the Old Testament, a curse has an objective power. Hence a deaf man would be unable to hear a curse and so unable to take preventive action, any more than would a blind man who could not see *an obstruction in the way* (cp. Deut. 27: 18). Again, 'the law of holiness' shows a special concern for the unfortunate.

15. *You shall not pervert justice:* this begins a series of instructions designed to safeguard the proper administration of the law. Justice is one of the key themes of the Old Testament, which sees it as the foundation of the whole social order (cp. Deut. 16: 20). *by favouring the poor or by subservience to the great:* the latter was obviously the greater danger, because of the possibility of bribery (cp. Exod. 23: 8; Deut. 16: 19). But strict impartiality was the ideal (cp. Deut. 1: 17) and it was recognized that sympathy could be as misleading as fear (cp. Exod. 23: 3). *You shall judge your fellow-countryman:* it is not a special class of judges that is referred to here, but the court which was held at the town-gate (cp. Job 31: 21 where the N.E.B. has 'in court' for the literal expression 'in the gate', which appears in the footnote) in which all the leading men of the local community took part.

16. *spreading slander:* this could prejudice a man's case when it came to be tried by his fellows (cp. Exod. 23: 1). *take sides:* that is, unfairly (cp. Exod. 23: 7).

17. *nurse hatred:* to nurse hatred against a man accused of a crime would make an impartial verdict difficult. *you will have no share in his guilt:* as the footnote indicates, the sense is not wholly clear, but the general meaning is plain. If you see a man doing wrong and do not try to stop him, you implicitly condone his offence and so share in his guilt.

18. *you shall love your neighbour as a man like yourself:* cp. verse 34. This is no doubt the best-known saying in Leviticus, because of its quotation in the New Testament. But, in this context, it means the sense of brotherhood which should be felt with every member of the Israelite sacral community. It does not have the universal application that Jesus gives it (cp. Luke 10: 25–37). *

DUTIES TO GOD AND NEIGHBOUR:
RELIGIOUS DEMANDS

You shall keep my rules. You shall not allow two different 19 kinds of beast to mate together. You shall not plant your field with two kinds of seed. You shall not put on a garment woven with two kinds of yarn.

When a man has intercourse with a slave-girl who has 20 been assigned to another man and neither ransomed nor given her freedom, inquiry shall be made. They shall not be put to death, because she has not been freed. The man 21 shall bring his guilt-offering, a ram, to the LORD to the entrance of the Tent of the Presence, and with it the 22 priest shall make expiation for him before the LORD for his sin, and he shall be forgiven the sin he has committed.

When you enter the land, and plant any kind of tree for 23

food, you shall treat it as bearing forbidden[a] fruit. For
24 three years it shall be forbidden and may not be eaten. In
the fourth year all its fruit shall be a holy-gift to the LORD,
25 and this releases it for use.[b] In the fifth year you may eat
its fruit, and thus the yield it gives you shall be increased.
I am the LORD your God.

26 You shall not eat meat with the blood in it. You shall
27 not practise divination or soothsaying. You shall not
round off your hair from side to side, and you shall not
28 shave the edge of your beards. You shall not gash yourselves in mourning for the dead; you shall not tattoo yourselves. I am the LORD.

29 Do not prostitute your daughter and so make her a
whore; thus the land shall not play the prostitute and be
30 full of lewdness. You shall keep my sabbaths, and revere
my sanctuary. I am the LORD.

31 Do not resort to ghosts and spirits, nor make yourselves
unclean by seeking them out. I am the LORD your God.

32 You shall rise in the presence of grey hairs, give honour
to the aged, and fear your God. I am the LORD.

33 When an alien settles with you in your land, you shall
34 not oppress him. He shall be treated as a native born
among you, and you shall love him as a man like yourself,
because you were aliens in Egypt. I am the LORD your God.

35 You shall not pervert justice in measurement of length,
36 weight, or quantity. You shall have true scales, true
weights, true measures dry and liquid. I am the LORD your
37 God who brought you out of Egypt. You shall observe
all my rules and laws and carry them out. I am the LORD.

[a] *Lit.* uncircumcised.
[b] and this. . .use: *so Sam.; Heb.* a festal jubilation.

✳ 19. The idea underlying this little group of three prohibitions is the same as that underlying the laws about
'uncleanness' (cp. the comment on 11: 1–8): creatures or
things of one nature are not to be mixed up with those having
another. *two different kinds of beast to mate together:* this is certainly a very early regulation, since it would exclude mules,
which were known in Israel but seem to have been introduced
comparatively late (the first reference to them is 2 Sam. 13:
29). In the parallel passage, Deut. 22: 9–11, this particular rule
is omitted.

20–2. In these verses, we have an isolated piece of case law,
of a kind not otherwise found in ch. 19, developed to deal
with a particular problem. *assigned to another man:* this refers to
the betrothal ceremony which, in the Old Testament, gives
the prospective husband the same rights as the actual marriage.
Hence any one who had intercourse with a betrothed girl was
guilty of adultery and liable to the death penalty (cp. Deut.
22: 23–7). The question is: 'does this apply to a slave-girl?'.
The answer is 'no', provided that she has been *neither ransomed* – that is, bought out from her servitude – *nor given her
freedom* – that is, by her owner, because in this case she still
belonged to her master, not to the future husband. *inquiry:* the
Hebrew word occurs only here, and perhaps really means
'compensation for damage', paid either to the owner or the
future husband. In addition, a cultic ceremony has to be performed, but again there is no suggestion that the ram was
sacrificed, rather than being understood as a monetary compensation (cp. the comments on 5: 15–16; 14: 12).

23–5. This is another very old taboo, which, like the laws
of verses 9–10 (cp. the comment there), was originally concerned with leaving the crop for the spirits of the ground, but
which has been assimilated to the worship of Israel's God.
forbidden: the literal meaning is given in the footnote. Anyone
'uncircumcised' was outside the holy community, so produce
not available to the community could be described in this way.
holy-gift to the LORD: here we have the distinctively Israelite

tradition of a further year's taboo, when the produce was specifically given to the LORD as 'firstfruits' (cp. the comment on 2: 12; Exod. 23: 19; 34: 26; Deut. 26: 2). *this releases it for use:* the reading of the Samaritan text (cp. the footnote) correctly expresses the purpose of the holy-gift to the LORD, but the Hebrew may be right. It would mean that the gift was made on the occasion of a joyful harvest festival (cp. Judg. 9: 27, where the same Hebrew word is used). This festival would have taken place in the autumn at the end of the year (cp. the comment on 16: 1–10, p. 124) and so in the following year the fruit would be available for ordinary use. *the yield it gives you shall be increased:* due recognition of God's rights in the crop, and the proper performance of the ritual, would win his favour and he would increase the yield (cp. 26: 3–5, 10).

26. *meat with the blood in it:* the basic law, more fully developed in 17: 10–11. *divination or soothsaying:* these practices were at one time perfectly legitimate in Israel (cp. Gen. 44: 4–5, 15; Judg. 9: 37), but here they are viewed as characteristic of heathen cults (cp. Deut. 18: 14).

27–8a. Various mourning-rites are forbidden here, which again were once the regular custom in Israel (cp. Isa. 22: 12; Jer. 16: 6; Mic. 1: 16). Since, however, their original purpose was to placate the spirits of the dead by a hair-offering (cp. Num. 6: 18), or drive them away by a blood-rite (cp. the comment on 14: 5–6), they were really heathen practices incompatible with true Israelite worship (cp. Deut. 14: 1–2).

28b. *you shall not tattoo yourselves:* probably this is not specifically a mourning-rite. Worshippers often bore some sort of mark on their skin, to show they were devotees of a particular deity (cp. Gen. 4: 15b; Ezek. 9: 4–6). Once again, a common custom of non-Israelite religion is condemned.

29. *prostitute your daughter:* the ground for the prohibition is primarily religious rather than moral. Cultic prostitution, with the object of promoting fertility (cp. *the land* in verse 29b), was, in Israelite eyes, the most striking feature of Canaanite worship: the denunciations of the prophets show

how widespread it became in Israel also (cp. Deut. 23: 18; Hos. 4: 13–14).

30. *keep my sabbaths:* cp. the comment on verse 3. *revere my sanctuary:* perhaps this has come in here because the sanctuary in particular would be defiled by the practice described in the preceding verse (cp. the comment on 12: 4).

31. *ghosts:* consulting the spirits of the dead is meant here (cp. 1 Sam. 28: 7–8). *spirits:* the word means literally 'those who have knowledge'. Typical Canaanite practices such as those described became especially common among the Israelites in the last years of the kingdom of Judah (cp. Deut. 18: 10–13; 2 Kings 21: 6; Isa. 8: 19).

32. Reverence for *the aged* is not primarily on humanitarian grounds. It is rooted in the divine ordering of society and hence is coupled with the injunction *fear your God.*

33–4. Cp. the comments on 17: 8–9 and verse 18. *because you were aliens in Egypt:* these words form part of the sermonic framework of the chapter (cp. p. 92), but they repeat an old formula which has its roots in a particular understanding of the nation's saving history (cp. Exod. 22: 21; 23: 9; Deut. 10: 19).

35–7. Dishonesty in commercial transactions would be a sign of injustice throughout the whole of society (cp. the comment on verse 15), generally at the expense of the poor, so it is often condemned in the prophets and elsewhere in the Old Testament (cp. Ezek. 45: 10–11; Amos 8: 5; Deut. 25: 13–15). The temptation to falsify weights and measures would be particularly strong in a time of scarcity such as the exile. Again, a well-developed economy is shown here (cp. the comment on verse 13). *who brought you out of Egypt:* cp. the comment on verses 33–4.

37. *all my rules and laws:* the final words of the sermon stress the all embracing range of the rules and laws set out in it. ✳

THE DEATH PENALTY

20 1, 2 The LORD spoke to Moses and said, Say to the Israelites: Any Israelite or alien settled in Israel who gives any of his children to Molech shall be put to death: the common 3 people shall stone him. I, for my part, set my face against that man and cut him off from his people, because he has given a child of his to Molech, thus making my sanctuary 4 unclean and profaning my holy name. If the common people connive at it when a man has given a child of his 5 to Molech and do not put him to death, I will set my face against man and family, and both him and all who follow him in his wanton following after Molech,[a] I will cut off from their people.

6   I will set my face against the man who wantonly resorts to ghosts and spirits, and I will cut that person off from 7 his people. Hallow yourselves and be holy, because I the 8 LORD your God am holy.[b] You shall keep my rules and obey them: I am the LORD who hallows you.

✳ The core of ch. 20 is verses 9–16, which list a series of sexual offences for which the punishment is the death-penalty inflicted by the human agents of the community. To these have been added various miscellaneous prohibitions, where the punishment is through direct divine intervention, such as to be 'cut off' (verses 17–18; cp. the comment on 17: 4), or some other procedure, such as to 'be proscribed' (verses 20–1). All this material is introduced (verses 7–8), and concluded (verses 22–6), by exhortations in the usual style of 'the law of holiness'. The unit thus created is prefaced by a quite independent section (verses 1–5), which has been loosely attached, probably

[a] *Or* in his lusting after human sacrifice.
[b] *So Sept.; Heb.* because I am the LORD your God.

because it dealt with another crime that involved the death-penalty and also because this particular crime was linked with sexual offences (cp. 18: 21). The repetition of several regulations that have appeared already shows that we have here the form in which parts of the basic covenant law were presented at another sanctuary.

2. The crime is child-sacrifice to a foreign deity. Other references in the Old Testament show that the children were transferred to the god by being burnt (Deut. 18: 10; 2 Kings 23: 10; Ezek. 20: 31). *Molech:* cp. 18: 21. The text and the footnote to verse 5 present two different ways of understanding this word:

(i) *Molech* is the personal name of a foreign deity. This is supported by 1 Kings 11: 7, where Molech appears as 'the god of the Ammonites'. Alternatively, it could mean 'king', Hebrew *melek*, which has the same consonants as Molech. 'King' as a divine title was common in the ancient Near East and so a number of different deities could be envisaged under the word.

(ii) *Molech* is a technical sacrificial term, meaning 'human sacrifice'. This is supported by a similar term in the sacrificial terminology of the Phoenicians, who were closely akin to the Canaanites. If this is correct, when they practised the rite, the Israelites may have intended to offer their children, not to a foreign god, but to the God of Israel.

In any case, from the standpoint of 'the law of holiness', this custom was a foreign intrusion. Moreover, shortly before the exile, it was practised at a place called 'Topheth' in the near vicinity of Jerusalem (cp. 2 Kings 23: 10). It had been suppressed in Josiah's reformation but from Jeremiah we learn that it had revived later (cp. Jer. 32: 35).

3. *making my sanctuary unclean:* cp. the comment on 19: 30. *profaning my holy name:* this might mean that the children were given over in the name of the LORD and so suggest the view that *Molech* is really a sacrificial term.

4–5. *man and family:* an individual's crime involved his

whole kin-group (cp. the comment on 14: 8). *I will cut off from their people:* the context clearly indicates the meaning of this expression (cp. the comment on 17: 4). If *the common people* fail in their duty, God himself will intervene.

6. Here we have a quite independent comment, repeating 19: 31: it has become attached to the preceding verse by the link-words *set my face* and *cut off.*

7–8. This is really the sermonizing introduction to the list in verses 9–21. *

SEXUAL CRIMES MERITING DEATH

9 When any man reviles his father and his mother, he shall be put to death. He has reviled his father and his mother;
10 his blood shall be on his own head. If a man commits adultery with his neighbour's wife,[a] both adulterer and
11 adulteress shall be put to death. The man who has intercourse with his father's wife has brought shame on his father. They shall both be put to death; their blood shall
12 be on their own heads. If a man has intercourse with his daughter-in-law, they shall both be put to death. Their deed is a violation of nature; their blood shall be on their
13 own heads. If a man has intercourse with a man as with a woman, they both commit an abomination. They shall be put to death; their blood shall be on their own heads.
14 If a man takes both a woman and her mother, that is lewdness. Both he and they shall be burnt; thus there
15 shall be no lewdness in your midst. A man who has sexual intercourse with any beast shall be put to death,
16 and you shall kill the beast. If a woman approaches any animal to have intercourse with it, you shall kill both woman and beast. They shall be put to death; their blood

[a] *So Luc. Sept.; Heb. adds* a man commits adultery with the wife of. . .

shall be on their own heads. If a man takes his sister, his 17
father's daughter or his mother's daughter, and they see
one another naked, it is a scandalous disgrace. They shall
be cut off in the presence of their people. The man has had
intercourse with his sister and he shall accept responsibility. If a man lies with a woman during her monthly 18
period and brings shame upon her, he has exposed her
discharge and she has uncovered the source of her discharge; they shall both be cut off from their people. You 19
shall not have intercourse with your mother's sister or
your father's sister: it is the exposure of a blood-relation.
They shall accept responsibility. A man who has inter- 20
course with his uncle's wife has brought shame upon his
uncle. They shall accept responsibility for their sin and
shall be proscribed and put to death. If a man takes his 21
brother's wife, it is impurity. He has brought shame upon
his brother; they shall be proscribed.

You shall keep all my rules and my laws and carry them 22
out, that the land into which I am bringing you to live
may not spew you out. You shall not conform to the 23
institutions of the nations whom I am driving out before
you: they did all these things and I abhorred them, and I 24
told you that you should occupy their land, and I would
give you possession of it, a land flowing with milk and
honey. I am the LORD your God: I have made a clear
separation between you and the nations, and you shall 25
make a clear separation between clean beasts and unclean
beasts and between unclean and clean birds. You shall not
make yourselves vile through beast or bird or anything
that creeps on the ground, for I have made a clear separation between them and you, declaring them unclean. You 26

shall be holy to me, because I the LORD am holy. I have
made a clear separation between you and the heathen,
27 that you may belong to me. Any man or woman among
you who calls up ghosts or spirits shall be put to death.
The people shall stone them; their blood shall be on their
own heads.

* The basic list, with its appendages (verses 9–21), clearly has
a close relationship with the list, and its similar appendages, in
18: 6–23. But there are important differences, quite apart from
the fact that this passage is in casuistic form (i.e. 'if...'), while
ch. 18 uses the apodictic form (i.e. 'you shall/shall not'). In
particular, the group in question here is much less wide than
that of ch. 18. It seems only to envisage the head of the family
with his parents and children, while the other list is concerned
with a considerably larger group. Again, the prohibitions here
include offences against marriage, which, as was seen, are not
dealt with in the original legislation of ch. 18. The two lists,
then, appear to have in mind two different types of social
organization and the one in this chapter is almost certainly a
later development than the one reflected in ch. 18.

9. *he shall be put to death*: this characteristic expression of
verses 9–21 is here an expansion of the basic unconditional
commandment, as found in 19: 3 and presupposes a developed
penal system, not present in ch. 18. *his blood shall be on his own
head*: this is another expression characteristic of this list. It is
the equivalent of a verdict of 'guilty', for these words were
pronounced by the spokesman of the 'court' (cp. the comment
on 19: 15) in giving judgement. The rule does not properly
belong with verses 9–21, which are concerned with sexual
offences, but was added because it too incurred the death
penalty.

10. This is a much stronger regulation than 18: 20 (see p.
148), involving the death of both the man and the woman.

11–12. The same prohibitions as in 18: 8 and 18: 15, but in

a casuistic, not an apodictic, form, and with a definite punishment specified.

13. Cp. the comment on 18: 22–3.

14. *takes:* this means 'takes in marriage', in contrast to 18: 17.

15–16. Cp. 18: 23 and the comment on verse 10.

17. *takes:* cp. the comment on verse 14 and contrast 18: 9. *they see one another naked:* that is, 'consummate the marriage'. Here and in the following verses, the formula 'be put to death' is absent, indicating that they are additions.

18. Cp. 18: 19.

19. Cp. 18: 12–13.

20. Cp. the comment on 18: 14. *be proscribed:* a related Arabic word suggests that this means 'cut off from the kingroup'. *put to death:* this is not the same Hebrew phrase as that so translated in verses 9–15, but is virtually identical with the expression 'shall accept responsibility' of the preceding verse.

21. *takes:* cp. the comment on verse 14 and contrast 18: 16.

22–4. The sequence of thought is again much the same as in 18: 24–9. *flowing with milk and honey:* a traditional expression to describe the promised land (cp. Exod. 3: 8), as it was seen by nomads from the inhospitable desert.

25–6. The regulations of ch. 11 are presupposed here (cp. the comment on 11: 47) but 'the law of holiness' adds its own distinctive reason to explain them, which is quite different from their original purpose (cp. the comment on 11: 1–8). The Israelites are to separate between *unclean and clean* animals because God has *made a clear separation between you and the heathen* (cp. the comment on 18: 3, 4).

27. An isolated prohibition, parallel to 19: 31, which has been loosely tacked on to what precedes it, because it too prescribed the death-penalty. *or woman:* perhaps the woman is expressly mentioned because women were reputed to be specially skilled in divination (cp. Exod. 22: 18; 1 Sam. 28: 7). ✳

THE HOLINESS OF THE PRIESTS

21 The LORD said to Moses, Say to the priests, the sons of
Aaron: A priest shall not render himself unclean for the
2 death of any of his kin except for a near blood-relation,
3 that is for mother, father, son, daughter, brother, or full
4 sister who is unmarried and a virgin; nor shall he make
himself unclean for any married woman[a] among his
father's kin, and so profane himself.

5   Priests shall not make bald patches on their heads as a
sign of mourning, nor cut the edges of their beards, nor
6 gash their bodies. They shall be holy to their God, and
they shall not profane the name of their God, because they
present the food-offerings of the LORD, the food of their
7 God, and they shall be holy. A priest shall not marry a
prostitute or a girl who has lost her virginity, nor shall he
marry a woman divorced from her husband; for he is
8 holy to his God. You shall keep him holy because he
presents the food of your God; you shall regard him as
holy because I the LORD, I who hallow them,[b] am holy.
9 When a priest's daughter profanes herself by becoming a
prostitute, she profanes her father. She shall be burnt to
death.

* In contrast to the four preceding chapters, there follows a
section consisting of various regulations for the priesthood. It
is a clearly distinct collection, made during the exile, as is
shown by the fact that a very similar set of rules is found in
Ezek. 44 (cp. also the comment on verse 10). Both this passage
and the chapter in Ezekiel look to the future and make

[a] for any married woman: *prob. rdg.*; *Heb.* husband.
[b] *So Sam.* (*cp. verse 23*); *Heb.* you.

arrangements for the new unified priestly body which had
come into being during the period of the exile (cp. p. 16).
As with most of 'the law of holiness', the regulations here
generally go back a long way into Israel's past but they are all
interpreted in the light of that law's overriding concern for
'holiness' (cp. the comment on verse 6). The whole is made
up of three separate units, each dealing with a particular topic,
and each provided by the compilers of 'the law of holiness'
with a reason for the commands laid down, in a concluding
formula 'I am the LORD who hallows' (verses 8, 15,
23).

1. *the sons of Aaron:* Aaron is mentioned only in opening
and concluding formulae (cp. verses 17, 24) and in verse 21
which, since it duplicates what is said in verse 17, is an obvious
addition. This is the work of the compilers of Leviticus, who
wished to set the regulations in the Mosaic age and also to
make them conform to the theory formulated after the exile,
of the Aaronic descent of the whole priesthood. In the older
material in this chapter only the *priest* is mentioned (cp. the
comment on 1: 5).

2. More stringent prohibitions to preserve 'cleanness' apply
to the priest than to the ordinary Israelite: the concept of
various degrees of holiness is characteristic of Leviticus (cp.
the comment on 2: 10). The layman was allowed to bury the
dead, an obvious practical necessity, although contact with the
corpse rendered him temporarily unclean (cp. Num. 19: 11,
14, 16). But, fundamentally, the priest was not, even in the
case of 'the death of any of his kin'. However, a supplementary expansion of the basic law permits an exception for
a near blood-relation, but what this covers is carefully defined
(cp. Ezek. 44: 25). In these cases, the priest incurred the same
degree of uncleanness as the layman (cp. Ezek. 44: 25).

3. *full sister:* in the Hebrew *full* is literally 'near to him',
and this gives the true sense. An *unmarried* sister would be
living with her brother, whereas one who was married would
be with her husband in a separate establishment.

4. *married woman:* as the footnote indicates, the original text is obscure. There seem to be three possibilities:

(i) this is a further clarification of verse 3, to make clear that a married sister was not included.

(ii) or it explains, as the N.E.B. translation would suggest, that the wife of any of the men listed in verse 2 is excluded.

(iii) this is to explain, as the Hebrew may imply, that a 'husband', if he is a priest, must not 'render himself unclean' for his dead wife. It is striking that the wife is not mentioned in the series in verses 2–3.

5. A further regulation dealing with funerals is here added. It reflects a period when the mourning-rites described were permitted for the ordinary Israelite (cp. the comment on 19: 27–28a), but they are forbidden to the priest.

6. This verse is the formulation of the compilers of 'the law of holiness' (cp. p. 134). *present the food-offerings:* cp. the comment on 1: 9. Priests are holy because of their sacrificial service to *the LORD. the food of their God:* the vestige of an old expression, indicating that sacrifices were once viewed as providing food for the deity (cp. the comment on 1: 9).

7. Stricter marriage rules apply to the priest than to the ordinary Israelite. *a prostitute:* probably, in contrast to *a girl who has lost her virginity*, this refers to a cultic prostitute (cp. the comment on 19: 29). *a woman divorced:* the priest, however, could presumably marry a widow, although Ezek. 44: 22 confines the permission to 'the widow of a priest' (contrast verse 14).

8. This verse is again the work of the compilers of chs. 17–26: its direct form of address indicates that it is intended for a group of hearers and thus it is characteristic of the sermon technique of 'the law of holiness'.

9. The form of the regulation is completely different from the rest of the section and belongs to the distinct class of legal material represented in 20: 9–16 (cp. 20: 14). But it is tacked on because verses 1–9 are concerned with how priests are to avoid uncleanness and when *a priest's daughter* becomes *a prostitute, she profanes her father.* *

THE HOLINESS OF THE CHIEF PRIEST

The high priest, the one among his fellows who has had 10
the anointing oil poured on his head and has been consecrated to wear the vestments, shall neither leave his hair
dishevelled nor tear his clothes. He shall not enter the 11
place where any man's dead body lies; not even for his
father or his mother shall he render himself unclean. He 12
shall not go out of the sanctuary for fear that he dishonour
the sanctuary of his God, because the consecration of the
anointing oil of his God is upon him. I am the LORD. He 13
shall marry a woman who is still a virgin. He shall not 14
marry a widow, a divorced woman, a woman who has
lost her virginity, or a prostitute, but only a virgin from
his father's kin; he shall not dishonour his descendants 15
among his father's kin, for I am the LORD who hallows
him.

* In turn, more stringent prohibitions, set out in the same
order as those in verses 1–9, are imposed on 'the high priest'
(cp. the comment on 4: 3), than on the ordinary priests.

10. *the one among his fellows:* the high priest has not yet
acquired the unique and outstanding position he afterwards
attained but is still rather the first among equals. The detailed
description of him which follows (cp. 8: 2, 30) also suggests a
period when the office was only just beginning to emerge and
needed precise definition. *consecrated:* cp. the comment on
8: 22–8. *neither leave his hair dishevelled nor tear his clothes:* cp.
10: 6. Again, these were ordinary mourning-rites (cp. the
comment on 13: 45–6) which were still permitted to the
priesthood in general.

11. *the place where any man's dead body lies:* cp. Num. 19: 14.
not even for his father and mother: the words naturally include
all the persons mentioned in verses 2–3.

12. *He shall not go out of the sanctuary:* this does not mean that the high priest was perpetually confined to the holy place, but only that he was not to leave it to participate in a funeral (cp. the comment on 10: 6–7).

13–14. The basic regulation is first given, then an expansion is added to clarify what is meant by a *virgin* and also to restrict the bride to the *father's kin* (cp. the comment on verse 7): in Ezek. 44: 22, the high priest is forbidden to marry a 'non-Israelite', but here the older kinship pattern is the governing factor. ✻

PHYSICAL DEFECTS OF THE PRIESTS

6, 17 The LORD spoke to Moses and said, Speak to Aaron in these words: No man among your descendants for all time who has any physical defect shall come and present 18 the food of his God. No man with a defect shall come, whether a blind man, a lame man, a man stunted or over-19, 20 grown, a man deformed in foot or hand, or with mis-shapen brows or a film over his eye or a discharge[a] from it, a man who has a scab or eruption or has had a testicle 21 ruptured. No descendant of Aaron the priest who has any defect in his body shall approach to present the food-offerings of the LORD; because he has a defect he shall not 22 approach to present the food of his God. He may eat the bread of God both from the holy-gifts and from the 23 holiest of holy-gifts, but he shall not come up to the Veil nor approach the altar, because he has a defect in his body. Thus he shall not profane my sanctuaries, because I am the LORD who hallows them.

24 Thus did Moses speak to Aaron and his sons and to all the Israelites.

[a] film. . .discharge: *the Heb. words are of uncertain mng.*

✷ We have here a situation where the priesthood is confined to a single hereditary family group. At one time, the defects listed would have prevented a man from becoming a priest at all but now they only debar a member of that family from performing priestly functions (cp. the comment on verse 22). Such defects destroyed the priest's wholeness and perfection and so rendered him unclean (cp. the comment on 11: 1–8).

17–20. *food for his God:* cp. the comment on verse 6. *has had a testicle ruptured:* this defect debarred the ordinary Israelite from public worship (cp. Deut. 23: 1). Again, a wider range of disabilities is imposed on priests because of their special 'hallowing' (cp. the comment on verse 2).

21. Cp. the comment on verse 1. Perhaps, however, on the analogy of verses 1–9 and 10–15, the compiler thought there should be a specific reference to the high priest and understood the phrase *descendant of Aaron the priest* to mean a member of the actual high-priestly line (cp. the comment on 16: 32).

22. This is an expansion to make clear that the disabled priest, although he could not function as a priest, was allowed to live off the sacrificial dues that went to the priesthood. *from the holy gifts:* that is, 'the special gift' and 'the contribution' (cp. the comment on 7: 34). *the holiest of holy gifts:* that is, the priest's share of the grain-, sin- and guilt-offerings (cp. 6: 17, 25–6; 7: 6).

23. *sanctuaries:* the plural is striking. Generally in Leviticus we only hear of a single sanctuary, but this verse is evidence of a period when there were many shrines in Palestine. ✷

THE HOLY-GIFTS

The LORD spoke to Moses and said, Tell Aaron and his **22** 1, 2 sons that they must be careful in the handling of the holy-gifts of the Israelites which they hallow to me, lest they profane my holy name. I am the LORD. Say to them: Any 3 man of your descent for all time who while unclean approaches the holy-gifts which the Israelites hallow to the LORD shall be cut off from my presence. I am the

4 LORD. No man descended from Aaron who suffers from a malignant skin-disease, or has a discharge, shall eat of the holy-gifts until he is cleansed. A man who touches anything which makes him unclean or who has an

5 emission of semen, a man who touches any vermin which makes him unclean or any human being who makes him

6 unclean: any person who touches such a thing shall be unclean till sunset and unless he washes his body shall not

7 eat of the holy-gifts. When the sun goes down, he shall be clean, and after that he may eat from the holy-gifts,

8 because they are his food. He shall not eat an animal that has died a natural death or has been mauled by wild beasts, thereby making himself unclean. I am the LORD.

9 The priests shall observe my charge, lest they make themselves guilty and die for profaning my name. I am

10 the LORD who hallows them. No unqualified person may eat any holy-gift; nor may a stranger lodging with a

11 priest or a hired man eat a holy-gift. A slave bought by a priest with his own money may do so, and slaves born

12 in his household may also share his food. When a priest's daughter marries an unqualified person, she shall not eat

13 any of the contributions of holy-gifts; but if she is widowed or divorced and is childless and comes back to her father's house as in her childhood, she shall share her father's food. No unqualified person may eat any of it.

14 When a man inadvertently eats a holy-gift, he shall make good the holy-gift to the priest, adding a fifth to

15 its value. The priests shall not profane the holy-gifts of

16 the Israelites which they set aside for the LORD; they shall

172

not let men eat their holy-gifts and so incur guilt and its
penalty, because I am the LORD who hallows them.

* In this chapter occur three separate sections, distinguished
by a fresh introduction at verses 1, 17, and 26, put together
because they all deal with aspects of sacrificial ritual. The first
section is connected with what immediately precedes it by the
link-words 'holy-gifts' (cp. 21: 22) and 'profane' (cp. 21: 23).
It deals exclusively with 'holy-gifts', but under two aspects:
first, in what circumstances may the priests eat them (verses
2–9) and secondly, who else is qualified to eat them (verses
10–16).

2: *the holy-gifts:* this includes both the 'gifts' specified in
21: 22.

3. First is given the basic regulation, which is amplified in
what follows. *from my presence:* the *unclean* priest is not said to
'be cut off from his kin', as was the layman, but from the
presence of the LORD, with whom, during his service in the
sanctuary, he was in daily close contact.

4–6. The object here was to make it clearly understood that
the regulations of chs. 11–15, which are concerned with the
layman, applied equally to the priest. *any person:* indeed, the
use of this general term, instead of the more specific *man
descended from Aaron*, shows that even the laws here were
originally framed for the layman.

8. This is an addition, since it has nothing to do with 'the
holy-gifts', which follows the theme of ch. 21, in that it im-
poses a stricter prohibition on the priest than on the layman
(cp. 17: 15).

10*a*. The fundamental law is given, and then expounded to
deal with doubtful cases.

10*b*–11. According to chs. 6–7, only male Aaronites could
eat the holy-gift (cp. 6: 18, 29; 7: 6) but at a later stage, this
was permitted to all members of the priest's family and
'household' (cp. Num. 18: 11). Thus the question arose: 'who
actually belongs to the household?' A lodger or a workman

hired by the day did not, but slaves, whether bought or born into slavery, were reckoned as members of the family.

12–13. Next a further problem is answered: 'what about a daughter who leaves home to get married to an *unqualified person* (that is, someone not a member of a priestly family) and only visits her father occasionally?' By her marriage, she has joined a different group, and so can no longer eat of the holy-gifts, but she can if circumstances compel her to return and live permanently with her father again.

14. An addition to mollify the absolute command of verse 13*b*, permitting an unqualified person who has *inadvertently* eaten a holy-gift to purge his offence by what is clearly a 'guilt-offering' (cp. 5: 15–16 and the comment on 5: 16).

15–16. But the priests are warned to do their utmost to prevent unqualified people eating the holy-gifts which they bring to the sanctuary. ✲

WHAT IS ACCEPTABLE AS A SACRIFICE

17,18 The LORD spoke to Moses and said, Speak to Aaron and his sons and to all the Israelites in these words: When any man of the house of Israel or any alien in Israel presents, whether in fulfilment of a vow or for a freewill offering, such an offering as is presented to the LORD for a whole-

19 offering so as to win acceptance for yourselves, it shall be

20 a male without defect, of cattle, sheep, or goats. You shall not present anything which is defective, because it

21 will not be acceptable on your behalf. When a man presents a shared-offering to the LORD, whether cattle or sheep, to fulfil a special*a* vow or as a freewill offering, if it is to be acceptable it must be perfect; there shall be no

22 defect in it. You shall present to the LORD nothing blind, disabled, mutilated, with running sore, scab, or eruption,

---

[*a*] fulfil a special: *or* discharge a. . .

nor set any such creature on the altar as a food-offering
to the LORD. If a bull or a sheep is overgrown or stunted, 23
you may make of it a freewill offering, but it will not be
acceptable in fulfilment of a vow. If its testicles have been 24
crushed or bruised, torn or cut, you shall not present it to
the LORD; this is forbidden in your land.

You shall not procure any such creature from a 25
foreigner and present it as food for your God. Their
deformity is inherent in them, a permanent defect, and
they will not be acceptable on your behalf.

✲ This section deals with defects in animals brought for
various kinds of sacrifice. It is really intended for the layman,
to inform him as to what defects in a beast would render it
unfit for sacrifice. We may note that most of these are the
same as those which, according to 21: 17–20, made a man
unable to officiate as a priest. In the situation of great poverty
brought about by the Babylonian invasions, there would be a
particular temptation to neglect the strict rules about the
perfection of sacrificial animals (cp. Mal. 1: 7–8).

18–21. The sacrifices considered here are those offered *in
fulfilment of a vow* (there is no real difference in meaning
between text and footnote in verse 21) or *as a freewill offering*,
which could either be a *whole-offering* (verse 19), or *a shared-
offering* (verse 21; cp. the comment on 7: 16). Perhaps they
alone are dealt with here, because in 7: 16–19 it is not explicitly
stated that the victims offered on these occasions had to be
'without blemish', as is the case with all the other sacrifices
listed in chs. 1–7. No actual punishment is laid down for a
person who brings a defective offering: it is only said that *it
will not be acceptable* (cp. the comment on 1: 3).

22. *food-offering:* this term is applied, as far as animal
sacrifices are concerned, to the 'whole-offering' and the
'shared-offering' (cp. the comment on 1: 9).

23. An additional regulation to answer the question: 'what

is the position of an animal that is not actually deformed but only abnormally large or abnormally small?' It can be used for a *freewill offering*, because that was purely voluntary, but not *in fulfilment of a vow*, because a vow represented a definite commitment to make a gift to God and he could not be fobbed off with anything that was not ritually perfect.

24. An animal with this deformity was forbidden in the territory of Israel, just as was a man in the same case (cp. Deut. 23: 1 and the comment on 21: 17–20). It was regarded as particularly imperfect because it was useless for breeding: the outlook of a largely agricultural society is seen here.

25. This verse belongs with verse 24 and refers to the same animal. It is another additional regulation to meet the problem: 'what if the animal with defective genitals does not come from the land of Israel, from our own flocks or herds, but has been procured from a foreigner outside the country?' The ruling is that the prohibition still applies. ✳

MISCELLANEOUS SACRIFICIAL REGULATIONS

26, 27 The LORD spoke to Moses and said: When a calf, a lamb, or a kid is born, it must not be taken from its mother for seven days. From the eighth day onwards it will be acceptable when offered as a food-offering to the LORD.
28 You shall not slaughter a cow or sheep at the same time
29 as its young. When you make a thank-offering to the LORD, you shall sacrifice it so as to win acceptance for
30 yourselves; it shall be eaten that same day, and none be left till morning. I am the LORD.

31 You shall observe my commandments and perform them. I am the LORD. You shall not profane my holy
32 name; I will be hallowed among the Israelites. I am the
33 LORD who hallows you, who brought you out of Egypt to become your God. I am the LORD.

✻ 27. This is a version of the ancient law by which the first-born of animals had to be given to God (cp. Exod. 22: 30). *seven days:* kindness to animals does not enter in. Domestic animals were part of the community (cp. the comment on 11: 3) and so their birth was surrounded by the same taboos as with humans (cp. 12: 2–3).

28. Probably this prohibits a rite from non-Israelite cults, although we do not know what its significance was (but cp. Exod. 23: 19*b*).

29–30. Cp. the comment on 7: 15.

31–3. The concluding exhortation, characteristic of 'the law of holiness' (cp. the comments on 19: 33–4). ✻

THE SACRED CALENDAR

✻ The purpose of the various sacred calendars in the Old Testament is to specify the occasions when all males had to make a 'pilgrim-feast' to the sanctuary, to take part in an act of worship which dedicated the different crops to God, who had provided them and to whom they therefore belonged, by giving him a representative part of them, thus releasing the remainder for human use. What represents the basic and simplest form of such a calendar is the cycle of three annual feasts in Exod. 23: 14–17 and all the later calendars are developments of this. Originally, therefore, these feasts were directly connected with agriculture and were taken over from the Canaanites by the Israelites when they settled in Palestine. But by the time of the exile, they had come to be regarded primarily as a solemn act of worship, as is shown by the key phrase of ch. 23, 'a sacred assembly', and, with the greater emphasis during and after the exile on the importance of the correct performance of the ritual, increasingly detailed regulations were developed to ensure their proper celebration. We can see this development by comparing the three calendars, which probably follow one another chronologically, in Deut. 16: 1–17, Lev. 23 and Num. 28: 16 — 29: 39. So, in later

Judaism, the festal calendar came to have great significance and questions about its proper observance often led to serious disputes: for example, one reason why the sect which produced the Dead Sea Scrolls broke with the Jerusalem priesthood was that it followed a calendar different from the official one.

However, as compared with Deut. 16 and Num. 28, the calendar of ch. 23 is much less clearly arranged, and once again, the reason is that it is an attempt to harmonize the practices of different sanctuaries at a single centre during the time of the exile, of which several other examples have already been noted. In fact, this chapter is basically made up of a combination of two distinct calendar systems:

(i) there are two sections which specify rather briefly a precise month and day for the celebration: verses 5–8 and 23–36. The months are numbered according to the Babylonian system (where the first month was mid-March to mid-April), which was introduced under the Judaean monarchy not long before the fall of Jerusalem and became the regular practice thereafter (cp. the comment on 16: 29–32). Probably, then, we have here the festal calendar of the Jerusalem temple. It appears to prescribe two great annual celebrations, one in spring and one in autumn, and this corresponds to the calendar in Ezek. 45: 21–5. The chapters of Ezekiel in which this calendar occurs, although set in the future, in fact largely seek to preserve the ritual of the temple built before the exile and it should be noted that Ezek. 45: 21–5 deal with the role of 'the prince', the counterpart of the Davidic king, in the two festivals.

(ii) on the other hand, there are sections, verses 9–21 and, originally, 39–43 (cp. the comment on verse 39), where no precise dates are specified. This is because here, in contrast to the urban Jerusalem cultus, the feasts are more directly connected with agricultural operations, which, owing to the vagaries of the weather, could not be precisely fixed. Hence these sections are closely linked to the old system of Exod.

23: 15-16 and reproduce its three-fold festal scheme. They almost certainly represent the customs of more than one sanctuary outside Jerusalem, for, as will be seen, verses 10-14 really parallel verses 6-8.

The material of this chapter has been given its existing form in two stages. First, the calendars of the different sanctuaries were combined by the compilers of 'the law of holiness' to form a unified set of instructions for the laity, with typical exhortatory comments (cp. verses 22, 43*b*). Secondly, the resulting collection has been worked over by the priestly theologians responsible for Leviticus as we now have it, who, among other supplements, added the section dealing with the sabbath (verses 2-3), extended the sabbath prohibition of abstention from work to the annual festivals also, and systematized all of them by a common description as 'sacred assemblies', verse 2. ✲

THE SABBATH

The LORD spoke to Moses and said, Speak to the Israelites **23** 1, 2 in these words: These are the appointed seasons of the LORD, and you shall proclaim them as sacred assemblies; these are my appointed seasons. On six days work may be 3 done, but every seventh day is a sabbath of sacred rest, a day of sacred assembly, on which you shall do no work. Wherever you live, it is the LORD's sabbath.

✲ 2. This is the priestly introduction to cover all the different regulations in the chapter: they are all to be observed as *appointed seasons* and *sacred assemblies*.

3. That the *sabbath* commandment is a later addition to the earlier material is shown by the fact that the rest of the chapter only deals with annual celebrations, while the sabbath was a weekly one. The distinctive feature of *every seventh day* was that *no work* was to be done on it and this is its most original

characteristic in Israel (cp. Exod. 20: 9–10; 23: 12; 34: 21), but perhaps the reason why the sabbath was attached to the annual festival cycle was that, by this time, it had also become *a day of sacred assembly*, an occasion of worship when special sacrifices were offered as on the other celebrations (cp. Ezek. 46: 4–5; Num. 28: 9–10 and cp. Lev. 24: 8). In any case, from the exile onwards the sabbath became one of the most binding and most distinctive marks of Israelite religion (cp. Isa. 56: 2–6; 58: 13–14): in priestly thought it was something observed even by God himself (cp. Gen. 2: 3) and failure to keep it was punished by death (cp. Exod. 31: 14*b*; Num. 15: 32–6). *Wherever you live:* this phrase has sometimes been taken to indicate those living in exile outside Palestine, but probably it only refers to keeping the sabbath commandment in the individual home (cp. Exod. 35: 3, where 'at home' translates the identical Hebrew expression as here). ✳

PASSOVER AND UNLEAVENED BREAD

4 These are the appointed seasons of the LORD, the sacred assemblies which you shall proclaim in their appointed
5 order. In the first month on the fourteenth day between
6 dusk and dark is the LORD's Passover. On the fifteenth day of this month begins the LORD's pilgrim-feast of Unleavened Bread; for seven days you shall eat unleavened
7 cakes. On the first day there shall be a sacred assembly;
8 you shall not do your daily work. For seven days you shall present your food-offerings to the LORD. On the seventh day also there shall be a sacred assembly; you shall not do your daily work.

9, 10 The LORD spoke to Moses and said, Speak to the Israelites in these words: When you enter the land which I give you, and you reap its harvest, you shall bring the
11 first sheaf of your harvest to the priest. He shall present

the sheaf as a special gift before the LORD on[a] the day
after the sabbath, so as to gain acceptance for yourselves.
On the day you present the sheaf, you shall prepare a 12
perfect yearling ram for a whole-offering to the LORD,
with the proper grain-offering, two tenths of an ephah of 13
flour mixed with oil, as a food-offering to the LORD, of
soothing odour, and also with the proper drink-offering,
a quarter of a hin of wine. You shall eat neither bread, nor 14
grain, parched or fully ripened, during that day, the day
on which you bring your God his offering; this is a rule
binding on your descendants for all time wherever you
live.

* Originally, Passover and Unleavened Bread were two quite
separate festivals, with a different background and purpose,
and in this section there is still a distinction between them. But
they became linked together because they were both cele-
brated at approximately the same time in the spring.

5. *in the first month:* cp. p. 178. *between dusk and dark:* this
expression occurs only in priestly material in the Old Testament and shows a concern for ritual precision. *the LORD's
Passover:* in origin, the Passover was a rite of a nomadic group
to ward off the powers of evil from the household (cp. the
comment on 14: 5–6 and Exod. 12: 7, 11–13). Notice that, in
contrast to all the other festivals, the Passover is not described
as 'a sacred assembly' nor are any sacrificial offerings
mentioned in connection with it. This is because Passover
always remained a celebration in the home and not in the
sanctuary.

6. *Unleavened Bread:* by contrast, this was a communal
agricultural festival characteristic of the settled Canaanite
population, marking the beginning of the barley harvest, the
first crop to be gathered: the Passover is not mentioned with

[a] Or from.

it in the oldest calendars (cp. Exod. 23: 15). *unleavened cakes:*
eating these was the ancient characteristic of the celebration.
Bread was normally made with leaven which came from
previously baked dough. Since the purpose of the rite was to
make available for food the new crop, nothing from the past
year could be associated with it, and so the cakes were made
from the grain in its natural state (cp. Josh. 5: 11–12).

7–8. These verses are the work of the priestly revisers. They
make the first and last days of the seven-day period into an
assembly for worship and assimilate them to the sabbath: they
also lay down that *food-offerings* (cp. the comment on 1: 9),
presumably the 'grain-offerings' of ch. 2, are to be presented
each day, thus converting the ancient Canaanite rite into a gift
of 'firstfruits' to the LORD (cp. the comment on 2: 14–16).

9–14. As verse 14 indicates, the purpose of the rite described
here is the same as that of the feast of 'Unleavened Bread'. But
the ceremonies are quite different and are mentioned nowhere
else in the Old Testament, which shows that we have here the
characteristic practice of a particular sanctuary. The rite
occupies only a single day for which no precise date is given
(cp. p. 178), and abstention from all cereal food is prescribed
until the presenting of the sheaf has been carried out: 'during
that day' (verse 14), is a somewhat misleading translation, for
the Hebrew really means 'until that day', implying that the
cereal food could be taken as soon as God had had his share.
The word 'parched' (verse 14), occurs elsewhere only at 2: 14
(cp. the comment on 2: 14–16) and Josh. 5: 11: since what is
described in Josh. 5: 10–12 took place on one day and mentions the same kind of food, it is possible that the sanctuary
where this distinctive rite originated was Gilgal.

10. *first sheaf:* for the significance of the *first*, cp. the
comment on 2: 12.

11. *on the day after the sabbath:* the Hebrew text suggests
that the footnote gives the better sense. Since the mention of
the sabbath indicates priestly revision, this may be an attempt
to assimilate 'the first sheaf' to the 'food-offerings' (verse 8),

thus ordering it to be presented on each of the days of the feast of Unleavened Bread. Since it was *a special gift*, it would ultimately go to the priest (cp. the comment on 7: 30-1). In this case, the sabbath here would be the same as the 'sacred assembly' of verse 7.

12-13. Again, these verses are a mark of priestly revision, in order that *a whole-offering*, which after the exile came to be sacrificed on all important occasions, should accompany the presenting of the *sheaf*. Marks of a comparatively late and developed ritual are that the *grain-offering* is only an accompaniment of the whole-offering (cp. p. 25) and that there is also an accompanying *drink-offering*, a libation poured out for God, although the custom is an old one with the idea of conveying nourishment to the deity (cp. Gen. 35: 14; Deut. 32: 38; 2 Kings 16: 13). *a hin of wine:* cp. p. 227. ✻

THE FEAST OF WEEKS

From the day after the sabbath, the day on which you 15 bring your sheaf as a special gift, you shall count seven full weeks. The day after the seventh sabbath will make 16 fifty days, and then you shall present to the LORD a grain-offering from the new crop. You shall bring from your 17 homes two loaves as a special gift; they shall contain two tenths of an ephah of flour and shall be baked with leaven. They are the LORD's firstfruits. In addition to the bread 18 you shall present seven perfect yearling sheep, one young bull, and two rams. They shall be a whole-offering to the LORD with the proper grain-offering and the proper drink-offering, a food-offering of soothing odour to the LORD. You shall also prepare one he-goat for a sin- 19 offering and two yearling sheep for a shared-offering, and 20 the priest shall present them in addition to the bread of

the firstfruits as a special gift before the LORD.[a] They shall
21 be a holy-gift to the LORD for the priest. On that same
day you shall proclaim a sacred assembly for yourselves;
you shall not do your daily work. This is a rule binding
on your descendants for all time wherever you live.
22 When you reap the harvest in your land, you shall not
reap right into the edges of your field, neither shall you
glean the fallen ears. You shall leave them for the poor
and for the alien. I am the LORD your God.

✲ This section, again from the non-Jerusalem tradition,
describes the second great annual feast. In contrast to Unleavened Bread, it marked the end of the wheat harvest, and
its oldest name was thus 'the pilgrim-feast of Harvest' (cp.
Exod. 23: 16). It too was taken over from the Canaanites and,
in Israel's early days, because of its agricultural importance, it
was a very special occasion (cp. Gen. 30: 14; Judg. 15: 1;
1 Sam. 6: 13; 12: 17). After the exile, however, it came to
have less significance than the other two great feasts, probably
because, unlike them, it only lasted a single day (cp. the
comment on verses 9–14).

15. *From the day after the sabbath:* the old regulation prescribed a period of seven times seven days, a specially sacred
number (cp. the comment on 4: 5–7), 'from the time when
the sickle is put to the standing corn' (cp. Deut. 16: 9). Thus
it was not precisely dated, but its celebration depended on the
course of agricultural operations. The priestly tradition, however, gave it a definite date by linking it with the presentation
of the 'first-sheaf', which in turn was probably exactly dated
to the sixteenth day of the first month (cp. the comment on
verse 11). *seven full weeks:* this explains another and somewhat
later title of the celebration 'the pilgrim-feast of Weeks' (cp.
Exod. 34: 22; Deut. 16: 10; Num. 28: 26).

[a] *So Vulg.; Heb. adds* in addition to the two sheep.

16. *The day after the seventh sabbath:* liturgical practice after the exile tended to add a further festival day to the traditional seven-day period (cp. verse 36 and contrast verse 8). *fifty days:* this explains the feast's later Greek name 'Pentecost' i.e. 'fiftieth' (cp. Tobit 2: 1; 2 Macc. 12: 32; Acts 2: 1).

17. *two loaves:* the offering of these was the particular rite of this festival, and as the feast of Unleavened Bread was the firstfruits of the barley harvest (cp. the comment on verses 7–8), so here we have *the LORD's firstfruits* of the wheat harvest. *baked with leaven:* but, by contrast with the feast of Unleavened Bread, the feast of Weeks marked an end, not a beginning, and so the ordinary bread that the farmer would eat in the coming year is brought. However, since leaven could not be given to God by being burnt on the altar (cp. the comment on 2: 11), it is made clear that the loaves were *a special gift*, that is, they went to the priest (cp. the comment on 2: 12).

18. Since the 'firstfruits' did not go directly to him, God is provided with his due sacrifice (cp. the comment on verses 12–13).

19–20. The sacrificial ritual is still further elaborated, as a result of developments after the exile, and as the words *in addition to* indicate. As the footnote shows, the Hebrew has 'in addition to the two sheep'. No doubt this is a gloss which has crept into the original text, but it was probably a note to make clear that, on this occasion, the whole of the *shared-offering* belonged to the priest, since normally, unlike the *sin-offering*, only a part of it went to him (cp. the comment on 7: 14–18): the same object is achieved by the last sentence of verse 20, but this was not sufficiently clear.

22. This has nothing to do with the calendar rules. It was added by the compilers of 'the law of holiness' because, like the feast of Weeks, it was concerned with *the harvest*. It repeats 19: 9–10, but omitting the statements there about the grape harvest, because only the wheat harvest is dealt with here. ✻

THE AUTUMN CELEBRATIONS

23, 24 The LORD spoke to Moses and said, Speak to the Israelites in these words: In the seventh month you shall keep the first day as a sacred rest, a day of remembrance and acclama-
25 tion, a day of sacred assembly. You shall not do your daily work; you shall present a food-offering to the LORD.

26, 27 The LORD spoke to Moses and said: Further, the tenth day of this seventh month is the Day of Atonement. There shall be a sacred assembly; you shall mortify yourselves
28 and present a food-offering to the LORD. On that same day you shall do no work because it is a day of expiation, to make expiation for you before the LORD your God.
29 Therefore every person who does not mortify himself on
30 that day shall be cut off from his father's kin. I will extir-
31 pate any person who does any work on that day. You shall do no work; it is a rule binding on your descendants
32 for all time wherever you live. It is for you a sabbath of sacred rest, and you shall mortify yourselves. From the evening of the ninth day to the following evening you shall keep your sabbath-rest.

33, 34 The LORD spoke to Moses and said, Speak to the Israelites in these words: On the fifteenth day of this seventh month the LORD's pilgrim-feast of Tabernacles*a*
35 begins, and it lasts for seven days. On the first day there shall be a sacred assembly; you shall not do your daily
36 work. For seven days you shall present a food-offering to the LORD; and on the eighth day there shall be a sacred assembly, and you shall present a food-offering to the LORD. It is the closing ceremony; you shall not do your daily work.

[a] Or Booths or Arbours.

These are the appointed seasons of the LORD which you 37
shall proclaim as sacred assemblies for presenting food-
offerings to the LORD, whole-offerings and grain-offerings,
shared-offerings and drink-offerings, each on its day,
besides the LORD's sabbaths and all your gifts, your vows, 38
and your freewill offerings to the LORD.

Further, from the fifteenth day of the seventh month, 39
when the harvest has been gathered, you shall keep the
LORD's pilgrim-feast for seven days. The first day is a
sacred rest and so is the eighth day. On the first day you 40
shall take the fruit of citrus-trees, palm fronds, and leafy
branches, and willows[a] from the riverside, and you shall
rejoice before the LORD your God for seven days. You 41
shall keep this as a pilgrim-feast in the LORD's honour for
seven days every year. It is a rule binding for all time on
your descendants; in the seventh month you shall hold
this pilgrim-feast. You shall live in arbours for seven days, 42
all who are native Israelites, so that your descendants may 43
be reminded how I made the Israelites live in arbours
when I brought them out of Egypt. I am the LORD your
God.

Thus Moses announced to the Israelites the appointed 44
seasons of the LORD.

* With verses 23–36, we return to the precise dating of the
Jerusalem calendar tradition. Originally, the three celebrations
of the 'seventh month' were parts of a single great festival
(cp. p. 124), celebrating both the end of the grape harvest and
the beginning of the year.

23–5. Before the exile, the year began in the autumn, in the
month later called *Tishri* (cp. the comment on 16: 29–34). Hence

[a] *Or* poplars.

the *first day* is New Year's Day. In addition to the regular features of all festivals (verse 25), it has two special features:

(i) it is *a day of remembrance*. In ancient Babylonia, New Year's Day was the occasion when the gods decided the nation's destiny for the coming year. Probably, then, the original significance of the phrase was that on this day God should be reminded of the needs of his people.

(ii) it was also a day of *acclamation*, a technical term, *terūʿāh*. This was a ritual shout (cp. Josh. 6: 5, where 'great shout' translates the same Hebrew word) to welcome the new year.

26–32. For these verses in general, cp. the comment on 16: 29–34.

29–30. The threat of the death penalty for anyone *who does not mortify himself* or who *does any work* (cp. the comment on verse 3) emphasizes the particular importance of the Day of Atonement.

32*b*. A priestly amplification of the foregoing regulations to define precisely the period covered by the Day of Atonement (cp. the comment on 11: 24–5).

33–6. The celebration described here is the third of the old annual festivals and again of Canaanite origin (cp. Judg. 9: 27). It was the climax of the agricultural year, when all the crops, including the grapes, had been harvested (cp. Deut. 16: 13) and hence its oldest title was 'the pilgrim-feast of Ingathering' (cp. Exod. 23: 16; 34: 22). It was an occasion of great rejoicing (cp. Deut. 16: 14) and in ancient Israel it was the main celebration of the year: so it is often referred to simply as 'the pilgrim-feast' (cp. 1 Kings 8: 2, 65; Ezek. 45: 25), the supreme feast.

34. *pilgrim-feast of Tabernacles:* cp. the comment on verse 42.

36. *the closing ceremony:* cp. the comment on verse 16.

37–8. A typical summarizing conclusion by the editors of Leviticus which shows that the account of the calendar originally ended at this point.

39–43. But another section dealing with the autumnal festival is now added, as the word *Further* shows, which does not belong to the Jerusalem cultic tradition, but is related to the material of verses 9–21. It stresses the original primarily agricultural nature of the celebration and preserves two ancient customs.

39. *from the fifteenth day:* this is a harmonizing addition of the priestly editors (cp. the comment on verse 15). The real occurrence of the festival is not precisely dated, but only takes place *when the harvest has been gathered. the LORD's pilgrim-feast:* cp. the comment on verses 33–6.

40. This is the first ancient custom mentioned in the section. Probably the original purpose of taking *the fruit* and *leafy branches* was for a great and joyful procession (cp. *rejoice before the LORD*), which was a particular feature of this festival (cp. 2 Macc. 10: 6–8). Later, however, the branches were used to make the 'arbours' referred to in verse 42 (cp. Neh. 8: 15–16). Here, again, the time of the procession would be dictated by nature, when the trees were in fruit.

42. Here we have the second ancient custom, from which the celebration gained its later title of Tabernacles (cp. verse 34 and the footnote). The word *sukkōth*, rendered *arbours*, properly means 'huts': huts made out of branches were, and still are, erected in the vineyards and orchards of Palestine, in which the agricultural labourers live while the fruit is being harvested.

43. But, for the compilers of 'the law of holiness', the living in *arbours* is no longer a mere agricultural necessity, but is a reminder of how God saved the Israelites from Egypt and of his presence with them in their nomadic existence in the desert, before they settled down and built houses (cp. the comments on 19: 33–4). *all who are native Israelites:* the 'aliens', for whom 'the law of holiness' otherwise shows such great concern (cp. the comment on 17: 8–9), had not experienced this divine deliverance, and so they are excluded here. ✳

THE LAMP AND THE BREAD OF THE PRESENCE

24 1,2 The LORD spoke to Moses and said: Command the Israelites to take pure oil of pounded olives ready for 3 the regular mounting of the lamp outside the Veil of the Tokens in the Tent of the Presence. Aaron shall keep the lamp in trim regularly from dusk to dawn before the LORD: this is a rule binding on your descendants for all 4 time. The lamps on the lamp-stand, ritually clean, shall be regularly kept in trim by him before the LORD.

5 You shall take flour and bake it into twelve loaves, two 6 tenths of an ephah to each. You shall arrange them in two rows, six to a row on the table, ritually clean, before the 7 LORD. You shall sprinkle pure frankincense on the rows,[a] and this shall be a token of the bread, offered to the LORD 8 as a food-offering. Sabbath after sabbath he shall arrange it regularly before the LORD as a gift from the Israelites. 9 This is a covenant for ever; it is the privilege of Aaron and his sons, and they shall eat the bread in a holy place, because it is the holiest of holy-gifts. It is his due out of the food-offerings of the LORD for all time.

✶ Ch. 24 begins with a set of directions for two particular details of the regular service of the sanctuary. They embody customs of the temple built before the exile, but they have been adapted to the situation after the exile, as is shown by the reference to Aaron, verses 3, 9 and cp. the comment on verse 4.

1–3. In these verses, a single *lamp* is mentioned, which was to be kept burning throughout the night. There was such a lamp in the Jerusalem temple (and also at other sanctuaries, cp. 1 Sam. 3: 3), which was a royal symbol, identified with

[a] *So Pesh.; Heb.* row.

the life of the king (cp. 2 Sam. 21: 15–17; Ps. 132: 17): this is the 'lamp', described in almost the same words as here, mentioned in Exod. 27: 20–1. Moses has to see that the *pure oil* for the lamp is provided and probably we should again understand by this the civil leader who, for a short time after the return from exile, took the place of the Davidic king (cp. p. 60). *of the Tokens:* cp. the comment on 16: 13.

4. By contrast, this verse deals with *The lamps on the lampstand*, something quite different from the 'lamp' of verses 2–3, described in detail in Exod. 25: 31–40. It was part of the equipment of the temple built after the exile and perhaps symbolized the divine gift of light.

5–6. In Exod. 25: 30, there is a brief mention of 'the Bread of the Presence': a fuller description of it is given here, although the actual term is not used. In the temples of Babylon, a tray, including twelve loaves, was prepared daily for the deities as their food (cp. Daniel, Bel and Snake, verses 3–7). The Israelite custom was similar, which is an indication of its age, but all trace of its original meaning has disappeared here. Note that, again, Moses apparently provides the loaves, as the king probably once did (cp. Daniel, Bel and Snake, verse 14).

7. *frankincense:* this looks like a specifically Israelite ritual development to make 'the Bread of the Presence' conform as closely as possible to the 'grain-offering' (cp. 2: 1–3). In this, 'all the frankincense' was burnt as *a token*, so it is not difficult to see how it came to be viewed, as here, as the token itself.

8. The 'loaves' were renewed every week. *he:* probably 'Aaron' is to be understood.

9. The previous week's bread belonged to the priesthood. For the phraseology here, cp. 7: 16–18.　　✳

LAWS AGAINST BLASPHEMY AND ASSAULT

Now there was in the Israelite camp a man whose mother 10–11
was an Israelite and his father an Egyptian; his mother's name was Shelomith daughter of Dibri of the tribe of

Dan; and he went out and became involved in a brawl with an Israelite of pure descent. He uttered the Holy
12 Name in blasphemy, so they brought him to Moses; and they kept him in custody until the LORD's will should be clearly made known to them.

13, 14 The LORD spoke to Moses and said, Take the man who blasphemed out of the camp. Everyone who heard him shall put a hand[a] on his head, and then all the community
15 shall stone him to death. You shall say to the Israelites: When any man whatever blasphemes his God, he shall
16 accept responsibility for his sin. Whoever utters the Name of the LORD shall be put to death: all the community shall stone him; alien or native, if he utters the Name, he shall be put to death.

17 When one man strikes another and kills him, he shall
18 be put to death. Whoever strikes a beast and kills it shall
19 make restitution, life for life. When one man injures and disfigures his fellow-countryman, it shall be done to him
20 as he has done; fracture for fracture, eye for eye, tooth for tooth; the injury and disfigurement that he has inflicted upon another shall in turn be inflicted upon him.

21 Whoever strikes a beast and kills it shall make restitution, but whoever strikes a man and kills him shall be put
22 to death. You shall have one penalty for alien and native alike. For I am the LORD your God.

23 Thus did Moses speak to the Israelites, and they took the man who blasphemed out of the camp and stoned him to death. The Israelites did as the LORD had commanded Moses.

[a] *Or* their hands.

✳ The framework of this section, verses 10–14, 23, is made up of a narrative of how a difficult legal case was once decided, thus creating a precedent for the future (cp. the comment on 10: 16–20). Into it, the compilers of 'the law of holiness' (cp. verse 22b) have loosely inserted a string of old regulations dealing with various cases of murder and assault, verses 15–22. They have been brought in at this point because the object was to make clear that they applied to the 'alien' as well as to the 'native' Israelite (verse 22), and this is exactly the purpose of the legal narrative. However, the narrative itself has been expanded to make it cover not only the case of 'blasphemy' but also the later problem of uttering 'the Holy Name'.

10–11. There was an ancient law forbidding *blasphemy* which is found in Exod. 22: 28, where 'revile' translates the same Hebrew word. Here the difficulty is: does the law apply also to a half-Israelite, especially to one who, although himself only an 'alien', would have descendants who would be reckoned as full Israelites (cp. Deut. 23: 7–8)? Mixed marriages, which would produce cases like this, appear to have become especially frequent in the disturbed period during and after the exile (cp. Mal. 2: 11; Ezra 9: 1–2; Neh. 13: 23–4). *of the tribe of Dan:* the priesthood at the tribal sanctuary of Dan claimed descent from Moses (cp. Judg. 18: 30), so this tradition of a decision given by their founder may well have grown up among the priests at that particular shrine. *uttered the Holy Name:* originally, the story was concerned with blasphemy, which alone is referred to in verses 14, 23, that is, using some kind of insulting language about the deity. But there has been added – *in blasphemy* is actually a separate verb in the Hebrew, 'and he blasphemed' – a statement which defines blasphemy as the pronouncing of the Holy Name, that is the personal name of Israel's God, the four letters or tetragrammaton YHWH, translated in the N.E.B. as 'the LORD'. In later Judaism, and to this day, the uttering of this Name is strictly forbidden and in the present passage we seem to have the earliest instance of the prohibition. Probably at this stage the prohibition only applied outside the sphere of public worship, although later again it was extended to that area as well. For the significance of the Name, cp. the comment on 19: 12.

12. No case law was available to cover this particular problem, so action had to wait on a direct divine verdict, given in answer to a ritual inquiry to God by Moses (cp. Exod. 18: 15–16).

14. *Everyone who heard him shall put a hand on his head:* the actual witnesses had to transfer to the offender the guilt they had incurred by hearing his blasphemy (cp. the comment on 1: 4). *all the community:* the entire nation was affected by the man's sin and had to take responsibility for removing it. *stone him:* this was the traditional punishment for blasphemy (cp. 1 Kings 21: 11–14).

15. *You shall say to the Israelites:* a new introduction indicates the beginning of a separate section. A general law is first stated.

16. *Whoever utters the Name:* a later addition (cp. the comment on verses 10–11). *alien or native:* this is the answer to the problem about the extent of the application of the general law, which the foregoing narrative has provided.

17. An ancient law, laying down the penalty for murder (cp. Exod. 21: 12), is attached to the preceding verse by the expression in both *he shall be put to death.*

18–21. There follows a little group of regulations which are all governed by the principle of the so-called 'law of retribution' (verse 20*b*, cp. Exod. 21: 23–5; Deut. 19: 21), which enshrines a very ancient concept. The idea is not to make the punishment fit the crime but to restore to the victim what he has lost. In the case of physical injury, this can only be done by the offender surrendering the organ of which the other has been deprived. But it is possible to *make restitution* for a domestic animal, which is considered as its owner's property, either by means of another animal, which is the meaning of *life for life* in verse 18, or by a monetary compensation (cp. Exod. 21: 33–4).

22. The purpose of repeating these old laws is to make clear that they apply to *alien and native alike*, and this reflects one of the special concerns of 'the law of holiness' (cp. the comment on 17: 8–9). ✻

THE SABBATH YEAR AND THE JUBILEE YEAR

The Lord spoke to Moses on Mount Sinai and said, Speak **25** 1, 2 to the Israelites in these words: When you enter the land which I give you, the land shall keep sabbaths to the Lord. For six years you may sow your fields and for six years 3 prune your vineyards and gather the harvest, but in the 4 seventh year the land shall keep a sabbath of sacred rest, a sabbath to the Lord. You shall not sow your field nor prune your vineyard. You shall not harvest the crop that 5 grows from fallen grain, nor gather in the grapes from the unpruned vines. It shall be a year of sacred rest for the land. Yet what the land itself produces in the sabbath year 6 shall be food for you, for your male and female slaves, for your hired man, and for the stranger lodging under your roof, for your cattle and for the wild animals in your 7 country. Everything it produces may be used for food.

You shall count seven sabbaths of years, that is seven 8 times seven years, forty-nine years, and in the seventh 9 month on the tenth day of the month, on the Day of Atonement, you shall send the ram's horn round. You shall send it through all your land to sound a blast, and 10 so you shall hallow the fiftieth year and proclaim liberation in the land for all its inhabitants. You shall make this your year of jubilee. Every man of you shall return to his

11 patrimony, every man to his family. The fiftieth year shall be your jubilee. You shall not sow, and you shall not harvest the self-sown crop, nor shall you gather in

12 the grapes from the unpruned vines, because it is a jubilee, to be kept holy by you. You shall eat the produce direct from the land.

13 In this year of jubilee you shall return, every one of you,

14 to his patrimony. When you sell or buy land amongst

15 yourselves, neither party shall drive a hard bargain. You shall pay your fellow-countryman according to the number of years since the jubilee, and he shall sell to you

16 according to the number of annual crops. The more years there are to run, the higher the price, the fewer the years,

17 the lower, because he is selling you a series of crops. You must not victimize one another, but you shall fear your

18 God, because I am the Lord your God. Observe my statutes, keep my judgements and carry them out; and

19 you shall live in the land in security. The land shall yield

20 its harvest; you shall eat your fill and live there secure. If you ask what you are to eat during the seventh year, seeing that you will neither sow nor gather the harvest,

21 I will ordain my blessing for you in the sixth year and the

22 land shall produce a crop to carry over three years. When you sow in the eighth year, you will still be eating from the earlier crop; you shall eat the old until the new crop is gathered in the ninth year.

* A very clear example of the aims and methods of the compilers of 'the law of holiness' is provided by ch. 25. Old laws concerned with economic and social relationships are collected, systematized and reinterpreted to take account of developments that had occurred in the course of Israel's history. One aim was to preserve ancient customs from the early days when the Israelites were settling as semi-nomads in Palestine. These had tended to fall into disuse when the monarchy brought in a new social order and had been even more drastically disrupted by the Babylonian invasions. Another aim was to revive them as a practical basis for the restored nation to which 'the law of holiness' looks. The basis of ch. 25 is legal material regulating property and labour relations (verses 23-55), but because such laws rested to a large extent on the 'year of jubilee' this is described first (verses 8-17). In turn, because the 'year of jubilee' came to have a number of features in common with 'the seventh year', a section dealing with this is prefixed to the whole (verses 2-7; cp. verses 20-2).

It has been questioned how far the sabbath year and the jubilee were really practical and actually observed. Certainly they both rest on practices attested before the exile. The sabbath year is a very old institution (cp. Exod. 23: 10-11) and, as will be seen, was quite practicable at least in its original form: again, cancelling of debts, reversion of property and freeing of slaves, which, in this chapter, are all associated with the jubilee, occurred under the monarchy (cp. Exod. 21: 2; Deut. 15: 1-15; Jer. 34: 13-16), although at this time they were linked with the seventh year. On the other hand, the jubilee year is found in the Old Testament only in Leviticus and in Num. 36: 4, a piece of late priestly material. It is possible, therefore, that the regulations for it were only framed after the exile, probably to meet more developed economic and social conditions, for which a seven-year period was too disturbing, although even these are based on an old arrangement of the calendar (cp. the comment on verses 8-10). It is also true that 'the law of holiness' gives to the sabbath and jubilee years an ideal and symbolic significance, which sometimes goes beyond the bounds of ordinary reality, and that the compilers were anxious to do all they could to persuade their contemporaries of the vital importance of observing those periods. Nevertheless, there is a considerable amount of evidence from Rabbinic sources that at least the sabbath year was actually operative in the period of the second temple.

3–4. Leaving the land fallow every *seventh year* corresponds to a widespread custom of early peoples and present-day primitive races. It should be noticed that when the period of *six years* began is not specified, and originally probably varied throughout the country so that all the land was not out of cultivation at the same time: such is the usual practice among the peoples just referred to. But 'the law of holiness' appears to envisage the prohibition as covering the entire land: this is no doubt an idealization but it may also reflect the situation of people living in a comparatively restricted area around Jerusalem during the exile. The law was a practical necessity in a farming system which knew nothing of the rotation of crops or the use of fertilizers and manure, but in origin its purpose was to leave a year's produce for the spirits of the soil (cp. the comment on 19: 9). Here, however, the seventh year is assimilated by the priestly revisers to the *sabbath* (cp. p. 179): it is regarded as a divine command, to give the land a time of *sacred rest*, corresponding to the weekly rest-day for human beings and animals.

5. According to the older law of Exod. 23: 11, what was produced by the untended crop and the vines could be eaten by 'the poor of your people' and 'the wild animals'. Here, however, the priestly concern for 'holiness' has made for greater stringency: everything from the agricultural land belongs in the seventh year to God and is therefore 'holy' and must be left strictly alone.

6–7. *what the land itself produces:* this refers to land which was not cultivated (cp. verse 12). Since what it produced was not the result of human labour it was not affected by the sabbath prohibition of work and could be *used for food* during the rest-year. This is a typical priestly expansion and clarification of the ancient law of Exod. 23: 10–11 which, as it stood, made no provision for sustaining life for the majority of the population during *the sabbath year*.

8–10. For the year of jubilee, a specially sacred period is calculated (cp. the comment on 23: 15), with the extra year characteristic of liturgical practice after the exile (cp. the comment on 23: 16).

9. *The Day of Atonement:* the fiftieth year began on this day. This indicates the period before the exile, when the year began in autumn, and also shows clearly the New-Year setting of the Day of Atonement (cp. p. 124). *the ram's horn:* the beginning of the jubilee year was called to people's attention by a blast from a horn in the different centres of the country. Here the Hebrew word for *ram's horn* is shōpār, but in some other places in the Old Testament it is designated by the word yōbēl (cp. Exod. 19: 13; Josh. 6: 5). The word translated 'jubilee' is also yōbēl: the year took its name from the blowing of the ram's horn which marked its opening.

10. *liberation:* in contrast to the sabbath year, this is the distinguishing mark of the year of jubilee. What is implied for both persons and property is explained in verses 25–8. *return to his patrimony:* as verses 27–8 show, this means that a man must recover his ancestral property which he has previously alienated. *every man to his family:* cp. verse 41.

11–12. But, because of the great priestly interest in the sabbath (cp. the comment on 23: 3), the *jubilee* is subject to the same prohibitions as the sabbath year.

13–17. A section is introduced here, giving the terms on which a man could temporarily alienate his 'patrimony'.

14. First, there is a general prohibition on the man in the stronger position driving an unfair bargain with the weaker partner.

15–16. Then, what constitutes a fair bargain is laid down. The price is determined by the number of annual crops which the property in question would produce before the next jubilee, when it had to be returned to its original owner (verse 28). *he is selling you a series of crops:* only the crops, and not the land, can actually be sold (cp. the comment on verse 23).

17–19. A typical sermonic addition from the compilers of 'the law of holiness', exhorting the hearers to keep the divine commandments, by using the stick (verse 17*b*), and the carrot (verses 18–19).

20–2. *If you ask:* this is a separate section, dealing not with the jubilee but with *the seventh year*, and is a good example of how priestly teaching developed in response to practical questions (cp. Exod. 12: 26; Deut. 7: 17; 18: 21; Josh. 4: 21). It explains that the rule of verse 6 does not exclude eating the crop of the year before during the sabbath year and goes on to paint an ideal picture, to reassure the questioners, of how God will so bless the harvest in the last year when agricultural operations are permitted that its crop will last until they can be resumed again. ✳

THE SALE OF PROPERTY

23 No land shall be sold outright, because the land is mine,
24 and you are coming into it as aliens and settlers. Throughout the whole land of your patrimony, you shall allow land which has been sold to be redeemed.

25 When one of you is reduced to poverty and sells part of his patrimony, his next-of-kin who has the duty of redemption shall come and redeem what his kinsman has
26 sold. When a man has no such next-of-kin and himself
27 becomes able to afford its redemption, he shall take into account the years since the sale and pay the purchaser the balance up to the jubilee. Then he may return to his
28 patrimony. But if the man cannot afford to buy back the property, it shall remain in the hands of the purchaser till the year of jubilee. It shall then revert to the original owner, and he shall return to his patrimony.

When a man sells a dwelling-house in a walled town, he 29
shall retain the right of redemption till the end of the year
of the sale; for a time he shall have the right of redemption. If it is not redeemed before a full year is out, the 30
house in the walled[a] town shall vest in perpetuity in
the buyer and his descendants; it shall not revert at the
jubilee. Houses in unwalled hamlets shall be treated as 31
property in the open country: the right of redemption
shall hold good, and in any case the house shall revert at
the jubilee. Levites shall have the perpetual right to redeem 32
houses of their own patrimony in towns belonging to
them. If one of the Levites does not redeem[b] his house in[c] 33
such a town, then it shall still revert to him at the jubilee,
because the houses in Levite towns are their patrimony
in Israel. The common land surrounding their towns shall 34
not be sold, because it is their property in perpetuity.

✻ 23. *No land shall be sold outright:* This is probably the old
basic law, going back to the days when property was held in
common by the large family group, and so no individual
could dispose of it (cp. 1 Kings 21: 3). But 'the law of holiness'
adds an explanation for the prohibition: the land of Palestine
belongs to God and the Israelites enter it only as *aliens*, that is,
permanent, but non-property owning, residents (cp. 1 Chron.
29: 15; Ps. 39: 12).

24. However, with the development of individual property
in the more advanced economic circumstances of the monarchy, it came to be recognized that ancestral land could be
sold, but there always remained the right to 'redeem' it, that
is, to buy it back. The succeeding verses lay down the conditions under which such 'redemption' could be made.

[a] *So Sept.; Heb.* unwalled.
[b] does not redeem: *so Vulg.; Heb.* redeems.
[c] *So Sept.; Heb.* and.

25. *reduced to poverty:* inherited property could only be sold when dire necessity demanded, not to make a profit. The *next-of-kin* had the specific duty of buying back the part of the patrimony that had been sold, on behalf of the family group to whom it really belonged (cp. Ruth 4: 1–4; Jer. 32: 7–8).

26–8. If there is *no such next-of-kin*, but the seller's financial circumstances improve, he may himself redeem what he has sold. The price must be fixed to compensate the purchaser for the crops he would have expected to obtain until the next *jubilee* (cp. the comment on verses 15–16), when, in any case, the property had *to revert to the original owner*.

29–31. There follows a further legal stipulation, to clarify the problem: 'does the right of redemption apply to *a dwelling-house* as well as to land?' *walled* towns, typical of Canaanite city culture, were a novelty to the Israelite farming population and their customary family law did not provide for them. So a house in such a town was considered more an individual than a family possession. A *right of redemption* remained for a strictly limited period, but, if it was not exercised, the house was alienated *in perpetuity* and did not revert even at the jubilee. But the agricultural Israelites were used to living in *unwalled hamlets*, so houses there were treated as landed property, and the old rules applied.

32–4. The Levites, however, formed a special case. Whatever their past history may have been, by the time of the exile, which is the situation here, the Levites had become a group of ministers performing certain duties in connection with the sanctuary, but distinct from, and subordinate to, the priesthood proper (cp. Ezek. 44: 10–14). At some period, probably towards the end of the monarchy, they had acquired a number of towns in which to reside (see the list in Josh. 21). Since these towns were regarded as a gift from the Israelites to the whole Levitical group (cp. Num. 35: 2, 8; Ezek. 45: 5), who had no landed property of their own (cp. Deut. 18: 1–2), they and their buildings were only held in trust from God (cp. verse 23) and were therefore 'holy' and could not be alienated in perpetuity (cp. verse 33*b* and Ezek. 48: 14). An individual Levite's house, therefore, was part of the patrimony and the rules of verses 26-8 applied. Agricultural land *surrounding their towns* could not be sold even temporarily because it was held in *common* (cp. the comment on verse 23). ✶

THE FATE OF THE POOR

When your brother-Israelite is reduced to poverty and 35 cannot support himself in the community, you shall assist him as*a* you would an alien or a stranger, and he shall live with you. You shall not charge him interest on a loan, 36 either by deducting it in advance from the capital sum, or by adding it on repayment. You shall fear your God, and your brother shall live with you; you shall not deduct 37 interest when advancing him money nor add interest to the payment due for food supplied on credit. I am 38 the LORD your God who brought you out of Egypt to give you the land of Canaan and to become your God.

When your brother is reduced to poverty and sells 39 himself to you, you shall not use him to work for you as a slave. His status shall be that of a hired man or a stranger 40 lodging with you; he shall work for you until the year of jubilee. He shall then leave your service, with his children, 41 and go back to his family and to his ancestral property: because they are my slaves whom I brought out of Egypt, 42 they shall not be sold as slaves are sold. You shall not drive 43 him with ruthless severity, but you shall fear your God. Such slaves as you have, male or female, shall come from 44 the nations round about you; from them you may buy

[*a*] as: *so Sept.; Heb. om.*

45 slaves. You may also buy the children of those who have
46 settled and lodge with you and such of their family as are
born in the land. These may become your property, and
you may leave them to your sons after you; you may use
them as slaves permanently. But your fellow-Israelites you
shall not drive with ruthless severity.

47 When an alien or a stranger living with you becomes
rich, and your brother becomes poor and sells himself to
the alien or stranger or to a member of some alien family,
48 he shall have the right of redemption after he has sold
49 himself. One of his brothers may redeem him, or his
uncle, his cousin, or any blood-relation of his family, or,
50 if he can afford it, he may redeem himself. He and his
purchaser together shall reckon from the year when he
sold himself to the year of jubilee, and the price shall be
adjusted to the number of years. His period of service
with his owner shall be reckoned at the rate of a hired
51 man. If there are still many years to run to the year of
jubilee, he must repay for his redemption a proportionate
52 amount of the sum for which he sold himself; if there are
53 few, he shall reckon and repay accordingly. He shall have
the status of a labourer hired from year to year, and you
shall not let him be driven with ruthless severity by his
54 owner. If the man is not redeemed in the intervening
years, he and his children shall be released in the year of
55 jubilee; for it is to me that the Israelites are slaves, my
slaves whom I brought out of Egypt. I am the LORD
your God.

* 35–8. The first section is full of the exhortatory terminology
characteristic of 'the law of holiness' (cp. verses 36*b*, 38),

because it is trying to commend an ideal pattern of behaviour to the Israelites.

35. If a *brother-Israelite is reduced to poverty*, what ought to happen is that he should be taken into a home, usually by one of his kinsfolk, and given the same hospitality *as an alien or a stranger* would be: here once more we see the particular outlook of 'the law of holiness' (cp. the comment on 19: 33-4).

36-7. But the original heart of this section is an ancient law forbidding charging interest on a loan (cp. Exod. 22: 25) to a 'fellow-Israelite', although by this period, when the Israelites had come into contact with a wider world, this was allowed in dealing with a foreigner (cp. Deut. 23: 20). Here again is to be seen the strength of the concept of the family and its common possessions. The old law has been expanded to stop any device for getting round the prohibition, such as advancing a smaller sum than had been agreed or exacting a larger sum on repayment (verse 36), or by making a loan in kind and then demanding a further monetary payment (verse 37*b*).

39-41. A less ideal situation is recognized here. An extra mouth to feed might be too much, without getting work in return. But the *brother* Israelite, although he is not being paid for his labour, must be treated as though he were (verse 40*a*). He must not be given the status of a slave, he must not be treated as a possession (contrast verse 46): in any event, he goes free at *the year of jubilee*. Originally, as has been noted, 'a fellow-Hebrew' was freed in 'the seventh year' (Deut. 15: 12) and a certain unreality has been introduced by the transfer of this to the jubilee: life-expectancy was not high among the Hebrews and, if a man had to wait for his freedom for forty-nine years, he would usually be dead, although at least his children would go free (verse 41*a*; contrast verse 46).

42. A reason for the law is given by 'the law of holiness', typically drawn from the saving history of Israel. Because God took the Israelites from slavery in Egypt, now they are only his slaves, and can belong to no-one else (cp. verse 55 and the comment on verse 23).

43. In any event, harsh terms of service must not be imposed, because, as an Israelite, the man is under God's protection.

44-6. Permanent slavery was allowed in Israel but only in two cases:

44. (i) Foreigners could be bought as such *from the nations round about*.

45. (ii) So could children of 'aliens', whether born before or after their parents settled in Palestine. In either case, it was a business transaction, unlike the Israelite who was forced into slavery by poverty (cp. verse 39), and incurred a permanent status (verse 46).

47-55. The final section deals with the case of a poor Israelite who is forced to sell himself to an alien. His situation is the same as if he had sold himself to a fellow Israelite (compare verses 53*a* and 40; 53*b* and 43; 54-5 and 41-2), with one exception:

48*b*. The Israelite who sells himself to the alien has *the right of redemption*.

49-52. This right operates in the same way as in the case of a sale of land (cp. verses 25-7), except that the kinsman who *may redeem him*, presumably because a human being is in question here, can be drawn from a much wider circle (verse 49). The redemption price is calculated according to the number of years left to run before the jubilee (cp. verses 15-16), reckoned at the rate of a hired labourer's annual pay (verses 50*b*, 53*a*). ✳

AGAINST IDOLATRY

26 You shall not make idols for yourselves; you shall not erect a carved image or a sacred pillar; you shall not put a figured stone on your land to prostrate yourselves upon, 2 because I am the LORD your God. You shall keep my sabbaths and revere my sanctuary. I am the LORD.

✶ Actually these verses are an isolated fragment, but the compilers of 'the law of holiness' have placed them here as a kind of 'text' for the great concluding exhortation which follows, to summarize what is to be understood by keeping God's commandments.

1. This verse is related to 19: 4, but it is much more detailed in order to emphasize that Israel's worship must be free from all heathen practices. *You shall not make idols:* in 19: 4 the Israelites are forbidden to 'resort to idols', but here they must not make them for use in their own worship (cp. Deut. 4: 28; Isa. 44: 9–20). *a carved image:* cp. Deut. 4: 16, 23, 25. Lev. 19: 4 and Exod. 34: 17 only prohibit 'gods of cast metal' and probably reflect a period when carved statues, such as the 'teraphim', were acceptable in the Israelite cult (cp. the N.E.B. footnotes on 1 Sam. 19: 13; Hos. 3: 4; Zech. 10: 2). *a sacred pillar:* this was a standing stone, representing the god Baal (cp. 2 Kings 3: 2), placed beside the altar in Canaanite shrines (cp. Deut. 16: 21–2). It too was once a regular feature at Israelite sanctuaries as well (cp. Gen. 28: 18; Hos. 3: 4). *a figured stone on your land:* this probably refers to the boundary stones, many examples of which have been found in Mesopotamia, which served for marking the boundaries of fields and were carved with emblems of gods. *upon:* the Hebrew could equally well be translated 'over'.

2. Here are presented what became the three fundamental characteristics of Judaism after the exile: keeping the sabbath, loyalty to the temple, as the sole *sanctuary*, and worship of the one true God. ✶

THE BLESSINGS

If you conform to my statutes, if you observe my com- 3 mandments and carry them out, I will give you rain at 4 the proper time; the land shall yield its produce and the trees of the country-side their fruit. Threshing shall last 5 till vintage and vintage till sowing; you shall eat your fill

6 and live secure in your land. I will give peace in the land, and you shall lie down to sleep with no one to terrify you. I will rid your land of dangerous beasts and it shall not be

7 ravaged by war. You shall put your enemies to flight and

8 they shall fall in battle before you. Five of you shall pursue a hundred and a hundred of you ten thousand; so shall

9 your enemies fall in battle before you. I will look upon you with favour, I will make you fruitful and increase your numbers: I will give my covenant with you its full

10 effect. Your old harvest shall last you in store until you

11 have to clear out the old to make room for the new. I will establish my Tabernacle among you and will not spurn

12 you. I will walk to and fro among you; I will become

13 your God and you shall become my people. I am the LORD your God who brought you out of Egypt and let you be their slaves no longer; I broke the bars of your yoke and enabled you to walk upright.

✶ 'The law of holiness' concludes with an adaptation of an ancient Near Eastern formal pattern. A section containing blessings and curses was often appended to law codes and to documents embodying state treaties made between a suzerain and his vassal. Their object was to ensure the observance of the laws or the terms of the treaty on the part of those who were bound to them, by calling in the deity to act as guarantor: he would reward those who obeyed the regulations and bring disaster on those who did not. In these documents, as in ch. 26, threats are always much more prominent than promises: for example, the famous law-code of Hammurabi of Babylon, dating from round about 1700 B.C., concludes with some 16 lines containing blessings but some 280 lines of curses, many of them with similar themes to those found in this chapter of Leviticus. The immediate source of the blessing and cursing pattern in 'the law of holiness', however, is the Israelite cultus. There, the law, which enshrined the provisions of the 'covenant', a kind of treaty between God, as Israel's lord, and his subjects, was read out in a solemn public ceremony at regular intervals (cp. Deut. 31: 10-13; 2 Kings 23: 2; Neh. 8: 1-8) and followed by an intoning (cp. Deut. 27: 14) of blessings and curses to secure its observance (cp. Josh. 8: 34; Deut. 27: 15-26; 28). In the Old Testament, this ceremony is located particularly on the two mountains Gerizim and Ebal in the neighbourhood of the great northern sanctuary of Shechem (cp. Deut. 11: 29; 27: 11-13; Josh. 8: 33) and thus it may be that 'the law of holiness' is making use of a distinctive tradition of the Shechem shrine, brought to Jerusalem by the priests from there when they migrated after the fall of the northern kingdom. There, the blessing element at least became linked with the tradition of the idealized Davidic king as the source of blessings for his country, as the close parallels between verses 3-13 and Ezek. 34: 23-31; 37: 24-8 clearly show (cp. Ps. 72; Isa. 9: 2-7; 11: 1-9). The compilers of 'the law of holiness' reshaped the old cultic formulae in their own outlook and language as a concluding exhortation to their preaching (cp. p. 136). In doing so, they sought to bring home to their hearers as powerfully as possible the absolute necessity of strict obedience to the commandments in chs. 17-25, if the disasters that had followed the nation's disobedience were not to fall on the future restored community which they were engaged in creating. A similar set of exhortations deriving from the blessing and curse pattern occurs in Deut. 4-11.

Verses 3-13 have as their basis five promises of divine favour if the divine commandments are observed (verse 3): they are strongly rhythmical in form, which indicates their origin in public worship. But they have been expanded by five rhetorical sermonic additions (verses 5, 6b, 8, 10, 13), typical of the method of 'the law of holiness'.

4. The first promise is of *rain* and of the good harvests which depended on it (cp. Ezek. 34: 26-7). *at the proper time:*

in a dry country like Palestine, regular rain was essential for successful agriculture (cp. Deut. 11: 10–11). The chief rainy season was from December to March, but equally vital were the 'autumn' and the 'spring' rains, which preceded and followed it: these were always viewed as special signs of God's favour (cp. Deut. 11: 14; Jer. 5: 24; N.E.B. footnote on Joel 2: 23).

5. The addition transforms the picture of a good harvest into a near miraculous one (cp. Amos 9: 13): the *Threshing* of grain in early summer (cp. the comment on 23: 6) will last until the grape harvest in autumn (cp. the comment on 23: 33–6) and the latter until the time for *sowing* in early spring. We have here the beginning of a line of thought which issues in the description of the miraculous fertility of the Messianic age common in apocalyptic literature (cp. Isa. 35; 65: 19–25).

6a. The second promise is of *peace* and security (cp. Ezek. 34: 25a, where 'prosperity' represents the same Hebrew word as *peace* here).

6b. A sermonic addition, promising the complete extirpation of *dangerous* wild *beasts* (cp. Ezek. 34: 25b), and introducing the third blessing.

7. This is victory in war.

8. The rhetorical, idealizing addition of 'the law of holiness' (cp. Deut. 32: 30; Josh. 23: 10; Isa. 30: 17).

9. The fourth promise is of a high birth-rate, an important consideration for a rudimentary society, where under-population was a real problem. *give my covenant with you its full effect:* in the priestly picture of God's covenant with Abraham, the promise of numerous descendants is very prominent (cp. Gen. 17: 1–6).

10. Again, an addition in the spirit of verse 5 (cp. 25: 22).

11–12. The fifth promise is that God will set up his *Tabernacle* (cp. Ezek. 37: 26, 28) and will dwell in a relationship of closest intimacy *among* his people (cp. 2 Sam. 7: 6, where 'made my journey' translates the same Hebrew word as *walk* here). Probably the reference to the establishment of the Tabernacle reflects an actual institution in Palestine during the period of the exile (cp. above p. 16). *I will become your God and you shall become my people:* here is repeated the regular basic statement which summarized the essential meaning of the divine covenant with Israel (cp. Exod. 6: 7; Ezek. 37: 27).

13. Again, a typical example of the appeal of 'the law of holiness' to the facts of the saving history (cp. 25: 38). *broke the bars of your yoke:* cp. Ezek. 34: 27*b*. ✳

THE CURSES

But if you do not listen to me, if you fail to keep all these 14 commandments of mine, if you reject my statutes, if you 15 spurn my judgements, and do not obey all my commandments, but break my covenant, then be sure that this is 16 what I will do: I will bring upon you sudden terror, wasting disease, recurrent fever, and plagues that dim the sight and cause the appetite to fail. You shall sow your seed to no purpose, for your enemies shall eat the crop. I 17 will set my face against you, and you shall be routed by your enemies. Those that hate you shall hound you on until you run when there is no pursuit.

If after all this you do not listen to me, I will go on to 18 punish you seven times over for your sins. I will break 19 down your stubborn pride. I will make the sky above you like iron and the earth beneath you like bronze. Your 20 strength shall be spent in vain; your land shall not yield its produce nor the trees of the land their fruit.

If you still defy me and refuse to listen, I will multiply 21 your calamities seven times, as your sins deserve. I will 22 send wild beasts among you; they shall tear your children from you, destroy your cattle and bring your numbers

23 low; and your roads shall be deserted. If after all this you
24 have not learnt discipline but still defy me, I in turn will
defy you and scourge you seven times over for your sins.
25 I will bring war in vengeance upon you, vengeance irrevocable under covenant; you shall be herded into your
cities, I will send pestilence among you, and you shall be
26 given over to the enemy. I will cut short your daily
bread[a] until ten women can bake your bread in a single
oven; they shall dole it out by weight, and though you
eat, you shall not be satisfied.

27 If in spite of this you do not listen to me and still defy
28 me, I will defy you in anger, and I myself will punish you
29 seven times over for your sins. Instead of meat you shall
30 eat your sons and your daughters. I will destroy your hill-
shrines and demolish your incense-altars. I will pile your
rotting carcasses on the rotting logs[b] that were your idols,
31 and I will spurn you. I will make your cities desolate and
destroy your sanctuaries; the soothing odour of your
32 offerings I will not accept. I will destroy your land, and
33 the enemies who occupy it shall be appalled. I will scatter
you among the heathen, and I will pursue you with the
naked sword; your land shall be desolate and your cities
34 heaps of rubble. Then, all the time that it lies desolate,
while you are in exile in the land of your enemies, your
35 land shall enjoy its sabbaths to the full. All the time of its
desolation it shall have the sabbath rest which it did not
36 have when you lived there. And I will make those of you
who are left in the land of your enemies so ridden with
fear that, when a leaf flutters behind them in the wind,

[a] *Lit.* I will break your stick of bread.
[b] rotting logs: *or* effigies.

they shall run as if it were the sword behind them; they
shall fall with no one in pursuit. Though no one pursues 37
them they shall stumble over one another, as if the sword
were behind them, and there shall be no stand made
against the enemy. You shall meet your end among the 38
heathen, and your enemies' land shall swallow you up.
Those who are left shall pine away in an enemy land 39
under their own iniquities; and with their fathers'
iniquities upon them too, they shall pine away as they did.

✶ This section, too, appears to be based on five originally
cultic threats of disaster for disobedience, arranged in an
ascending order of severity, but, as already noted, they have
been much more expanded than the blessings and hence their
basic outline is not so easy to discover. Further, in the preaching of 'the law of holiness', they have been combined with a
formally expressed threat of punishment 'seven times over for
your sins' (verses 18, 21, 24, 28): the number 'seven' is not to
be understood literally but expresses the completeness and
irrevocability of the divine judgement. We have here a form
of a tradition of a series of calamities sent by God to bring
Israel back to obedience, which is found in the prophets (cp.
Isa. 9: 8–21; Amos 4: 6–11) and particularly, with a number
of parallels to Lev. 26, in Ezek. 5: 10–17: the narrative of the
'plagues of Egypt' (cp. Exod. 7–11) has probably been
moulded on the same tradition.

16–17. The first threat is of military defeat, at the hands of
a foreign invader, with its accompanying disasters.

16. *sudden terror:* when God fought in battle on the side of
his people, he was believed to send supernatural terror into the
hearts of the enemy, so that they fled in disorder (cp. 1 Sam.
7: 10; 14: 15), but now God becomes the enemy of Israel
(cp. Deut. 28: 25–6 and Lev. 26: 17*a*). *plagues that dim the sight
and cause the appetite to fail:* a regular expression (cp. 1 Sam.

2: 33). The effect of these plagues would obviously be to render the Israelites incapable of fighting. *to no purpose:* cp. Deut. 28: 33, 51.

19–20. The second threat is of famine, resulting from the failure of the crops. *the sky above you like iron:* in Israelite thought, rain came from the 'water above the vault of heaven' (cp. Gen. 1: 7). If the sky became hard, the essential rains (cp. the comment on verse 4) could not get through and soften *the earth beneath* for sowing.

22. The third threat is of a plague of *wild beasts* (contrast verse 6*b*), which would ravage humans and cattle and make movement on the roads impossible (cp. Ezek. 5: 17*a*; 14: 15).

25–6. The fourth threat is of an actual occupying force, which besieges the cities and causes *pestilence* and famine: the trio war, literally 'sword' here, pestilence and famine forms a common description of the effects of the Babylonian invasions in Jeremiah (cp. Jer. 21: 7, 9), and was an ancient prophetic formula threatening disaster (cp. Jer. 28: 8).

25. *vengeance irrevocable under covenant:* God is not acting arbitrarily, but is rightly punishing Israel for its neglect of its covenant obligations. Since the nation has completely cut itself off from God, the divine judgement is irrevocable.

26. *ten:* the figure is symbolic, indicating the small number who remained (cp. Zech. 8: 23). *daily bread:* a literal translation is given in the footnote. The reference is to the 'stick' on which flat cakes, with a hole in the middle, were strung. *a single oven* is all that will be required to bake the small amount of bread available. *dole it out by weight:* even this will have to be strictly rationed (cp. Ezek. 4: 16–17).

28–39. The fifth threat is much fuller than the others, because it involves the complete destruction of the nation and the exiling of its people. No doubt it reflects the actual circumstances of the catastrophe of 587 B.C. Five features of the disaster are picked out:

29. (i) The famine of verse 26 will cause cannibalism (cp. Ezek. 5: 10).

30. (ii) The *hill-shrines* and their cultic objects, which were characteristic of Canaanite worship and a constant temptation to the Israelites (cp. Deut. 12: 2–3), will be swept away and shown to be completely worthless. *rotting logs:* this refers to the wooden pole, representing the fertility goddess (cp. Exod. 34: 13; Judg. 6: 25; Isa. 17: 8), found in Canaanite sanctuaries alongside the 'sacred pillar' (cp. the comment on verse 1).

31. (iii) *cities* and the official *sanctuaries* – note that there are a number of these – will be destroyed. *I will not accept:* the cessation of worship is caused not so much by enemy invasion as by God's refusal any longer to accept the sacrifices of his faithless people (cp. Isa. 1: 11–15).

32–3. (iv) The countryside too will be devastated and depopulated.

34–5. But now 'the law of holiness' introduces a note of hope and grace, which is further developed in verse 43. The *desolation* of the land is punishment but also purification. While it lies empty, the country will recover its holiness (cp. the comment on 25: 5) through an extended *sabbath rest* (cp. the comment on 25: 3–4), which it could never enjoy while it was defiled by the sins of the Israelites and the heathen practices which they tolerated. These verses provide the basis for the interpretation of the exile in 2 Chron. 36: 21.

36–9. (v) An ultimate catastrophe awaits those who have survived the foregoing horrors: this is exile in miserable circumstances in a foreign land (cp. Deut. 28: 64).

38. Nor will the survivors remain long even in this condition. Complete annihilation is to be Israel's fate. In this section, no hope at all for the exiled people is envisaged. This suggests that the setting is in Palestine rather than in Babylonia.

39. *with their fathers' iniquities upon them:* the final destruction of the nation is seen as the outcome of a long period of repeated disobedience and rebellion (cp. Exod. 20: 5; 34: 7). ✻

HOPE FOR THE FUTURE

40 But though they confess their iniquity, their own and their fathers', their treachery, and even their defiance of
41 me, I will defy them in my turn and carry them off into their enemies' land. Yet if then their stubborn[a] spirit is
42 broken and they accept their punishment in full, I will remember my covenant with Jacob and my covenant with Isaac, yes, and my covenant with Abraham, and I
43 will remember the land. The land shall be rid of its people and enjoy in full its sabbaths while it lies desolate, and they shall pay in full the penalty because they rejected my
44 judgements and spurned my statutes. Yet even then, in their enemies' land, I shall not have rejected nor spurned them, bringing them to an end and so breaking my
45 covenant with them, because I am the LORD their God. I will remember on their behalf the covenant with the men of former times whom I brought out of Egypt in full sight of all the nations, that I might be their God. I am the LORD.

46 These are the statutes, the judgements, and the laws which the LORD established between himself and the Israelites on Mount Sinai through Moses.

* In spite of the apparently irrevocable doom envisaged in verses 38–9, the compilers of 'the law of holiness', whose characteristic language is noticeable in this section, were yet led to catch a glimpse of hope for their compatriots in exile. God will not completely reject his people and will keep the nation in being even in a foreign country where, according to the general outlook of the ancient world, he would not be

[a] *Lit.* uncircumcised.

expected to have any power. There is even a hint that the exiles might one day hope to return to Palestine, but it is faint and allusive (cp. the comments on verses 42 and 45), and this suggests a time shortly after the fall of Jerusalem when there seemed little prospect of any return, in contrast to the later period during the exile when 'Second Isaiah' could hope for such a return in the near future (cp. Isa. 40–55).

40–1. Since God is a God of justice, the Israelites' repeated *iniquity*, *treachery* and *defiance* must be punished. But the aim of the punishment is remedial, to bring Israel to repentance and amendment. *stubborn:* cp. the footnote, the comment on 19: 23–5, and Deut. 10: 16; Jer. 4: 4; Ezek. 44: 7, 9.

42. If the Israelites 'accept their punishment in full', God *will remember* his covenant with the patriarchs. 'Remember' in the Old Testament means not only 'to recollect' but also to take action on the basis of what is recalled. The covenant with the patriarchs included the divine promise to give them the land of Canaan (cp. Gen. 17: 7–8; 26: 3; 35: 12). Hence it is here hinted that God would in due course do the same for the exiles.

44. This verse gives the ground for God's merciful action. Whatever the Israelites might have done, God would never break his *covenant with them*, which would of necessity bring the nation *to an end*, because he was 'ever constant and true' (cp. Exod. 34: 6–7).

45. Rather, he will *remember...the covenant* made at Mount Sinai after the exodus. This, too, included the promise of the land of Canaan (cp. Exod. 23: 28–31) and so again the restoration of the exiles is hinted at. *in full sight of all the nations:* there is a clear contrast between the people of God and all other nations. The phrase is a favourite one in Ezekiel (cp. Ezek. 20: 9, 14, 22).

46. A summarizing conclusion marks the close of 'the law of holiness'. ✶

VOWS, GIFTS AND DUES TO GOD

✳ Ch. 27 has no real connection with what precedes it but is a separate, self-contained section dealing with a single topic: what gifts or dues to the sanctuary (cp. Num. 18: 8–19) could be commuted into a money payment. It may have been tacked on to 'the law of holiness' when that was incorporated into the rest of Leviticus, because it presupposes the rules for 'the year of jubilee' (cp. verses 17–25), which 'the law of holiness' contained in its final form (ch. 25). The fact that the gifts in question can be given a monetary value, but that such is not universally the case (cp. the comment on verses 9–10), suggests that the passage comes from the period shortly after the exile, when the process was beginning but had not progressed as far as it was later to do (cp. above p. 14). ✳

VOWS

27 1,2 The LORD spoke to Moses and said, Speak to the Israelites in these words: When a man makes a special*a* vow to the
3 LORD which requires your valuation of living persons, a male between twenty and sixty years old shall be valued at fifty silver shekels, that is shekels by the sacred standard.
4,5 If it is a female, she shall be valued at thirty shekels. If the person is between five years old and twenty, the valuation
6 shall be twenty shekels for a male and ten for a female. If the person is between a month and five years old, the valuation shall be five shekels for a male and three for a
7 female. If the person is over sixty and a male, the valuation shall be fifteen shekels, but if a female, ten shekels.
8 If the man is too poor to pay the amount of your valuation, the person shall be set before the priest, and the priest

---

[a] makes a special: *or* discharges a. . .

shall value him according to the sum which the man who
makes the vow can afford: the priest shall make the
valuation.

If the vow concerns a beast such as may be offered as 9
an offering to the LORD, then every gift shall be holy to
the LORD. He shall not change it for another, or substitute 10
good for bad or bad for good. But if a substitution is in
fact made of one beast for another, then both the original
beast and its substitute shall be holy to the LORD. If the 11
vow concerns any unclean beast such as may not be
offered as an offering to the LORD, then the animal shall
be brought before the priest, and he shall value it whether 12
good or bad. The priest's valuation shall be decisive; in case 13
of redemption the payment shall be increased by one fifth.

✻ 2. A *vow* was a promise to make a gift to the deity to
persuade him to show favour to the man so promising: it
could take the form of a regular sacrifice (cp. the comment on
7: 16), or of a particular course of action (cp. 2 Sam. 15: 8) or
often of a special gift (cp. Gen. 28: 20–2). Such a promise,
being made to God, was absolutely binding (cp. Num. 30: 2)
and had to be 'discharged' (cp. the footnote) in due course.
Verses 2–8 deal with the case where a man has promised to
give a human being to God. Originally this meant that the
person became a permanent slave for the sanctuary (cp. 1 Sam.
1: 28; 2: 18), but as the idea grew up that such a status was
improper for an Israelite (cp. the comment on 25: 39–41), it
became possible to make a monetary payment to the sanctuary
instead and this was clearly obligatory by the time when the
passage here was formulated. The question then arose, how
is a person's equivalent in money to be calculated?, and this is
what is regulated here. *your valuation:* at first, no doubt, the
sum to be paid was determined by the priest, but in course of
time a fixed tariff was established (cp. above p. 218).

3–7. Payments are not calculated according to the number of years' work the sanctuary might expect to receive from a particular person (contrast the comment on 25: 49–52), but by that person's status in the Israelite social order. So a man in the prime of life is at the top, followed by the young man who would be marrying and beginning to take his place in society, then by the man whose active life was nearly over (verse 7), and lastly by the infant (verse 6): in accordance with the outlook of a patriarchal society (cp. the comment on 1: 3), in each case *a female* is less highly valued. *shekels:* cp. the comment on 5: 15.

8. So clear is now the principle that a human being cannot be given to the sanctuary, that some compensation must be paid even if the full amount cannot be afforded.

9–10. By contrast, an animal which could be *offered as an offering* according to the regular ritual had to be sacrificed. Since it was made over to God, it was *holy to the LORD*, and it was not possible to change it or substitute even a better animal for it. Verse 10b expands the regulation by a piece of case-law; if a man deceitfully attempts such a substitution, then both the original animal *and its substitute* must be given to God.

11–12. Any other animal vowed to the deity had to be compensated for. The standard for 'uncleanness' here is simply whether or not the beast may be *offered as an offering*. *shall be decisive:* here *the priest's valuation* is still final for each particular case (cp. the comment on verse 2).

13. A priestly expansion, in answer to the question: 'what if the animal has actually been presented at the sanctuary, but the offerer wants it back?' (cp. verses 15, 19). In this case, he must pay the compensation fee, plus a fine of *one fifth* (cp. the comment on 5: 16). ✳

GIFTS AND TITHES

14 When a man dedicates his house as holy to the LORD, the priest shall value it whether good or bad, and the priest's

valuation shall be decisive. If the donor redeems his house, 15 he shall pay the amount of the valuation increased by one fifth, and the house shall be his.

If a man dedicates to the LORD part of his ancestral land, 16 you shall value it according to the amount of seed-corn it can carry, at the rate of fifty shekels of silver for a homer of barley seed. If he dedicates his land from the year of 17 jubilee, it shall stand at your valuation; but if he dedicates 18 it after the year of jubilee, the priest shall estimate the price in silver according to the number of years remaining till the next year of jubilee, and this shall be deducted from your valuation. If the man who dedicates his field 19 should redeem it, he shall pay the amount of your valuation in silver, increased by one fifth, and it shall be his. If he does not redeem it but sells the land to another 20 man, it shall no longer be redeemable; when the land 21 reverts at the year of jubilee, it shall be like land that has been devoted, holy to the LORD. It shall belong to the priest as his patrimony.

If a man dedicates to the LORD land which he has 22 bought, land which is not part of his ancestral land, the 23 priest shall estimate the amount of the value for the period until the year of jubilee, and the man shall give the amount fixed as at that day; it is holy to the LORD. At the 24 year of jubilee the land shall revert to the man from whom he bought it, whose patrimony it is. Every valuation you 25 make shall be made by the sacred standard (twenty gerahs to the shekel).

Notwithstanding, no man may dedicate to the LORD 26 the first-born of a beast which in any case has to be offered as a first-born, whether an ox or a sheep. It is the

27 LORD's. If it is any unclean beast, he may redeem it at your valuation and shall add one fifth; but if it is not
28 redeemed, it shall be sold at your valuation. Notwithstanding, nothing which a man devotes to the LORD irredeemably from his own property, whether man or beast or ancestral land, may be sold or redeemed. Every-
29 thing so devoted is most holy to the LORD. No human being thus devoted may be redeemed, but he shall be put to death.

30 Every tithe on land, whether from grain or from the fruit of a tree, belongs to the LORD; it is holy to the LORD.
31 If a man wishes to redeem any of his tithe, he shall pay its
32 value increased by one fifth. Every tenth creature that passes under the counting rod shall be holy to the LORD;
33 this applies to all tithes of cattle and sheep. There shall be no inquiry whether it is good or bad, and no substitution. If any substitution is made, then both the tithe-animal and its substitute shall be forfeit as holy; it shall not be redeemed.

34 These are the commandments which the LORD gave Moses for the Israelites on Mount Sinai.

✻ This section deals with voluntary gifts, often in gratitude for God's favour, as opposed to those required in fulfilment of a vow (cp. the comment on 7: 16), which a person 'dedicates to the LORD'.

14–15. Cp. the comments on verses 11–12, 13 and 25: 29–31.

16. A gift of *ancestral land* is governed by the regulations laid down in 25: 15–16. *a homer:* according to Ezek. 45: 11, this was equal to ten 'ephahs' (cp. p. 227).

17–18. If the land is dedicated during any particular *year of jubilee*, the full price as determined by the priest has to be paid. But if it is dedicated in any year following that year, the priest must calculate how many annual crops it will produce *till the next year of jubilee* (cp. the comment on 25: 15–16) and only charge for these in his valuation.

20–1. Another priestly expansion, to deal with another example of dishonesty (cp. the comment on verse 10*b*), when a man *sells...to another* what he has in fact already given to God. In this case, he loses the land permanently. It is now regarded as *devoted* (cp. verses 28, 29), a technical Hebrew term, *ḥerem*, meaning something that must be entirely withdrawn from human use to be made over to the deity (cp. verse 28*b*). The meaning of the term is seen most clearly in Israel's military practice: all booty taken in war was *ḥerem*, so all prisoners and cattle had to be killed (cp. Josh. 6: 21, where 'Under the ban' represents the word *ḥerem*; 1 Sam. 15: 14–33; Lev. 27: 29) and inanimate objects given to the sanctuary (cp. Josh. 6: 19), as is to be the case with *the land* here (verse 21*b*).

22–4. If a man *dedicates to the LORD land which he has bought* from someone else, so that it *is not part of his ancestral land*, the monetary compensation is again fixed by the rules of 25: 15–16. But the land is still another man's patrimony: it cannot be 'redeemed' by the dedicator (contrast verse 19) but must revert to the original owner *At the year of jubilee*.

26–9. Next three special cases are discussed:

26–7. (i) It was not possible to dedicate to the LORD the first-born of animals, because by an ancient law (cp. Exod. 13: 2, 12; 22: 30; 34: 19) these were his due in any case (cp. the comment on 2: 12).

27. *any unclean beast:* in contrast to verse 11, this means the 'first-born' of such a beast. Since it could not be offered to God (cp. the comment on verse 11), it had to be *redeemed*. Originally this was done by substituting an animal that could be offered in sacrifice (cp. Exod. 13: 13; 34: 20) but here it is done by a monetary payment. *if it is not redeemed:* after the exile, the 'first-born' was considered to belong to the priests

(cp. Num. 18: 15), so with an *unclean beast* (cp. Num. 18: 16), if the offerer did not wish to buy it back, the priest could sell it.

28-9. (ii) The mention of the 'redemption' procedure in verse 27 leads on to a further expansion to make clear when this procedure was not applicable. If a man devotes someone or something to God, as opposed to simply 'dedicating' (cp. the comment on verses 20-1), it is lost to him irredeemably.

29. *he shall be put to death:* cp. the comment on verses 20-1, but probably the compiler of this chapter is only repeating an old rigorous law which, by his time, was no longer in force and had been replaced by excommunication (cp. Ezra 10: 7-8).

30-3. (iii) Like the 'first fruits', the tithe already belongs to the LORD by ancient custom (cp. Deut. 14: 22) and so could not be 'dedicated'. In origin, the tithe was another old rite, closely akin to 'firstfruits' (cp. the comments on 2: 12; 23: 6), which freed the produce of land and animals for human use (cp. Deut. 14: 23). But after the exile, *the tithe on land* came to be regarded as a gift to God, specifically for the maintenance of the priests and Levites, for whom provision had to be made in a time of economic stringency (cp. Num. 18: 21, 24). Hence, it could easily be commuted for money (cp. Deut. 14: 24ff.) and this is presupposed here.

31. *wishes to redeem:* cp. the comment on verse 13.

32-3. Tithes of domestic animals could not be redeemed: cp. the comment on verses 9-10.

34. Cp. the comment on 7: 38. The final words of the book sum up its purpose – to record the divine covenant laws given to Moses during Israel's stay on Mount Sinai, before the priestly account of their subsequent journey through the desert is resumed in the following book of Numbers. ✶

A NOTE ON FURTHER READING

The two standard commentaries in English on Leviticus, both based on the Revised Standard Version, are those by Martin Noth, *Leviticus*, Old Testament Library (S.C.M., 1962) and N. H. Snaith, *Leviticus and Numbers*, The Century Bible (new edition, Nelson, 1967). The former is invaluable for its analysis of the way in which Leviticus reached its present form: unfortunately, the English translation is often unreliable. The latter is useful for its citation of Rabbinic evidence to illustrate the text of Leviticus. A full treatment of the religious institutions mentioned in Leviticus will be found in Part IV of R. de Vaux, *Ancient Israel* (Darton, Longman and Todd, 1961): the earlier parts of this book also contain much information about Israelite society which bears on Leviticus.

For the sacrificial system, the older works of G. Buchanan Gray, *Sacrifice in the Old Testament* (Clarendon Press, 1925) and W. Robertson Smith, *The Religion of the Semites* (3rd ed., A. & C. Black, 1927) are still essential: the former also contains a section on the priesthood. A shorter and more recent book is R. de Vaux, *Studies in Old Testament Sacrifice* (University of Wales Press, 1964). The most up-to-date book on the Israelite priesthood is A. Cody, *A history of Old Testament priesthood* (Pontifical Biblical Institute, 1969). Important discussions of the 'purity laws', on which the treatment in the present commentary is based, will be found in Mary Douglas, *Purity and Danger* (3rd impression, Routledge and Kegan Paul, 1970) and Jacob Neusner, *The Idea of Purity in Ancient Judaism* (Leiden, E. J. Brill, 1973). For the priestly work and 'the law of holiness', the standard Introductions to the Old Testament may be consulted, such as O. Eissfeldt, *The Old Testament: an Introduction* (Basil Blackwell, 1965). The historical background of the period of the exile and the relationship of the 'law of holiness' and the priestly work to it are discussed in P. R.

Ackroyd, *Exile and Restoration*, Old Testament Library (S.C.M., 1968).

For illustrative material from the ancient Near East, reference may be made to J. B. Pritchard, *Ancient Near Eastern Texts relating to the Old Testament* (2nd ed., Princeton University Press, 1955) and the supplementary volume *The Ancient Near East* (1969): cp. especially, for blessings and curses, pp. 178–80; for the Babylonian New Year Festival, pp. 331–4; for sacrificial rituals, pp. 343–5; for Phoenician lists of priestly sacrificial dues, pp. 656–7.

APPENDIX

MEASURES OF LENGTH AND EXTENT

	span	cubit	rod[a]
span	1	...	...
cubit	2	1	...
rod[a]	12	6	1

The 'short cubit' (Judg. 3: 16) was traditionally the measure from the elbow to the knuckles of the closed fist; and what seems to be intended as a 'long cubit' measured a 'cubit and a hand-breadth', i.e. 7 instead of 6 hand-breadths (Ezek. 40: 5). What is meant by cubits 'according to the old standard of measurement' (2 Chron. 3: 3) is presumably this pre-exilic cubit of 7 hand-breadths. Modern estimates of the Hebrew cubit range from 12 to 25·2 inches, without allowing for varying local standards.

Area was measured by the 'yoke' (Isa. 5: 10), i.e. that ploughed by a pair of oxen in one day, said to be half an acre now in Palestine, though varying in different places with the nature of the land.

MEASURES OF CAPACITY

liquid measures	equivalences	dry measures
'log'	1 'log'	...
...	4 'log'	'kab'
...	7⅕ 'log'	'omer'
'hin'	12 'log'	...
...	24 'log'	'seah'
'bath'	72 'log'	'ephah'
'kor'	720 'log'	'homer' or 'kor'

[a] Hebrew literally 'reed', the length of Ezekiel's measuring-rod.

According to ancient authorities the Hebrew 'log' was of the same capacity as the Roman *sextarius*; this according to the best available evidence was equivalent to 0·99 pint of the English standard.

WEIGHTS AND COINS

	heavy (Phoenician) standard			light (Babylonian) standard		
	shekel	mina	talent	shekel	mina	talent
shekel	1	...	...	1	...	...
mina	50	1	...	60	1	...
talent	3,000	60	1	3,600	60	1

The 'gerah' was $\frac{1}{20}$ of the sacred or heavy shekel and probably $\frac{1}{24}$ of the light shekel.

The 'sacred shekel' according to tradition was identical with the heavy shekel; while the 'shekel of the standard recognized by merchants' (Gen. 23: 16) was perhaps a weight stamped with its value as distinct from one not so stamped and requiring to be weighed on the spot.

Recent discoveries of hoards of objects stamped with their weights suggest that the shekel may have weighed approximately 11·5 grammes towards the end of the Hebrew monarchy, but nothing shows whether this is the light or the heavy shekel; and much variety, due partly to the worn or damaged state of the objects and partly to variations in local standards, increases the difficulty of giving a definite figure.

Coins are not mentioned before the exile. Only the 'daric' (1 Chron. 29: 7) and the 'drachma' (Ezra. 2: 69; Neh. 7: 70-2), if this is a distinct coin, are found in the Old Testament; the former is said to have been a month's pay for a soldier in the Persian army, while the latter will have been the Greek silver drachma, estimated at approximately 4·4 grammes. The 'shekel' of this period (Neh. 5: 15) as a coin was probably the Graeco-Persian *siglos* weighing 5·6 grammes.

INDEX

Aaron: consecration of 60–8; on Day of Atonement 122–5, 128–31; as high priest 5, 70–6, 81, 83, 170–1; priests descended from 16–18, 21, 24, 37, 54, 166–7

Abihu, son of Aaron 75–8, 122

alien settler 140–1, 149–50, 153, 156, 184, 189; regulations involving 160, 174, 192–5, 204, 206

altar 22; fire 17–18, 47, 49, 75; hearth 46, 48–9; horns of 34–6, 38, 64, 70, 73, 129; of incense 128, 130; of whole-offering 64, 73, 131

Ark 38; cover over 12, 122–3, 126, 128, 130

assault, law on 192–5

assembly, sacred 177, 179-84, 186–7

blasphemy, law against 191–4

blessings 207–11, 213

blood: containing life 20, 26, 38, 108, 139–42; as expiation 33, 64, 66, 126, 129–30, 140–1; flung on altar 17–18, 21, 28; given to God 21, 139, 141; on horns of altar 34–6; taboo on 48, 51, 57–8, 138, 140–2, 156, 158

Bread of the Presence 190–1

burnt-offering 29

calendar, sacred 177–89, 195–200; autumn festival 186–9; feast of Weeks 183–5; Passover and Un-leavened Bread 29, 55, 180–3, 184–5; sabbath 179–80; see also Day of Atonement; Tabernacles

Canaan: legal traditions of 6; practices assimilated 28, 38, 177, 181–2, 184, 188; warnings against cults of 80, 136–8, 142–3, 147–50, 158–9, 161, 207, 215

cherubim as attendants of God 126

childbirth, rules concerning 82, 93–5

circumcision 93–4

commandments 9, 37, 134, 143–5, 150–9, 209, 211; apodictic 14, 135, 145, 151, 164–5; casuistic 14, 91, 96–7, 138, 157, 164–5

covenant 94, 208, 216–17; as basis of faith 9, 27; obligations of 8, 10, 37, 44, 151–3, 161, 212, 214; renewal of 142–3, 209–11

curses 208–9, 211–15

Day of Atonement 81; ceremonies of 128–33, 195, 199; goat of 108, 112, 123–4, 127, 129–31; preparation for 122–8; ritual 20, 66, 71, 186–9

death penalty, crimes involving 37, 160–1, 192, 194; for blasphemy 192; for breaking sabbath 180, 188; for sexual crimes 157, 162–5, 166

Decalogue 151–2

Deuteronomy 5, 7, 15, 19, 38

drink-offering 181, 183, 187; see also libations

Egyptian cults, warnings against 143

Eleazar, son of Aaron 16, 76, 78, 79

Elzaphan 75–6, 78

exile: and law of holiness 135–7, 139, 153, 159; priests' reaction to 5, 7–8, 15–17, 25; reconstruction of Israel after 5, 7

expiation 36–7, 39–44, 52, 126, 140–1; animal as 17, 20, 43–5, 123, 127–8; blood as 33; Day of Atonement 123–32; for altar 64, 66, 128–9, 132; for house 115; for people 70, 79, 110–11, 128, 132, 140, 186, for men 118, 120, 155, for women 93, 121; for priests 48, 68–70, 123, 126, 128, 132; for Tent of the Presence 128–30, 132; priestly concern with 11–12, 14, 16, 73, 134

Ezekiel 5, 7, 178, 217